The London Confederates

ALSO BY JOHN D. BENNETT
AND FROM McFARLNAD

Placenames of the Civil War: Cities, Towns, Villages, Railroad Stations, Forts, Camps, Islands, Rivers, Creeks, Fords and Ferries (2012)

The London Confederates

The Officials, Clergy, Businessmen and Journalists Who Backed the American South During the Civil War

JOHN D. BENNETT

McFarland & Company, Inc., Publishers
Jefferson, North Carolina, and London

The present work is a reprint of the illustrated case bound edition of The London Confederates: The Officials, Clergy, Businessmen and Journalists Who Backed the American South During the Civil War, *first published in 2008 by McFarland.*

LIBRARY OF CONGRESS CATALOGUING-IN-PUBLICATION DATA

Bennett, J.D. (John D.), 1937–
The London Confederates : the officials, clergy, businessmen
and journalists who backed the American South
during the Civil War / by John D. Bennett.
  p.   cm.
Includes bibliographical references and index.

ISBN 978-0-7864-6901-7
softcover : acid free paper ∞

1. Confederate States of America — Relations — England — London.
2. London (England) — Relations — Confederate States of America.
3. London (England) — History — 1800–1950. 4. Confederate
States of America — Foreign public opinion, British. 5. Public opinion —
England — London — History — 19th century. 6. Confederate States
of America — Relations — Great Britain. 7. Great Britain —
Relations — Confederate States of America. 8. United States —
History — Civil War, 1861–1865 — Foreign public opinion, British.
9. United States — Foreign relations — 1861–1865. I. Title.
E488.B46 2012   973.7'1— dc22   2007026097

BRITISH LIBRARY CATALOGUING DATA ARE AVAILABLE

© 2008 John D. Bennett. All rights reserved

No part of this book may be reproduced or transmitted in any form or by any means, electronic or mechanical, including photocopying or recording, or by any information storage and retrieval system, without permission in writing from the publisher.

On the cover: *foreground,* the offices of Overend, Gurney & Company, who lent money to London shipbuilders for the construction of blockade runners and were themselves involved; *background* © 2012 Shutterstock

Manufactured in the United States of America

*McFarland & Company, Inc., Publishers
Box 611, Jefferson, North Carolina 28640
www.mcfarlandpub.com*

Table of Contents

Preface	1
Introduction	3
1 — London in the 1860s	5
2 — A Diplomatic Presence	25
3 — The Propaganda War	39
4 — Supplies for the Confederate Army	51
5 — Vessels Suitable for Our Purposes	62
6 — The Spying Game	78
7 — The Cotton Loan	87
8 — Business with the Southern States	95
9 — Artistic Reflections, Literary Echoes	110
10 — Support for the South?	135
Epilogue	152
Appendix A. London Firms with Confederate Links	161
Appendix B. Pro-Confederate Publications and Their Publishers	164
Appendix C. Confederate Music Published in London	166
Appendix D. The Southern Lobby in Parliament	167
Appendix E. The Southern Independence Association of London	168
Appendix F. The British Jackson Monumental Fund	169
Appendix G. A Note on British Currency	170
Chronology	171
Gazetteer	175
Chapter Notes	183
Bibliography	195
Index	199

Preface

In spite of the enormous interest in the American Civil War which exists on both sides of the Atlantic, there is relatively little awareness of Confederate activity overseas, especially the quest for diplomatic recognition by Britain and France, then the leading European powers, and the procurement of armaments and ships which Britain in particular could supply.

This study of Confederates in London grew out of my interest in the Confederate Navy. The *Official Records of the Union and Confederate Navies in the War of the Rebellion*, Second Series, contain the published Confederate secret service correspondence, and I noticed that some of the letters bore London addresses. Wondering if any of these still existed, I went along to have a look.

It was to be the start of a long process of investigation and research, some of which was carried out in London — at the British Library, the Guildhall Library and the Institute of Historical Research — and elsewhere — at the libraries of Sussex University, Reading University, Leicester University, Cambridge University, John Rylands University, Manchester, and Sheffield Archives.

Although some of the activities described here — the efforts in the fields of diplomacy and propaganda, the purchasing operations for the Army, the attempts to obtain vessels for the Navy, and the raising of a foreign loan — have been previously chronicled by Frank L. Owsley in *King Cotton Diplomacy*, Charles P. Cullop in *Confederate Propaganda in Europe*, Richard I. Lester in *Confederate Finance and Purchasing in Great Britain*, and Warren F. Spencer in *The Confederate Navy in Europe*, I have taken a fresh look at them in the context of the London of the 1860s in which the Confederates found themselves, for one or two of them a relatively familiar place, but for most, a foreign environment. In addition, there are other aspects of the Confederate presence here which have so far received little or no attention. As far as I am aware, there has been no detailed examination of Federal surveillance and espionage operations, nor any recent account of British business relations with the Confederacy, and the cultural impact of the Civil War has gone largely unnoticed.

I owe a special debt of gratitude to the late Professor Peter J. Parish, formerly Director of the Institute of United States Studies, University of London, and subsequently Mellon Senior Research Fellow in American History at Cambridge University, who found time, in a very busy schedule, to read and comment on an earlier version of this manuscript; I was much encouraged by his remark, "there is plenty of scope for a book-length study of Confederate activity in London."

As well as reading several drafts of the text and making valuable observations, John G.

Cox helped me obtain two important university theses. I also had help from Undine Concannon, archivist at Madame Tussaud's; Tracey Earl, archivist at Coutts & Company; Tony Kelly, sales manager of Firmin & Sons plc; Ray L. Marshall, consultant archivist of De La Rue; the Rev. Prebendary Donald Barnes, formerly vicar of St. Peter's, Belsize Park; and the Manuscripts Department of the Wilson Library at the University of North Carolina at Chapel Hill, which supplied a microfilm of the unpublished diary of James H. North, C.S.N., in the Southern Historical Collection.

Acknowledgments are also due those publishers and organizations that kindly gave permission to use material from their books, periodicals and manuscripts: Royden Harrison, "British Labour and the Confederacy," *International Review of Social History,* 2 (1957) © Internationaal Instituut voor Sociale Geschiedenis, Cambridge University Press; excerpts from *The Education of Henry Adams: An Autobiography,* Boston: Mariner Books, 2000; Douglas F. Forrest, *Odyssey in Gray: A Diary of Confederate Service, 1863–1865,* Library of Virginia; *Murray's Modern London 1860,* reprinted by Old House Books; Douglas H. Maynard, "The Forbes-Aspinwall Mission," and Harriet C. Owsley, "Henry Shelton Sanford and Federal Surveillance Abroad," from *Mississippi Valley Historical Review,* © Organization of American Historians *http://www.oah.org/,* reprinted with permission; Sir John Trelawney, *Parliamentary Diaries, 1858–1865,* Royal Historical Society; Head of Sheffield Libraries, Archives and Information for letters in the Wharncliffe Muniments, which have been accepted in lieu of Inheritance Tax by HM Government and allocated to Sheffield City Council; Colin Narbeth, Robin Hendy, and Christopher Stocker, *Collecting Paper Money and Bonds,* Stanley Gibbons Publications; James Heyward North Papers #862, Southern Historical Collection, Wilson Library, University of North Carolina at Chapel Hill; Richard I. Lester, *Confederate Finance and Purchasing in Great Britain during the American Civil War,* © 1975 University of Virginia Press; C. Vann Woodward, ed. *Mary Chesnut's Civil War,* Yale University Press; extract from George Augustus Sala, *Twice Around the Clock,* by kind permission of Continuum International Publishing Group; Charles Shain, "The English Novelists and the American Civil War," *American Quarterly* 14:3 (1962), 420–421, © The American Studies Association, reprinted with permission of The Johns Hopkins University Press.

Introduction

The American war has of necessity occupied a large share of the attention of the people of this country, as was to be expected of two nations so closely connected as the English and the Americans in many of their sympathies and their institutions, as well as in their language, literature, race and religion.
— *London Journal*, August 22, 1863

    The American Civil War was of great interest to the people of Britain, with their historical, cultural and linguistic links with the United States. The progress of the war occupied much space in the newspapers and magazines of the day, though public attention was inevitably distracted later by events in Europe—the Polish revolt of 1863, and the brief war between Denmark and Prussia over Schleswig-Holstein in 1864.

    The war was also the cause of much concern to the British government. Should it intervene? Should it declare the Federal blockade of Southern ports illegal and break it? And most importantly, should it recognize the Confederate States? In the event, the Liberal government of Lord Palmerston declared its neutrality and declined to intervene in any way. Furthermore, it remained unwilling to recognize the Confederacy until the military course of the war became clearer. The events of September 1862—the failure of Lee's invasion of the North at Antietam, followed by Lincoln's preliminary Emancipation Proclamation, which added a moral dimension to the original aim of saving the Union—postponed, and ultimately ended, the likelihood of intervention and diplomatic recognition. On more than one occasion there was also the possibility of armed conflict with the United States—at the time of the *Trent* incident in 1861 and over the building of the Laird rams in 1863.

    Hopes that the war would leave the United States permanently weakened as a mercantile power were coupled with the willingness of British firms to supply both sides, and particularly the embattled Confederacy, with whatever they needed and could pay for. Support for the South came not only from the business community, but also most of the aristocracy, some of the professional middle classes, members of Oxford and Cambridge universities, Church of England clergymen, officers in the army and navy, and even some working men, who were by no means all pro–Union.

    The port of Liverpool became a center for Confederate shipbuilding and blockade-running, and the base for the South's chief naval purchasing agent, as well as housing the offices of Fraser, Trenholm & Company, the Confederacy's bankers in Europe, and its importance should not be underestimated. But it was to London, the center of power and influence, that the Confederates inevitably looked. The home of Parliament and the government, London, with its diplomatic, commercial, industrial and financial significance, became a principal focus of Southern activity in Britain and Confederates began to arrive there within weeks of the outbreak of hostilities.

One problem they faced was how to avoid infringing, or at least being seen to infringe, the laws of the host country, particularly the Foreign Enlistment Act and the Proclamation of Neutrality; another was avoiding the attentions of Federal spies. As the war progressed, the Federals became increasingly proficient at the surveillance and infiltration of Confederate activities, particularly shipbuilding and blockade-running.

Another difficulty, for both Confederates and Federals, was the time it took to learn of events in America.[1] In the absence of a transatlantic telegraph — it was not successfully laid until 1866 — it took nearly a fortnight for news to reach Europe.[2] Telegrams, dispatches and newspapers came by mail steamer to Liverpool, Plymouth or Southampton, where newspaper and news agency representatives were waiting, and initial reports were then telegraphed to London, with other items forwarded by post. In 1863, to speed up news-gathering, Reuter's News Agency constructed a telegraph line from Cork to Crookhaven, some 60 miles away on the southwest tip of Ireland, where the mail steamers could be intercepted and the news telegraphed to Cork, and from there to London.[3]

There was also the problem of communicating with the Confederacy. Letters and dispatches were carried through the blockade by purchasing agents, naval officers and emissaries, and the regular mail service between Liverpool and New York was sometimes used by Confederate agents in disguise, but whichever method was resorted to, it was slow and hazardous, with no guarantee of safe receipt.[4] Several attempts were made to overcome the problem, but none were successful.

The men described in these pages served the Confederacy, not on the battlefield — although several of them did have military experience — but in other ways: seeking diplomatic recognition for the South, attempting to put across her point of view, and obtaining much-needed arms and equipment, even warships. Some of them became minor public figures, while others, particularly those involved in purchasing and propaganda activities, preferred to keep a much lower profile. Whatever their role, their task would not be an easy one.

1

London in the 1860s

> *There is not a more striking sight in London than the bustle of its great streets — the perpetually rolling tide of people, carts, carriages, gay equipages, and omnibuses, in its great thoroughfares.*
> —*Murray's Modern London*, 1860

In 1861 London was the greatest city in the world, both in extent and population. It was several times the size of New York, and many times that of New Orleans, the largest city in the Confederacy, as well as Richmond, its capital. In an area encompassing about 78,000 acres, or nearly 121 square miles, were upwards of 10,500 streets, squares, crescents, terraces, courts and alleys, containing 362,890 houses. Beyond the ancient cities of London and Westminster and the parliamentary boroughs of Marylebone, Finsbury, Tower Hamlets, Southwark and Lambeth, the suburbs stretched as far as Hampstead, Holloway, Highgate, Kilburn, Tottenham and Edmonton to the north; Camberwell, Brixton, Dulwich, Peckham, Norwood, Lewisham and Sydenham to the south; Limehouse, Poplar, Blackwall and Greenwich to the east; and Battersea, Wandsworth, Putney, Fulham, Hammersmith and Acton to the west.

The metropolis was indeed vast, and on October 9, 1863, James Glaisher, an astronomer and meteorologist who had made a number of previous balloon ascents over London, described what he saw as he passed over London Bridge at 7,000 feet in a particularly clear atmosphere:

> The scene around was probably one that cannot be equaled in the world at one glance — the homes of 3,000,000 people were seen, and so distinctly that every large building at every part was easily distinguished; while those almost under us — viz., the Bank and Newgate [Prison], the Docks and surrounding buildings, &c., in such detail that their inner courts were visible, and their ground-plans could have been drawn. Cannon Street was easily traced; but it was difficult to believe at first sight that small building to be St Paul's. Looking onward, Oxford Street was visible; the Parks, the Houses of Parliament, and Millbank Prison, with its radiating lines from the centre, at once attracted notice. In fact, the whole of London was visible, and some parts of it very clearly. Then all around there were lines of detached villas, imbedded as it were in shrubs; and beyond, the country, like a garden, with its fields well marked, but becoming smaller and smaller as the eye wandered further away.[1]

The census of London, taken on April 7, 1861, recorded a total population of 2,803,921, which included those in workhouses, hospitals and prisons, as well as an estimate of the numbers living in vessels on the river or sleeping under railway arches or in doorways. Out of a foreign population of 40,909, 4.68 percent (1,914) were American citizens.[2] Some of these no doubt went home when the Civil War began, to be replaced by new arrivals of the kind described here.

There had been an American presence in London since at least the eighteenth century. Benjamin Franklin first lived there in 1724–1726, and again in 1757–1775, as colonial agent and postmaster for the colonies, while John Adams served as the new republic's first "minister plenipotentiary" in 1785–1788. In the first half of the nineteenth century London attracted American writers like James Fenimore Cooper and Ralph Waldo Emerson, painters such as John James Audubon and George Catlin, and famous actors like Edwin Forrest and Ira Aldridge (who became a naturalized Englishman). In 1842–1845 the short-lived Republic of Texas maintained a legation in London. The Great Exhibition of 1851, held in the Crystal Palace in Hyde Park, had many Americans among its six million visitors. The exhibits included such famous products as Samuel Colt's revolvers and Cyrus McCormick's reaper, the display of which was subsidized by the London-based American banker George Peabody, after the United States Congress had declined to do so.

Some of the Confederates who came to London during the Civil War had been there before, but for many of them it was an unfamiliar place. At this particular time it must also have seemed like a city in turmoil, with the disruption caused by the building of London's main drainage system, as well as the new underground railway, both of which were under construction when the war began.[3] In addition, in 1864 work also started on the Victoria Embankment along the north bank of the Thames.

The metropolis was not only an enormous place, it was also a very confusing one, with many street names repeated in different areas. There were, for instance, no fewer than 37 King Streets, 27 Queen Streets, 22 Princess Streets, 17 Duke Streets, 35 Charles Streets, 29 John Streets, 15 James Streets and 21 George Streets, not to mention 24 New Streets, 16 York Streets, 14 Cross Streets, 16 Union Streets and 10 Gloucester Streets.

To help both strangers and natives find their way around this vast city, there were many pocket maps available. Mounted on linen and folded in covers, they were issued colored and uncolored, priced accordingly, and usually included a street index. Mapmakers copied each other shamelessly and up-to-dateness was not a matter of great concern; sometimes the only features revised were the title and date. The publication of street maps was greatly stimulated by the International Exhibition of 1862, which brought millions of British and foreign visitors to London. Charles Cheffins' *Visitors' Railway Station Map of London and its Environs*, Charles Smith's *Exhibition Map of London, with Omnibus Routes and Cab Fares*, William Tweedie's *Picture Map of London*, Ward & Lock's *New Handy Pocket Map of London, containing all Railways and Proposed Lines, Railway Termini &c.*, and Josiah Whitbread's *Map of London, extending Four Miles round Charing Cross* all appeared in or about 1862, along with others published by George Cruchley, Benjamin Davies, James Dolling, George Philip and George Welland.

Two large-scale maps also appeared, the first proper surveys of London since the 1820s. The *Environs of London*, drawn and engraved by Edward Weller, at nine inches to the mile, was first issued in parts in 1861–1862 as supplements to the *Weekly Dispatch* newspaper and then reissued as the *Dispatch Atlas* in 1863. Edward Stanford's *Library Map of London and Its Suburbs*, at six inches to the mile, was also published in 1862. As well as in sheets, both maps were available on rollers or folded in a case.[4]

Although a street atlas of London had been produced in the late 1840s by James Wyld,

"Geographer to the Queen and H.R.H. Prince Albert," it was too large for use out-of-doors, and it was not until 1854 that the first pocket-sized one appeared. *Collins' Illustrated Atlas of London* was published by a little-known mapseller called Henry George Collins, and had specially drawn plates, a detailed index of streets, and supplementary lists of public buildings, museums and other places of interest. It covered most of the continuously built-up area, though not the sparsely populated outer suburbs. Collins had gone bankrupt by the time a second edition was issued in 1859, and it was brought out by another publisher, Thomas Hodgson. That, and the third edition, called *London at a Glance. A Guide for Visitors to the International Exhibition*, published by Darton & Hodge in 1862, also included a list of hotels, the new postal districts (introduced in 1856) and the railways.[5]

The difficulties faced by strangers trying to find their way around the capital were made worse by the dense winter fogs, caused by the burning of millions of coal fires. Fogs had been a feature of London for centuries but they had become progressively thicker and more frequent as the capital's population increased. Sometimes they appeared to be bottle-green in color, at other times pea-soup yellow, through which the street gas lamps at night could barely be seen. Charles Dickens described fog as a "London particular" and the yellow variety came to be known as a "pea-souper." The American historian John Lothrop Motley, who came to London in 1858, wrote to his mother in Massachusetts in November of the following year, describing a London fog:

> I do not object to fog always excepting a black, thick London fog. I was obliged to pass a day in town yesterday and to breathe unmitigated coal smoke for six hours. When the fog settles down in London the smoke from millions of chimneys settles down with it. It cannot escape upwards and so every breathing being is turned for the time into a chimney. I was a chimney all day yesterday and rejoiced that I was not born in that station in life in London, not finding it exhilarating. London is not attractive in November.[6]

Motley went back to America when the Civil War started, but he was to return to London in the late sixties as United States minister to Great Britain.

Where did people live in this great metropolis? Mayfair was still the traditional home of the aristocracy, but between about 1825 and 1850 a new aristocratic quarter — Belgravia — had come into being, "whose houses, palatial in character and size, denote the high social position of their occupants."[7] An attempt to create a second, or South, Belgravia a decade later — what we now know as Pimlico — was less successful. No sooner was it completed than the railway arrived: Victoria Station, opened in 1860, brought noise, dirt, greatly increased pedestrian and vehicular traffic, and the sort of undesirables who were attracted to London's railway terminals.

Another new area, north of Hyde Park, was Tyburnia, "principally inhabited by professional men, the great City merchants, and by those who are undergoing the transitional state between commerce and fashion."[8] Regent's Park and Marylebone were desirable middle-class areas, though further east, Bloomsbury was now chiefly occupied by lawyers, merchants and rooming house keepers, "its noble mansions no longer holding, as formerly ... the rank and fashion of the town."[9] Further out, once rural Islington was mostly inhabited by middle-class families.

The City of London, the center of trade and commerce, had already lost most of its resident population. "Teeming by day with its hundreds of thousands, its streets gorged by carriages, cabs, and carts, [it] presents at night ... the spectacle of a deserted city ... the railway

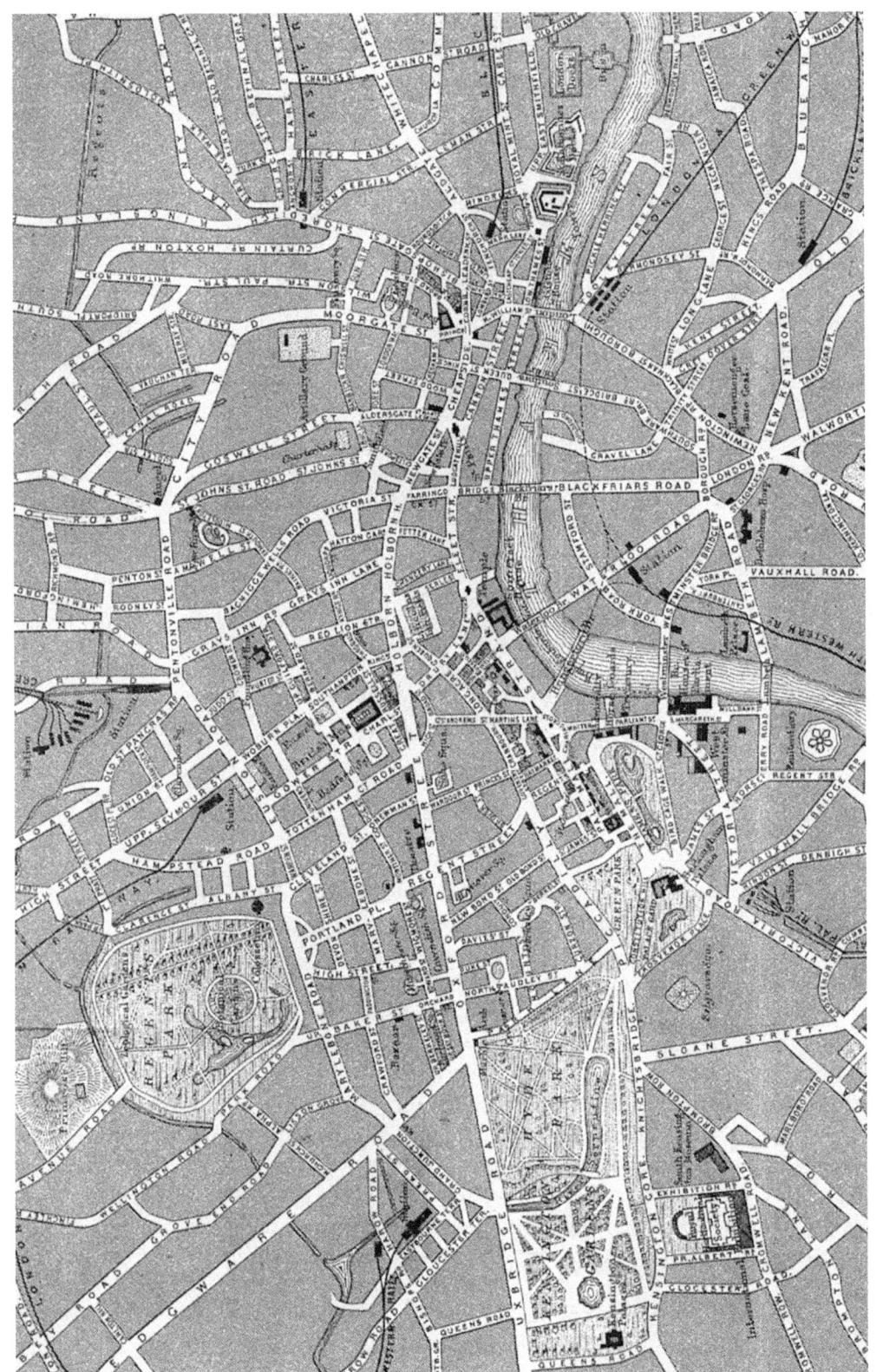

Map of central London in 1862. Present-day thoroughfares like Shaftesbury Avenue, Charing Cross Road, the Aldwych and Kingsway did not yet exist. (*Routledge's Popular Guide to London and its Suburbs*, 1862)

carriage, the omnibus, and the steam-boat carry the clerks to the outskirts, and the merchants and principals to their villas and mansions at Clapham, Hackney or the West End."[10]

Those following a particular calling tended to favor certain areas. Authors, journalists and publishers often chose St. John's Wood; artists and engravers, Kensington and Camden Town; and musicians, singers, actors and dancers, Brompton; physicians and surgeons frequently set up their practices in Savile Row or Brook Street, Mayfair; printers could be found in Fleet Street and the Strand; medical students in Southwark, near to Guy's Hospital; Members of Parliament in Westminster; diplomats sometimes resided in Belgravia; stockbrokers and merchants inhabited Bayswater, Brixton and Clapham, as well as Tyburnia; and clerks, Islington and Highgate. At a less respectable level, large numbers of "pretty horse-breakers"— well-dressed courtesans who rode in Hyde Park — had taken up residence in Lower Brompton and the area between Sloane Street and the International Exhibition site in South Kensington.

And what of those who worked with their hands? Watchmakers and jewelers were concentrated in Clerkenwell; silk and velvet weavers in Spitalfields and Bethnal Green; and cabinetmakers and carvers around Old Street and Aldersgate Street; iron-founders, shipwrights and boilermakers could be found in Blackwall, Poplar, Millwall and the Isle of Dogs; sugar bakers and refiners in Whitechapel and Commercial Road; and tanners, parchment makers and skin dressers in Bermondsey; potters and glassmakers were located in Lambeth; tailors in Golden Square and Burlington Gardens; boot and shoemakers in Shoreditch and around Drury Lane; hatters worked in Southwark; carriage builders in and around Long Acre; boat builders in Lambeth and Chelsea; and toy makers and doll-dressers in Hoxton.

The writer of a guidebook aimed at visitors to the International Exhibition of 1862, and intended to show the metropolis in the best possible light, was obliged to admit that "it is not pretended that London is all fair to look upon and bright with cleanliness and godliness," and he went on to paint a suitably lurid picture of another London, inhabited by what the Victorians regarded as the dangerous poor:

> Of course we do not pretend that London has not its squalid quarters — its dens of poverty and its sinks of iniquity, its horrible lanes and fever-haunted courts, its close, unhealthy streets, and its dark wretched bye-ways, its misery-filled alleys and its sinful slums, where the ginshop and the pawnbroker's stand side by side; its Whitechapel and its St Giles, where thieves and costermongers herd with debased women, whose most familiar word is an oath, and children whose earliest education has been picked up in the streets; and its hundreds of squalid lurking-places, known only to their wretched degraded inhabitants.[11]

For anyone arriving in London, the first requirement was somewhere to live. Hotels where Confederates are known to have stayed included the Albemarle, the Berners, the Brunswick, the Burlington, the Euston, Fenton's, the Grosvenor, Hatchett's, Haxell's, Morley's, the Tavistock, the Westminster Palace and Wood's.

The Burlington Hotel, which was owned by James Breach, had its main entrance in Cork Street, just off Piccadilly, but there was another entrance in Old Burlington Street, which was parallel to Cork Street. It had been a hotel since about 1823, and one of its residents in 1861 was the celebrated Florence Nightingale, who had made it her base for her campaign to reform the Army's medical services. Even older was Fenton's Hotel in St. James's Street, which had been established since about 1800. It was now owned by Francis Fenton, and though it was still regarded as a fashionable establishment, its rooms were described as being "small and dark, furnished like a common lodging house." Hatchett's Hotel, on the corner of Piccadilly and Dover Street, run by Joseph Bowles, was a former coaching inn; a guidebook described it as "a long-established and most respectable house" and it claimed to have been "established 100 years."

"Happily placed in the centre of the West Strand, Haxell's Hotel is one of the most complete and comfortable in London," announced a contemporary advertisement.[12] "It comprises numerous suites of apartments ... spacious coffee rooms, ladies' or family coffee room, etc. The improvements ... comprise a new entrance, noble hall, wide, light and commodious staircases and passages throughout the building, and the establishment now consists of upwards of one hundred rooms ... The hotel is much patronised by families and gentlemen arriving from the Confederate States of America." Run by Edward Nelson Haxell, it now also incorporated the adjacent Exeter Hall Hotel, and was not expensive by West End standards. Single bedrooms cost two shillings and sixpence, double rooms, four shillings, and a drawing room, with bedroom *en suite*, ten shillings and sixpence.

The Tavistock was one of a number of hotels in Covent Garden. It was popular with sea captains on leave, and had a huge dining room occupying the whole of the first floor and as many as two hundred bedrooms, but was thought "a miserable concern for all its reputation" by one Confederate who stayed there. Wood's Hotel, "for families and gentlemen," was part of Furnival's Inn, on the north side of High Holborn, and was owned by William Wood.

Most of these hotels had been converted from one or more private houses, and sometimes provided rather indifferent accommodation, which impressed neither European nor American visitors. The difficulty experienced by strangers in finding good hotels in London, where the accommodation was satisfactory and the charges moderate, was alluded to by guidebooks and newspapers. Some Confederates, particularly those accompanied by their families, undoubtedly found the high cost of living in London's West End a worry, and one army purchasing agent is known to have moved from lodgings in Jermyn Street to cheaper and more spacious accommodation on the western outskirts at Notting Hill, probably following the arrival of his wife and family.

It was the new railways which pioneered hotels built for the purpose in the capital, as they began to provide them at the main railway stations to accommodate travelers. The Euston, one of a pair of hotels situated on either side of the entrance to Euston Station, was opened in 1839 by the London & Birmingham Railway. The Great Northern Hotel at King's Cross and the Great Western Hotel at Paddington both opened in 1854. The Grosvenor Hotel, built next to Victoria Station in 1861 by the London, Brighton & South Coast Railway, contained "every convenience for the comfort of visitors." These were followed by railway hotels at London Bridge (1862) and Charing Cross Stations (1865).

At least one hotel already existed in the West End. Morley's Hotel, at the corner of Trafalgar Square and the Strand, had opened in 1831. It had a hundred bedrooms and in the early 1860s was owned by Thomas and George James; one Confederate who stayed there pronounced it "an excellent house — the best I've seen in London." In 1859 the Westminster Palace in Victoria Street, London's first luxury hotel, was built to provide accommodation for members of Parliament, people frequenting the law courts, foreign visitors and the public at large. It had "thirteen sitting-rooms, gentlemen's and ladies' coffee rooms (the latter an exceedingly fine apartment), several committee and dining rooms, with one hundred and thirty bedrooms, besides servants. apartments."[13] Managed by William Cowell, it was also the first hotel in London to have an elevator, or "rising room" as it was called, and it was noted for its good

THE COSTER-GIRL.

"Apples! An 'aypenny a lot, Apples!"

[*From a Daguerreotype by* BEARD.]

A coster-girl. Costermongers were street sellers of vegetables and fruit, particularly apples. (Mayhew)

English food. Another impressive hotel was the Palace in Buckingham Gate, containing "costly and luxurious suites of rooms," which opened in 1861 and also belonged to James Breach, the owner of the Burlington Hotel.

The year the Civil War ended saw the opening of the magnificent Langham Hotel in Portland Place, which was inaugurated in June 1865 with a reception for 2,000 guests, including the Prince of Wales. The hotel cost £300,000, had forty private sitting rooms and three hundred bedrooms, and provided every conceivable facility. Its second manager was James M. Sanderson, a former hotel owner in prewar Philadelphia and a wartime Union lieutenant colonel, who while an inmate of Libby Prison in Richmond had endeavored to instill some order into its catering arrangements. The Langham soon became a firm favorite with Americans in London.

Other hotels which catered to Americans included the Arundel Private Hotel, off the Strand, the Cavendish Hotel, Jermyn Street, the New York Hotel and the Prince of Wales Hotel, off Leicester Square, the Queen's Family Hotel, Bayswater, the Royal Opera Colonnade Hotel, Haymarket, the Villafranca Hotel, Covent Garden, and Woodall's Commercial and Private Hotel, Euston Road.

As well as hotels, there were innumerable rooming houses, and visitors planning a long stay were advised to rent an apartment. Moderately priced ones could be found in suburbs like Islington and Kensington, while "at the West End, apartments may be obtained from ten shillings a week for a single bed-room, use of sitting-room and attendance, to two or even three guineas a day for accommodation of a more pretentious character," advised a guidebook.[14] The best places to look for these were the streets leading off Piccadilly, Oxford Street, Regent Street and St. James's Street. One rooming house in Bury Street, St. James's, advertised in the *Index*, the South's propaganda newspaper, and several Confederates stayed there.

In addition, many "persons of respectability" were only too happy to let spare rooms. These could usually be found through house agents, as well as advertisements in newspapers like the *Times*, which "will often open to the stranger the doors of very respectable families, where he will get all the quiet and comfort of a home, so difficult to be found in the noisy, and often extortionate ... lodging-house."[15] One of the Confederate commissioners found rooms with a hosier and glover in Half Moon Street, off Piccadilly, while another lodged with a wine and spirit merchant in Albemarle Street in the same area.

There were hundreds of dining rooms and coffeehouses where meals could be obtained, and London guidebooks of the early 1860s were full of advice on where to eat. "A good, plain, cheap dinner or lunch, quickly served" or "a capital dinner, well served" were available at many places. "The visitor may dine well and respectably for a shilling, or luxuriously for a guinea. He has all the choice between a quiet chop or dish of meat and vegetables ... for about a shilling or fifteen pence; and a 'three-course and dessert' spread..."[16] Writing a few years after the Civil War, the American journalist Daniel Joseph Kirwan, the London correspondent of the *New York World*, observed, "at Blanchard's [a well-known restaurant in Soho] you may dine for a pound upon the choicest variety of dishes, cooked by a French *chef*."[17] Many hotels and inns, particularly in the Strand, Fleet Street, Cheapside and Holborn, also had lunch-bars, where "a chop or a snack and a glass of ale for sixpence, or a plate of hot meat, with vegetables and bread, for about eightpence" could be found.[18]

Most of the important institutions were on the north side of the Thames. Linking the north and south banks were ten bridges, the oldest of which were Blackfriars Bridge (1769), which was replaced in the 1860s, and Battersea Bridge, a wooden structure dating from 1772.

Vauxhall Bridge (1816) and Southwark Bridge (1819) were the first iron bridges to be built over the Thames. Waterloo Bridge (1817) was appropriately named as it had been opened on the second anniversary of the battle. The medieval London Bridge was rebuilt in 1831 and the eighteenth-century Westminster Bridge in 1862. The first suspension bridge in London was constructed at Hammersmith in 1827; Chelsea Bridge (1858) and Lambeth Bridge (1862) were also suspension bridges.

The Grosvenor Bridge (1860), serving Victoria Station, was the first railway bridge to be built across the Thames. Further west, at Battersea, the West London Railway constructed a wrought-iron bridge in 1861, while other railway bridges were built in 1864 at Blackfriars, for the London, Chatham & Dover Railway, and at Charing Cross for the South Eastern Railway.

There were a number of ways of getting around this vast metropolis. Horse-drawn cabs had first appeared in the 1830s, and by 1860 there were 4,600 of them on the streets of London. "Travelling in that most rapid and convenient of London vehicles, the cabriolet — or cab, as it is now universally called — is very common," readers of a contemporary guidebook were told. "Remember that the fare for one or two persons is sixpence a mile, by day or night."[19] A reasonable quantity of luggage could be carried free of charge, and to avoid any dispute with the cabdriver, passengers were advised to purchase the Red Book of fares, published by the Metropolitan Police (price one shilling), which told them how much they should pay for a particular journey.

From Mondays to Saturdays, between 9:00 A.M. and 12:00 midnight, as many as 1,200 brightly colored horse buses connected central London with the inner and outer suburbs, running to Bayswater, Brompton, Camberwell, Chelsea, Clapham, Hammersmith, Hampstead, Holloway, Islington, Kensal Green, Kensington, Kilburn, Pimlico, Putney, Richmond and St. John's Wood. In central London they ran between places like Paddington and Charing Cross, and Regent's Circus (now Oxford Circus) and the Bank of England. Usually drawn by a pair of horses, they could accommodate twelve passengers facing each other inside, and ten more on the roof, sitting back-to-back. At busy times they ran every five minutes, with a flat-fare system of fourpence for part of the way and sixpence for the whole distance, and were compelled by law to have a table of fares inside the vehicle. Many of them belonged to the London General Omnibus Company and their fame spread abroad, though foreign visitors were sometimes disappointed:

> We had heard so much about the London omnibuses, with their velvet upholstery and veneered panelling, that we were anxious to see these wonderful conveyances. So our amazement was great on boarding one in the Strand to find it narrow, rickety, jolting, dusty and extremely dirty. The only advantage of these vehicles is that they are closed by a door. The conductor stands outside on a small footboard, incessantly hailing the passers-by.[20]

London's first horse streetcars appeared in 1861, introduced by the American entrepreneur George Francis Train. A line of track laid along the Bayswater Road, between Marble Arch and Notting Hill, opened in March, followed by a second line down Victoria Street, between Westminster Abbey and Victoria Station, in April, and a third, from Westminster Bridge to Kennington Park, south of the river, in August. The single-deck cars, drawn by two horses, had room for twenty sitting and twelve standing passengers. Promising as it seemed, Mr. Train's scheme proved to be short-lived. Not only did the rails project well above the level of the street, creating a hazard for other horse traffic, but Train also met with strong

A cab driver. There were some four and a half thousand horse cabs plying for hire by the 1860s. (Mayhew)

opposition from a body called the Metropolis Road Commissioners, who objected to the inconvenience the streetcars caused to other road users. His case cannot have been helped by a fatal accident which took place in August 1861, when one boy was killed and two others injured "by climbing on the projections." In February 1862 he was ordered to remove his streetcars and ended up being fined £500.

The Thames, or "Silent Highway," still an important means of travel for many Londoners, was "traversed by a number of regular steamers. Eastward there are boats to ... Greenwich, Woolwich, Blackwall and Gravesend, from the piers at London Bridge. Westward, the Citizen [Steamboat] Company and the Iron Boat Company run steamers between London Bridge and Chelsea. These call at intermediate piers, and make a large number of trips daily, at fares varying between a halfpenny and sixpence."[21] There were the halfpenny boats, running between London Bridge and the Adelphi, the penny boats going to and from London Bridge, Hungerford Market and Westminster, and the twopenny and threepenny boats from London Bridge to Chelsea and Battersea. At times, the river could be almost as congested as the city streets themselves, not only with passenger steamers but also with merchant ships.

Work had begun on what was to be the world's first underground passenger railway in February 1860. It was built on the cut-and-cover system and caused enormous disruption, most of the trenches having to be dug along the main thoroughfares. Chancellor of the Exchequer W. E. Gladstone and his wife were among those who took part in the first trial trip on the steam-hauled trains in May 1862. The Metropolitan Railway ran from Paddington to Farringdon Street, with five intermediate stations, at Edgware Road, Baker Street, Portland Road (now Great Portland Street), Gower Street (now Euston Square) and King's Cross. In spite of the *Times'* disparaging observation that it was "an insult to common sense to suppose that people ... would ever prefer ... to be driven amid palpable darkness through the foul subsoil of London," it was an instant success when it opened in January 1863 — 30,000 passengers traveled on it on the first day — and it was soon extended, west to Hammersmith and east to Moorgate Street.[22] A Confederate naval officer sampled it in August 1863:

> Descended into the bowels of the earth, and tried this underground railroad. It passes through the city & when its proposed ramifications are completed, it will be as pervading as the upper highways ... The stations are lighted from above. The coaches are very nicely upholstered & arranged — each being supplied with two gas burners which in turn are supplied from a reservoir that runs along the top of the cars. Fare six pence to ride about 2½ miles.[23]

By the beginning of the 1860s London was connected by rail to all the main towns and cities in Britain. It then had eight railway terminals: London Bridge, Euston, Shoreditch, Fenchurch Street, Waterloo, King's Cross, Paddington and Victoria. London Bridge was built for the London & Greenwich Railway in 1836, but soon came to be used by the South Eastern Railway (with which it merged) and the London, Brighton & South Coast Railway as well. Euston was opened the following year by the London & Birmingham Railway (later part of the London & North Western Railway). As the station for Liverpool, it saw a number of Confederates coming and going during the war, while London Bridge was used by ones traveling to the Continent. Six years after it opened in 1840, the Shoreditch terminal of the Eastern Counties Railway was renamed Bishopsgate in an attempt to disguise the fact that it was situated in the wrong place — too far from the City and West End and in the middle of a festering slum. Fenchurch Street, the first railway terminal in London, was built in 1841 by the London & Blackwall Railway, which became part of the much larger London, Tilbury &

Southend Railway, and was also used by the Eastern Counties Railway and the North London Railway. Waterloo, the terminal of the London & South Western Railway and the station for Southampton, was opened in 1848. When it was built in 1852 by the Great Northern Railway, King's Cross was the largest station in England; the Midland Railway also used it until St. Pancras station was completed in the late sixties. Paddington, opened in 1854, was the Great Western Railway's London terminal. Victoria was a joint station for the London, Brighton & South Coast Railway and the London, Chatham & Dover Railway and was constructed in 1860–1862; like London Bridge, it was used by Confederates going across to the Continent. To these eight must be added Charing Cross, opened in 1864 as the West End terminal of the South Eastern Railway, and used by passengers wishing to travel to Europe.

London in the early 1860s was still mainly a city of small and medium-sized shops, often with their own speciality, though department stores, aimed at middle-class customers, were beginning to make their appearance. Many of these, such as Dickins & Jones in Regent Street, Swan & Edgar in Piccadilly, James Shoolbred in Tottenham Court Road, and Peter Robinson and Marshall & Snelgrove in Oxford Street, were drapers who, by the 1850s, had started to expand by opening other departments. Shoolbred's, founded in 1817, added carpets and soft furnishings, groceries and toys, and by mid-century had several hundred employees who either lived on the premises or in nearby hostels. Between 1854 and 1860, Peter Robinson (established in 1833) acquired no fewer than five adjacent shop premises in Oxford Street, offering "court millinery, mantles, and dressmaking; widows', families' and children's mourning," among other commodities. The prices of the goods were clearly displayed in the windows of these new stores, which operated on a cash rather than credit basis, as was often the case with older, more traditional shops.

William Whiteley, a Yorkshire draper, opened a shop in 1863 selling ribbons, lace and fancy goods in the new suburb of Bayswater, which was now served by the Metropolitan Railway as well as by horse buses. He started with just two assistants, but within a year had eighteen staff; three years later he was starting to expand, adding linens, furs, drapery, millinery, gloves, jewelry and umbrellas to his stock, to become eventually the self-styled "Universal Provider." John Lewis, a Somerset man who had been a buyer for Peter Robinson, bought a job lot of silks and set himself up in a small shop in Oxford Street in 1864; working on the principle of "buying cheap and selling cheap," he never looked back, soon expanding into neighboring shop premises.

In the West End, many shops were open from 8:00 A.M. until 8:00 P.M., though by the mid-sixties a number of the larger ones were closing at 2:00 P.M. on Saturdays as a result of the efforts of the Early Closing Association, formed in 1842 to campaign for the earlier closing of shops and a Saturday half-holiday. Their windows, often now of plateglass, were lit by gas at night. Gas lighting had been introduced in London in the early nineteenth century, and shopkeepers had quickly realized its potential for window displays and storefronts. It was impossible not to be impressed by the appearance of London at night, with its countless gas lamps, its broad streets and its wonderful shops, full of every item that could possibly be imagined. And of all the shopping streets, Regent Street, said the journalist George Augustus Sala, who several years later was to report the Civil War for the *Daily Telegraph*, was "an avenue of superfluities — a great trunk-road in Vanity Fair. Fancy watchmakers, haberdashers and photographers; fancy stationers, fancy hosiers and fancy staymakers; music shops, shawl shops, jewellers, French glove shops, perfumery and point lace shops, confectioners and milliners: ... these are the merchants whose wares are exhibited in this bezesteen of the world."[24]

There were also a number of shopping arcades which contained clusters of small shops. The first of these was the Royal Opera Arcade (1817), which was originally built as an adjunct to the Italian Opera House (later Her Majesty's Theater) in the Haymarket. A place where patrons could leave their hats and coats, rent opera glasses, and stroll during intervals, it gradually assumed the character of a shopping arcade, its shops reflecting the masculine world of nearby clubland.

Writing in 1865, the journalist Henry Mayhew described the Burlington Arcade in Piccadilly (1819) as "one of the brightest, pleasantest, and most aristocratic provinces of modern Arcadia," and it has always been renowned for its luxury goods or "expensive knick-knacks," as he called them.[25] In the 1860s it was also a haunt of what Mayhew calls "Cyprians of the better sort," or high-class prostitutes, who could be seen parading there each day between 3:00 and 5:00 P.M. The Lowther Arcade in the Strand (1831) was equally famous, though for a more innocent reason: its toy shops. It was often thronged with ladies and children buying toys at the French, German and Swiss shops.

When it opened in 1850, the *Lady's Newspaper* called the Royal Arcade, in the recently constructed New Oxford Street, "one of the chief attractions to the resident and stranger among the many that grace our gigantic metropolis," but it seems to have declined fairly quickly.[26] The early optimism had certainly departed by 1865, when Mayhew described its "dreary collection of shops," selling such things as stoves, furniture, kitchen ranges and baby linen. Some of the other early shopping arcades were equally unsuccessful and correspondingly short-lived. The Hungerford Arcade in Hungerford Market, the site of Charing Cross Station, the Exeter Arcade in Wellington Street, on the fringes of Covent Garden, and the South Eastern Arcade at London Bridge Station all closed and were demolished in the early 1860s.

Another feature of London's West End, then as now, were the gentlemen's clubs of Pall Mall and St. James's. Standing in Waterloo Place, at the bottom of Regent Street, the visitor would see:

> On our right hand the Athenaeum, chiefly frequented by literary men; on the left, and exactly opposite it, the United Service Club, whose members are naval and military veterans. Next to the Athenaeum ... is the Travellers'. The Reform, which is observable from its great size and from its Italian architecture, stands next in order. To the Reform succeeds the Carlton, the headquarters of the Conservatives, a stately building, and the last erected. The Oxford and Cambridge and the Guards' club houses complete this side of clubland. On the north, or opposite side, turning into St James's Square, is the Army and Navy Club ... Ascending [St James's Street] on the left hand side are seen the Conservative Club, Arthur's, and Brooks's (the Whig headquarters), whilst near the top is the once famous or infamous Crockford's ... White's and Boodle's, once fashionable political clubs, but now principally resorted to by elderly country gentlemen, stand on the opposite side near the top ... The stranger should endeavour to procure orders (given by members) to see some of these clubs, especially the Reform, famous for its central hall, and its kitchens planned by M. Soyer. The staircases and apartments of the Carlton, Reform, Conservative and Army and Navy Clubs are very beautiful.[27]

Most London theaters at this time offered a mixed fare, which might include drama, tragedy, melodrama, comedy, farce, spectacle and pantomime, usually in a double or triple bill, and they were often managed by actors who were themselves also dramatists. Programs were long, usually starting at 7:00 P.M. (7:30 P.M. for opera) and ending about midnight. In the West End, the cheapest theater seats cost a shilling, the most expensive, five or six shillings; after 9:00 P.M. they were usually half price. Private boxes at Covent Garden and Her Majesty's, where opera and ballet were performed, however, were from two or three guineas upwards and even seats in the stalls cost twenty-one shillings. At Her Majesty's, gentlemen were not admitted unless in black or white neckcloths, black pantaloons and dress coats. Several Confederates who kept diaries described their theater visits, which included the Theater Royal, Haymarket; the Adelphi in the Strand; the Olympic, Wych Street; the Princess's, Oxford Street; and further out, the Britannia, Hoxton.

Regarded as the leading theater in London, the Theater Royal, Haymarket, was run by the comic actor and playwright John Baldwin Buckstone. The American actor Edwin Booth (brother of John Wilkes Booth) made his London debut at the Haymarket in 1861, the same year that Tom Taylor's *Our American Cousin* was staged there. The Adelphi Theater in the Strand was owned and managed by another actor-dramatist, Benjamin Webster, and had seating for 1,300 people. The famous American actor Joseph Jefferson appeared there in a new version of Washington Irving's *Rip Van Winkle* in 1865.

Reconstructed after its predecessor had burnt down, the Olympic Theater, Wych Street, had witnessed the first stage version of *Uncle Tom's Cabin* in 1852 and also saw the production in 1862 of Horace Wigan's *A Southerner Just Arrived*, a play inspired by the Civil War. Two years later its author took over the running of the Olympic on the sudden death of actor-manager Frederick Robson. The Princess's Theater, Oxford Street, also managed by Benjamin Webster, had originally been built for concerts, but came to be used for operas and plays, and the American actress Charlotte Cushman made her London debut there in 1845. Disturbances in theaters still sometimes occurred, and in 1865 it was the scene of a riot during the first night of Charles Reade's *It's Never Too Late to Mend*, caused by an over-realistic flogging scene.

Other West End theaters included the Theater Royal, Drury Lane, the oldest in London, where the nautical extravaganza *The Alabama* was staged in 1864; the Royal Lyceum, Wellington Street, renowned for its interior decorations; the St. James's, King Street; and the Strand Theater, Strand.

Outside central London, the Britannia Theater, Hoxton, where Colin H. Hazlewood's play, *The Confederate's Daughter,* was performed in 1865, was owned and managed by Sam and Sara Lane. It was extremely large, with a total capacity (seated and standing) of nearly 4,000, though this was later reduced to some 3,000. Sadler's Wells Theater, Finsbury, sometimes put on plays by Shakespeare and his contemporaries; the Royal Victoria Theater, Lambeth (the "Old Vic"), which had a huge gallery, and where the most expensive seat cost a shilling, presented lurid melodramas which tended to attract unruly audiences; and the Surrey Theater, Blackfriars Road, offered an intriguing mixture of melodrama, farce and pantomime, and occasionally tragedy, comedy and even opera.

Music halls, providing food and drink in the auditorium, along with singing acts and comedy turns, had originated in the inner suburbs in the 1840s. They appealed to audiences which the *Observer* newspaper described scathingly as "mixed crowds of folly and vice," while *Punch* wondered "whether the music hall was the place for a gentleman to go to, or even for a greengrocer, a chimney-sweep, or costermonger, or any man who entertained a liking to be thought respectable."[28]

By the early 1860s more sophisticated ones were starting to appear in the West End. Among the first were Weston's in High Holborn and the Oxford in Oxford Street. Another was the London Pavilion in Tichborne Street, near what is now Piccadilly Circus. It had a capacity of 2,000 and had only been open two years when a Confederate diarist went there in 1863. He described it thus:

> A great cafe, at the upper end a stage, a gallery too, fronting the stage and on the right side; but on the left a wall hung with mirrors ... The acting on the stage was capital — a sort of ballet — a burlesque opera ... Had nearly expired when some women came out with abbreviated dresses & much muslin & ankle who gyrated around ... The lower floor was filled with people sitting at tables with their hats on & their pipes & cigars alight, drinking beer or strong drink, eating Welsh rarebits & chatting...[29]

The same diarist found Evans' Supper Rooms in Covent Garden, an older establishment, to be more decorous than the London Pavilion. It was housed in a seventeenth-century building, which was now a hotel, whose basement dining saloon had been turned into a song-and-supper room. Run by a man called John Greenmore, better known as "Paddy Green," the entertainment there consisted of selections of madrigals, glees, choruses and songs, with an occasional comic turn, sometimes supplemented by contributions from members of the audience.

Among other London music halls were the Middlesex, Drury Lane; the Metropolitan, Edgware Road; Collins', Islington; the Grecian Saloon, City Road; Wilton's, Whitechapel; the Bedford, Camden Town; and the Canterbury, Westminster Bridge Road. The Alhambra Palace, Leicester Square, which started life as the Royal Panopticon of Science and Art, had been converted into the Great United States Circus in 1858, then became a music hall in 1860, where the following year Charles Blondin, who had recently crossed Niagara Falls on a tightrope, appeared.

Casinos in the 1860s were places for music and dancing rather than gambling. The two best-known ones were the Holborn Casino in High Holborn and the Argyll Rooms in Great Windmill Street, at the top of the Haymarket. One Confederate agent, visiting London in 1861, was taken after dinner to the Holborn Casino, whose real name was the Casino de Venise. It cost a shilling to gain admittance to a large, brilliantly lit hall, where people were dancing to polkas and quadrilles. Among its clientele were medical students, clerks, apprentice lawyers and young ships' officers, as well as a large number of prostitutes. In spite of its doubtful reputation, it was a surprisingly sober establishment, where the main drinks served were beer and soda water.

A day or two later, on his way home from the theater, the same agent stopped for a brandy and soda at one of the bars in the Haymarket. He found it crowded with rough and rowdy individuals and, as soon as he had swallowed his drink, realized that it had been drugged. Fortunately, one glass was not enough to stupefy him, and he wisely resisted the temptation of a second drink.[30]

During the daytime the Haymarket, with its theaters, hotels, restaurants, cigar divans, coffeehouses and shops selling shellfish, had a half-deserted air, but it took on a very different aspect once darkness fell, when it and the adjacent streets became the center of London's nightlife. It was a tourist sight in itself and a guidebook recommended that the visitor should see it "between ½ past 11 and 12 of a night in the thickest of the London season; when the crush of carriages and cabs, the crowd of orderly and disorderly people, the brilliant appearance of the taverns and shell-fish shops, form an extraordinary picture."[31] Henry Mayhew also observed: "A stranger on his coming to London ... seldom leaves the capital before he makes an evening visit to the Haymarket and Regent Street." He drew attention to "the brilliant illumination of the shops, cafes, Turkish divans, assembly halls and concert rooms," as well as "the troops of elegantly dressed courtesans, rustling in silks and satins ... promenading along these superb streets among throngs of fashionable people, and persons apparently of every order and pursuit, from the ragged crossing-sweeper and tattered shoe-black to the high-bred gentleman of fashion and scion of nobility."[32] When the theaters closed at midnight, many of their patrons helped to swell the jostling crowds heading for the bars and oyster shops, cafes where it was not difficult to get one's pocket picked, and high-class night houses like the Cafe Royal, off Leicester Square, better known as Kate Hamilton's.

For those in search of more refined pleasures, there were a number of places where concerts, advertised in the *Times* and some of the other daily papers, were held. These included the Hanover Square Rooms, Exeter Hall, in the Strand, which could easily accommodate 3,000 people, St. Martin's Hall, Long Acre, and Willis's Rooms, King Street; in addition, weekly concerts were held at the Crystal Palace, Sydenham, which could be reached by train from Victoria or London Bridge.

And there were other diversions. Burford's Panorama ("The Views are varied every Season") still lingered on in Leicester Square, where it had been since 1793, though it was about to close, as was also James Wyld's Great Globe, which had been there for the previous decade, "exhibiting the different divisions of the world on its concave or interior surface." Unusual sights could often be seen at the Egyptian Hall, Piccadilly; John Banvard's moving "Panorama of the Mississippi, Missouri and Ohio Rivers," twelve feet high and 1,320 feet long, had caused a sensation when it was shown there in 1848–1849, and the Hall offered an ever-changing program of illustrated lectures and exhibitions. The evening was suggested as the best time to visit Madame Tussaud's Waxworks, which had been on Baker Street since the 1830s; admission cost one shilling and the Chamber of Horrors was sixpence extra.

Among London's other attractions were its parks. St. James's Park, its lake frequented by waterfowl, was the oldest, dating from the sixteenth century; Hyde Park, the largest of the London parks, had been opened to the public at the beginning of the seventeenth century; and Green Park was created by King Charles II in the second half of the seventeenth century. A notable feature of Hyde Park was Rotten Row (supposedly a corruption of the French *Route du Roi*), a carriage drive where, "from May to August ... may be seen all the wealth and fashion and splendid equipages of the nobility and gentry of Great Britain. As many as 800 equestrians ... have been seen assembled at Hyde Park in the height of the season."[33] For twenty-four weeks in 1851, Hyde Park had also been the setting for the Great Exhibition, held in the Crystal Palace, now moved to Sydenham.

Regent's Park, laid out in the early nineteenth century, housed the zoo. Kensington Gardens, next to Hyde Park and originally the grounds of Kensington Palace, had been opened to the public on a daily basis in the 1830s. Victoria Park was created in the 1840s to serve the people of the East End, and Battersea Park, south of the river, was opened in 1853. Further out, Greenwich Park and Richmond Park both dated from the seventeenth century and Kew Gardens, with its great variety of plants, was laid out in the eighteenth century.

Visitors to London in the early 1860s would have found the main streets extremely crowded. At certain times of day traffic congestion had reached epic proportions, with cabs, horse buses, private carriages, coal carts, railway vans, country wagons, drays and handbarrows all jostling for space, along with hordes of pedestrians. Until the introduction of cheap workmen's fares on the railways, many people walked to and from work; bus fares were simply too expensive for the thousands earning less than a pound a week. The situation was made even worse by the herds of cattle and flocks of sheep which were driven through the streets, bound for the Metropolitan Cattle Market at Islington. A few new thoroughfares had been built in an attempt to improve the traffic flow — Farringdon Road and New Oxford Street in the 1840s, Victoria Street and an extended Cannon Street in the 1850s, and Garrick Street in the early 1860s — but they had done little to alleviate the problem.

Central London was not only very congested, it was also remarkably noisy, with thousands of iron-rimmed wheels and iron-shod horses. hooves passing through streets laid with granite sets. The huge volume of horse traffic also made it very dirty, particularly in wet weather, hence the need for that legendary Victorian street character, the crossing sweeper.

Anyone visiting the metropolis for the first time would have been amazed by the street life. Hundreds of people made a living of sorts as street entertainers. A few years previously, Henry Mayhew had recorded a number of them in his *London Labour and the London Poor*. They included "Punch and Judy" men, exhibitors of mechanical figures, acrobats, strong men, jugglers, conjurers, snake, sword and knife swallowers, fire-eaters, clowns, jesters, tightrope dancers and stilt walkers, reciters, exhibitors of dancing dogs, "Ethiopian serenaders" (black-faced minstrels playing banjos, tambourines and fiddles), whistling men and ballad singers.

Even more numerous were the street vendors, who constituted about one-fortieth of the working population of the metropolis. An astonishing range of items could be bought on the streets of London, from fruit and vegetables, oysters, hot eels, fried fish, ham sandwiches, pea soup, roasted chestnuts, baked potatoes, ice cream, cakes, pastries and sweets, boiled puddings, milk, ginger beer, lemonade and coffee, to flowers, stationery, hardware, crockery, walking sticks, combs, matches, shoelaces, cigars, second-hand clothing and even birds and dogs.

Although there seems to have been no London equivalent of the gangs of the Five Points and the Bowery who plagued New York at this time, an outbreak of violent street robberies in 1862–1863 nevertheless spread alarm and panic throughout the metropolis. Attacks were being reported as early as March 1862 and were usually carried out by teams of three men using a technique known as garroting, whereby their victims were half-throttled with a rope or cloth from behind, while their pockets were rifled. At first the attacks took place at night, but soon they were occurring in the daytime as well, and in the heart of the capital. Garroting was not an entirely new phenomenon — there had been an outbreak of it in 1856 — but what made it different this time was its persistent and widespread nature.

No one, it seemed, was safe. In mid–July 1862, James Pilkington, M.P. for Blackburn in Lancashire, was garroted and robbed in an "open well-lighted place" while walking from the House of Commons to his club in Pall Mall, and on the same night Edward Hawkins, the former Keeper of Antiquities at the British Museum, was attacked in a similar manner between St. James's and Bond Street. Several of the garroters' victims were so badly injured that they died. Many attributed this ferocious crime wave to the ending of transportation (the sending of criminals to the penal settlements in Australia), and the ticket-of-leave system (the release of prisoners on license before their sentences were completed), which meant that London was full of former convicts.

The excitement and hysteria generated by the outbreak produced antigarroting collars, antigarroting societies and cartoons in *Punch*. There were some arrests: in November 1862, for instance, a number of men accused of garroting were tried at the Central Criminal Court, in the Old Bailey, and given sentences of penal servitude varying from four years to life. The public disquiet over the wave of garrotings led to the setting up of a government commission to inquire into the legislation relating to transportation and penal servitude. It recommended stricter penal discipline in the convict prisons and the surveillance of ticket-of-leave men by the police. Finally, in July 1863, there was what was known as the "Garroting Act," which amended the criminal law to make robbery with violence punishable by flogging.

Although Henry Mayhew refers to previous instances of garroting in his survey of London's criminal population (1862), the research for this probably took place before the main outbreak occurred.[34] In the course of his investigations he met and interviewed madams, pimps and prostitutes, thieves, swindlers, pickpockets, shoplifters, horse and dog stealers, burglars and housebreakers, receivers of stolen goods, forgers of banknotes and checks, embezzlers, card sharps, and many types of beggars, both real and sham; among this criminal fraternity were many juvenile thieves, who in due course graduated from stealing from stores to become pickpockets or burglars. They all had their own descriptions: "cracksmen" were housebreakers; "rampsmen" were footpads, criminals who rob pedestrians; "bludgers" were street thugs; "buzzers" were pickpockets; "snoozers" booked a room at a hotel, then burgled the rooms of the other guests; "area sneaks" called at the kitchen doors of big houses in the hope of finding something to steal; "skinners" were women who enticed children into their homes and then stripped them of their clothing; "shoful men" were counterfeit coiners, "smashers" those who passed the coins; and "drummers" were men who put knockout drops into their victims' drinks before robbing them.

Visitors to London certainly needed to be on their guard, and a guidebook which appeared in the year the garroting scare began advised its readers not to linger in crowded thoroughfares or relieve beggars, to avoid byways and poor neighborhoods after dark, to carry no more money than was necessary for the day's expenses, and to take care of their pockets at the entrances to theaters, exhibitions and churches, on buses and the streets. The interiors of buses, in particular, where people sat very close together, offered excellent opportunities for pickpockets. Many of these were well-dressed women, and Mayhew described in some detail the techniques they employed.

In spite of the best efforts of the police, the criminal underworld was still very active in the 1860s, and criminals were quick to seize the opportunities which new developments like railways presented. The railway terminals attracted swarms of prostitutes, pickpockets and confidence tricksters, and, in addition, London criminals could now travel all over the country, and even abroad, to pursue their particular callings.

London had had a uniformed police force since 1829, when the Metropolitan Police were established, though the City chose to be excluded from their jurisdiction and set up its own separate force a decade later, in 1839. The Metropolitan Police, whose headquarters were at Scotland Yard, were originally organized in seventeen divisions — in central London these covered the districts of Whitehall, Westminster, St. James's, Covent Garden, Marylebone and Holborn — and there were separate divisions to police the river and the shipyards. A major advance was the establishment of a detective branch in 1842.

In the early 1860s policemen in London still wore the dark blue, swallowtail coats and black top hats which had been their uniform since 1829, though these were replaced by short tunics and helmets in 1864, and they were issued with a baton, a whistle and a lantern. Average pay was about eighteen shillings a week, in addition to which officers were given a clothing and coal allocation. In 1863 the total establishment of the Metropolitan Police was 6,590, and the City Police, 743, or about one officer for every 382 inhabitants of London.

There was certainly no lack of prisons to accommodate criminals once they had been caught, tried and convicted; every year upwards of 30,000 prisoners were said to pass through London's jails and houses of correction (prisons for those serving short sentences, usually with hard labor). The oldest prisons were Newgate, in the City, Horsemonger Lane, Southwark, and Cold Bath Fields, Clerkenwell, which all dated from the late eighteenth century. By the

1860s Newgate was being used for prisoners awaiting trial or execution, which still took place in public just outside its walls; Horsemonger Lane, the Surrey County jail, housed mainly petty criminals; and Cold Bath Fields was a house of correction, notorious for its severe regime.

A number of London prisons were built or rebuilt in the nineteenth century. Millbank, the largest in London, was the first penitentiary, but now housed convicts awaiting transfer to other prisons. Pentonville, a "model prison" based on the Eastern Penitentiary, Philadelphia, was described as "bright and cheerful and airy." The Clerkenwell House of Detention, a remand prison used for prisoners awaiting trial, received unwelcome publicity in 1867 when, in an unsuccessful attempt to rescue Irish Fenian prisoners, part of it was blown up and six people were killed. The most remarkable feature of the City House of Correction, Holloway, was its appearance: it was built to resemble a medieval castle. Tothill Fields, Westminster, contained females and juveniles. Brixton, originally a house of correction, now housed only female convicts, whose tasks included washing all the clothes for Pentonville, Millbank and Brixton Prisons. Wandsworth was also built as a house of correction.

The early sixties were not uneventful years in London. In March 1861 Charles Spurgeon, one of the most popular preachers of the nineteenth century, opened the Metropolitan Tabernacle, near the Elephant & Castle in south London; it could accommodate 6,000 people. An American ship, the *Hortense*, caught fire in the London Docks in April; and a strike of London building workers, which had begun the previous month, ended with the men accepting the hourly system of payment and a Saturday half-holiday. One of the greatest fires London had ever seen broke out in June in a hemp warehouse in Tooley Street, Southwark, near London Bridge. It soon spread to neighboring warehouses containing tallow, cotton, sugar and saltpeter and continued for several days, attracting thousands of spectators. In the course of it, James Braidwood, the superintendent of the London Fire Engine Establishment Brigade, was killed when a wall collapsed on him. That same month the Royal Horticultural Society opened its ornamental gardens in South Kensington to the public. There was a huge meeting in Exeter Hall, Strand, in July to welcome the fugitive slave John Anderson, who had arrived in London the previous month. In September two trains collided at Gospel Oak, near Kentish Town, in north London, killing 16 people and injuring 321. Deerfoot, a Seneca Indian, ran a six-mile course against three Englishmen in December, before the Prince of Wales, and was declared the winner; he ran again later that month against a man called Mills at Hackney Wick. The death from typhoid fever of the prince consort, the husband of Queen Victoria, at Windsor Castle later that month caused "general gloom and consternation throughout the metropolis," and his funeral a week later took place "amidst universal demonstrations of mourning."

In January 1862 the queen was reported to be in a state of nervous collapse and her royal duties were carried out by her uncle, King Leopold of the Belgians, who was in temporary residence at Buckingham Palace. Deerfoot ran again in February, this time against Job Smith, of Hulme, near Manchester, at the Copenhagen Grounds, Wandsworth, for a purse of £50. The following month, to mark his twenty-five years in London, and "as a token of gratitude to the English nation," another American, the banker and philanthropist George Peabody, gave the enormous sum of £150,000 to improve the condition of the "artisan and labouring poor," a gesture which the queen described as a "noble act of more than princely munificence" and one "wholly without parallel." In May the International Exhibition opened in South Kensington; one of the more unusual exhibits was a mechanical bullfinch which later sang for the benefit of the Lancashire distress fund, in aid of victims of the Cotton Famine, "producing a considerable sum." A number of convicts escaped from London prisons in May and June: one from Newgate, three from Millbank and three more from Horsemonger Lane. George Peabody became the first American citizen to be given the Freedom of the City of London in July. That same month there was an explosion at a match factory in Bethnal Green, causing injuries and some fatalities. The International Exhibition closed in November after more than six million people had visited it, while the following month 20,000 people came to see the first cattle show held at the new Agricultural Hall, Islington.

There was "an immense demonstration" at Exeter Hall in the Strand "in favor of Negro Emancipation" in January 1863. Several persons were injured in an accident on the newly opened Metropolitan Railway in February. The following month there were celebrations to mark the wedding of the Prince of Wales and Princess Alexandra of Denmark, which took place at Windsor Castle. The day was observed as a general holiday but it was not without incident: eight women and a child were crushed to death in the crowds during the London celebrations in honor of the marriage. In April there was a crowded meeting at St. James's Hall, Piccadilly, organized by the Freedom Aid Society, to raise money to assist escaped slaves in the United States. The famous explorers John Speke and James Grant, discoverers of the source of the Nile, were present at a special meeting of the Royal Geographical Society at Burlington House, Piccadilly, in June.

The first dwellings built by the Peabody Trust for the industrious poor were opened in Whitechapel in February 1864. The Italian patriot, General Garibaldi, received an enthusiastic reception on his eleven-day visit to the capital in April and was granted the Freedom of the City of London. Work began on the Albert Memorial in Hyde Park in May, though it would not be completed until 1876. London's first railway murder took place in July when Thomas Briggs, a senior bank clerk, was killed in a carriage on the North London Railway, causing alarm among the commuting middle classes. In September Karl Marx helped to organize a meeting of the London Trades Council and the First International at St. Martin's Hall, Long Acre, which was attended by many European delegates. Franz Muller, the murderer of Thomas Briggs, was hanged outside Newgate Prison in November before an enormous and unruly crowd of spectators.

Savile House, Leicester Square, once a royal residence but in recent years used for a variety of miscellaneous entertainments, was destroyed by fire in February 1865. The metropolitan drainage system, begun in 1855 by Joseph Bazalgette, was finally completed, and opened by the Prince of Wales in April. Lord Palmerston died in October while still prime minister and was succeeded by Lord John Russell; at Queen Victoria's request, there was a public funeral later that month when he was buried in Westminster Abbey. Another funeral the following month, at Highgate Cemetery, also turned into a public event when an estimated 10,000 people attended that of the celebrated pugilist Tom Sayers, who in 1860 had fought the American John C. Heenan to a draw.

Much of the London the Confederates knew — the London of the 1860s — has inevitably disappeared, but there are still houses in Half Moon Street, Sackville Street and Savile Row where some of them lodged; nearby, the church in Piccadilly where one of them was married; and further afield, in Notting Hill, a house where a purchasing agent lived; and in Belsize Park, the church where a Confederate parson presided and houses where other Confederates stayed.

2

A Diplomatic Presence

Though with the North we sympathise,
It must not be forgotten,
That with the South we've stronger ties,
Which are composed of cotton.
—*Punch*, March 30, 1861

This rhyme might have been written for the leaders of the newly formed Confederate States of America, the cornerstone of whose foreign policy was the importance of cotton in the European economy. About 80 percent of the cotton used in British factories came from the South, and it was generally believed that withholding it would bring about British intervention and diplomatic recognition. In the event, an embargo on the export of cotton in the first year of the war was not the result of Confederate government legislation, but of voluntary action on the part of planters and shipowners, strongly supported by newspapers like the *Charleston Mercury*, which confidently assured its readers in June 1861: "The cards are in our hands, and we intend to play them out to the bankruptcy of every cotton factory in Great Britain and France or the acknowledgement of our independence." The power of King Cotton, however, would turn out to be illusory.[1]

In March 1861, Jefferson Davis, provisional president of the Confederate States of America, appointed three commissioners to represent the Confederacy's diplomatic interests in Europe. The men selected for this difficult mission were William L. Yancey, Pierre A. Rost and A. Dudley Mann.

They were not the first Southern representatives to be sent overseas. In January 1861, as soon as Georgia seceded, Thomas Butler King, a lawyer, planter and congressman, was appointed "Commissioner to the government of Queen Victoria, to the Emperor Napoleon III, and to the government of the King of the Belgians" by Governor Joseph E. Brown and sent to Europe to explain his state's new situation and gain recognition of her independence. King left for Europe at the beginning of March, but his role as a state commissioner, apparently a unique one, does not seem to have been particularly fruitful. His attempts, by means of negotiations in London and Paris, to establish a steamboat service between Savannah and European ports were thwarted by the blockade and he returned to Georgia early in 1862.

Jefferson Davis's emissaries were, meanwhile, on their way to London. The first to arrive was Dudley Mann, the only one of the three commissioners with any previous diplomatic experience. Born in Virginia in 1801, Ambrose Dudley Mann had attended West Point, but, deciding against a military career, had opted instead for the legal profession. Between 1842 and 1853 he had held a series of government appointments as consul or commercial agent in various European countries, then, back home, had served as assistant secretary of state from 1853 through 1855 during Franklin Pierce's administration. This seemed a promising background, and together with his known advocacy of states rights, Southern economic independence and the establishment of a Southern merchant marine, no doubt helped secure his appointment as one of the first Confederate commissioners.

Dudley Mann reached London on April 15, having traveled via New York, but did not get off to a good start. He caused astonishment when, three days later, he called at the U.S. legation in Portland Place, where the outgoing minister, George Mifflin Dallas, was an old friend. Though less well-known than his successor, Charles Francis Adams, George Dallas had actually had a more distinguished career, having served as U.S. minister to Russia in 1837–1839 and as vice president to James Polk in 1845–1849; in addition, Dallas, Texas, had been named after him.

Mann's appearance at the legation was recorded in his journal by Benjamin Moran, the assistant secretary there, who was well-placed to observe events. He noted disapprovingly:

> Dudley Mann is nearly 60 years of age. He is not more than 5 feet 5, is thick, short and rather heavy. His voice is soft and enunciation slow, with a decided Southern accent. He has a rather good head, but there is not much in him, being like most Southern men, a mere talker...[2]

Despite his previous experience, Dudley Mann was not a particularly good choice as a diplomat. Verbosity was not his only failing; he was tactless, as his presumptuous appearance at the U.S. legation demonstrated, credulous, indecisive and not overendowed with common sense. One historian has described him as "full of words and wind" and having "great vanity and ego."[3]

Benjamin Moran had further reason to exercise his disapproval when, nine days later, a telegram came, addressed to Mann, announcing that his colleagues, William Yancey and Pierre Rost, had also arrived. Yancey and Rost, who had left New Orleans at the end of March, reached London on April 29, where William Thompson, the American consul at Southampton, had obligingly engaged rooms for them, an act for which he was later to be severely censured.

William Lowndes Yancey was born in Georgia in 1814. Like Dudley Mann, he had studied law and in 1836 established a practice in Dallas County, Alabama, where he also rented a cotton plantation. In the 1840s he served in both the Alabama state legislature and the U.S. House of Representatives. Well-known for his support for states rights, he had advocated secession as early as 1858, and had come to be regarded as one of the most important orators in the South. At the inauguration of Jefferson Davis at Montgomery, Alabama, in February 1861, Yancey had introduced him with the words: "The man and the hour have met."

However, as a leading defender of slavery, he was an even worse choice than Dudley Mann, and certainly not the man to send to a country renowned for its dislike of the "peculiar institution." Robert Bunch, the British consul at Charleston, had met both Mann and Yancey; he dismissed the former as having no special merit of any kind, and described the latter as "impulsive, erratic and hot-headed, a rabid Secessionist."[4]

Pierre Adolph Rost was the oldest, but least well-known, of the three men. He was born in Lot-et-Garonne, in southwest France, about 1797, educated in Paris, and emigrated to

Louisiana in 1816, then settled in Natchez, Mississippi. Like Mann and Yancey, he had also read law and after qualifying, practiced for a while in Louisiana, but by the 1850s was managing his plantation there. One of his fellow law students had been Joseph E. Davis, the brother of the future president of the Confederate States, and this, together with his French birth, appears to have been largely responsible for his appointment as a commissioner in 1861. He based himself in Paris, but found he could achieve very little there. The fact that he appeared to have turned his back on France in early life, coupled with his poor French accent, did not create a very good impression in Parisian society, and his boundless optimism and continual use of the phrase "tout va bien" (everything is going well) in answer to every question about the war, soon made him into a figure of fun.

Back in London, one of the commissioners' first visitors was William H. Gregory, M.P. for County Galway, Ireland, through whom an unofficial meeting with Lord John Russell, the foreign secretary, was arranged for May 3, at his house in Chesham Place, Belgravia. William Yancey conducted the interview on their behalf; it lasted an hour, and Russell's response was cautious and noncommittal. A second meeting followed on May 9, which the foreign secretary terminated by saying that he would take up the matter of diplomatic recognition with the cabinet as soon as possible.

That same day Yancey was called on by Joshua Bates, the senior partner at Baring Brothers, an old, established merchant bank in Bishopsgate, which did business with both the Federal government and the Confederate government. Within the bank itself, Bates supported the North, while another partner, Russell Sturgis, favored the South. Bates, a Bostonian who eventually became a British citizen, had been with the bank since 1826 and directed its affairs with "great nerve, self-possession and self-confidence, with prudence and in the main, good judgement." Later that month a report appeared in an American newspaper that the commissioners had approached Barings in search of a loan, but had met with a frosty reception; Bates left them in no doubt about his low opinion of Jefferson Davis, and reminded them of the

A. Dudley Mann was the first Confederate commissioner to arrive in London. (*Illustrated London News*)

millions of dollars owed to the Federal government by the states of Alabama, Mississippi and Florida in prewar repudiated bonds. A second approach, made about the same time by Dudley Mann to another American banker, George Peabody in Old Broad Street, was equally unsuccessful, for much the same reason.[5]

On May 4, William Yancey and Pierre Rost moved to a hotel in Victoria Street. "The Southern commissioners ... [have] recently taken up their quarters at the Westminster Palace Hotel," reported a London newspaper.[6] Twelve days later Yancey moved again, this time to 15 Half Moon Street, off Picadilly, where furnished rooms cost 3 1/2 guineas per week, including such extras as coal fires and gas lights.[7] Dudley Mann had been installed in lodgings in nearby Albemarle Street since at least May 1, and was joined there by his son, William Grayson Mann, who had arrived on May 17 with dispatches, and was to serve as his private secretary. Yancey's secretary, John Walker Fearn of Alabama, was already in London, having traveled with him and Rost. An experienced and able man, before the war Fearn had been secretary to the United States legation in Belgium and Mexico. Rost, meanwhile, proceeded to Paris.

Yancey had a letter of introduction to William S. Lindsay, another leading pro–Confederate M.P., by whom he was invited to the Houses of Parliament, where he met a number of members. Some sightseeing was not ruled out, and included visits to the Zoological Gardens in Regent's Park, the Tower of London, and trips downriver to Greenwich for a traditional whitebait supper, and Woolwich, with its great dockyard and arsenal. Early June saw him in Paris, where a number of Confederates were already living.

The new U.S. minister, Charles Francis Adams, reached London on May 13 and took over from George M. Dallas. The son of John Quincy Adams, sixth president of the United States, who was himself a former U.S. minister to Great Britain, he had practiced as a lawyer before being sent to London, and had been a congressman in the three years prior to the Civil War. His arrival coincided with the issue of a Proclamation of Neutrality, which granted belligerent status to the Confederate States, and did little to improve relations between Great Britain and the United States.

Five days after Adams' arrival, the U.S. legation moved from Portland Place to nearby Duke Street; at the beginning of June it moved again, this time to St. George's Place, Hyde Park Corner; then at the end of July, to

William L. Yancey was another of the Confederate commissioners sent to London. (*Illustrated London News*)

The house in Half Moon Street, Mayfair, where Yancey lodged in 1861–1862, during his time in London. (Author's photograph)

Mansfield Street, in the vicinity of Portland Place; finally, after all this upheaval, in April 1862 it relocated to Upper Portland Place, close to Regent's Park, where it was to remain until after the war.

The first reports of the Federal rout at Manassas (Bull Run), which appeared in the *Times* on August 5, caused a great stir. "The sensation produced by those great events both here and in Paris was profound, and has tended to produce a conviction that the Confederate States cannot be brought back into the Union by arms," Yancey wrote to Secretary of State Robert M.T. Hunter.[8] Rost, who was now in Paris, was telegraphed to rejoin his colleagues in London, with a view to another meeting with Lord John Russell about diplomatic recognition.

Russell refused to see them and asked them to put any further communication in writing.[9] This they did on August 14, in a long letter written from Half Moon Street, which embodied the Confederacy's desire for recognition by the British government. The foreign secretary's carefully worded reply, ten days later, was that Britain must wait until a military solution or a negotiated settlement resolved the present situation, and in the meantime must maintain her neutrality.

Benjamin Moran was disgusted by the way in which William Yancey and Dudley Mann were being made welcome in London, and wined and dined. On November 9 they were guests of honor at a dinner at Fishmongers' Hall, in London, and Yancey's speech, punctuated by cries of "hear, hear" and cheers, was reported in the *Times*:

> One thing is clear, and that is that the contest now going on is upon the people of the Confederate States for the right to govern themselves, and to resist subjugation by the North ... In defence of their liberties and sovereign independence, the Confederate States and people are united and resolute. They are invaded by a power numbering 20,000,000; yet for eight months has the Confederate Government successfully resisted — aye repelled — that invasion, along a frontier of 1,000 miles.[10]

He went on to deny any wish for foreign intervention. Earlier he had expressed his thanks for the granting of belligerent status to the Confederate States. He understood there might be delays in recognition, but that each nation would grant it when the time was right. Peace with the North would come, he felt, when it recognized the Confederate States as a belligerent power, and not as rebels.

By early autumn, the Confederate government having decided to disband the original commission, Pierre Rost had been appointed commissioner to Spain and Dudley Mann to Belgium; William Yancey, who had been reluctant to come to Europe in the first place, had concluded that the Confederates could never expect any sympathy or help there, and decided to resign and return to the Confederacy. Two new commissioners, James M. Mason and John Slidell, both states-rights Democrats, were appointed for London and Paris. Until they arrived, Yancey, Rost and Mann were to remain in their present posts.

Born in the District of Columbia in 1798, James Murray Mason was a lawyer who had practiced in Winchester, Virginia, before entering the realm of politics in 1826. He served at both local and national levels and became a senator in 1847. John Slidell was born in New York in 1793, but moved to New Orleans in 1819, where he also became a lawyer as well as a prominent figure in Louisiana politics; he was elected to the Senate in 1853. Unlike Mason, Slidell had previously traveled abroad, having been sent to Mexico on a diplomatic mission in the 1840s, and England in 1853, as a financial agent for the New Orleans & Nashville Railroad.

Fishmongers' Hall. William Yancey and Dudley Mann were guests at a dinner here given by the Fishmongers' Company in November 1861. (Author's photograph)

In October 1861 Mason and Slidell successfully ran the Union blockade of Charleston in the *Theodora* and sailed for Havana, Cuba. From here they were to travel in the British mail steamer *Trent* to St. Thomas, in the British West Indies, where they would catch a connecting steamer for England. The news of the stopping of the *Trent* by the USS *San Jacinto*, the forcible removal of the two commissioners and their secretaries, on the middle leg of their journey, and their subsequent imprisonment at Boston reached London on November 27.

It provoked a wave of indignation, and was almost universally condemned; only one London paper, the *Morning Star*, thought the action of the *San Jacinto* was justifiable.[11] This violation of the British flag created an international crisis, which threatened to erupt into war with the United States. Troops were dispatched for the defense of Canada — it was reported that as one troopship left the Mersey, a regimental band was playing "Dixie"— and a royal proclamation prohibited any further exports of arms, ammunition and military stores.

Pierre Rost was again in Paris when he learned of the incident and he returned to London at once. Further letters were sent by the commissioners to Lord John Russell about this, and the effectiveness of the blockade, to be answered by a tart little note stating, "in the present state of affairs, he must decline to enter into any official communication with them."[12] In the meantime, a false sense of optimism had been created in Confederate circles, both in London and elsewhere; South Carolina diarist Mary Chesnut thought that something good was bound to come from such a stupid blunder on the part of the United States, while Dudley Mann felt that recognition by the British government could not be far away, and said so in a letter to Richmond at the beginning of December.

The possibility of war, however, was averted when the American cabinet ruled the stopping of the *Trent* to be illegal, and the prisoners were released into British custody at the end of December to continue their journey to Europe. When news of Mason's release and imminent arrival in the metropolis became known, the humorous weekly magazine, *Punch,* marked the occasion with a rhyme:

A Masonic Ditty
Sing high diddle diddle
The colleague of Slidell,
Released from the stone-jug, or basin,
And by England received,
May now be believed,
A free, and an accepted Mason.[13]

Commissioner James M. Mason, who was sent to replace William Yancey and Dudley Mann. (*Illustrated London News*)

James M. Mason and John Slidell, together with their secretaries, James E. McFarland and George Eustis, finally arrived at Southampton on January 29, 1862 in the steamer *La Plata*. In spite of their recent fame as the focus of an international incident, "There was no demonstration whatever when these gentlemen, whose capture in the *Trent* has been the subject of so much discussion, landed at Southampton, there being nothing more than the ordinary assemblage on the arrival of the mail-steamers. A moderate crowd, as is usual, was collected outside the barriers which are always placed until the specie [coinage] and mails are landed," reported the *Illustrated Times*. "Mr Mason," it added, "is rather tall and stout, of tolerably well-formed figure, full colour, and determined and severe expression of countenance. Mr Slidell is a little shorter and stouter, with a round face, and white hair and beard." Confederate propagandist Henry Hotze, who came to England on the same ship as the commissioners, also noted the absence of comment on their arrival; attributing this to their earlier notoriety, he imagined that "it was thought necessary to discourage and prevent manifestations and demonstrations to which a political significance might be attached."[14]

The commissioners proceeded to London, Mason taking rooms at Fenton's Hotel in St. James's Street; from there he would subsequently move to addresses in Piccadilly, Devonshire Street and finally Upper Seymour Street. Slidell, meanwhile, made arrangements to continue his journey to Paris.

With the arrival of their replacements, the original commissioners departed. While abroad, William Yancey had been elected to the Confederate Senate and he returned to the South in February 1862 to take his seat. Disillusionment had set in. As early as July 1861 he had written to a friend: "The anti-slavery sentiment is universal. 'Uncle Tom's Cabin' has been read and believed"; and someone who knew him described him as "the most broken-up, demoralized, and wretched-looking man I ever saw."[15]

Pierre Rost, accompanied by John Fearn, departed for Madrid, but found no more success there than in Paris. The Spanish foreign minister refused to see him, and this, together with poor health, led to his resignation in May 1862. He retired to Fumel, a small town in southwest France, where he remained until the end of the war, and Fearn returned to the Confederacy.

Though appointed to Brussels, Dudley Mann decided to remain in London for the time being, thinking that, as Parliament was about to meet, he might be of more use there. When he did finally proceed to the Continent, he found the Belgian government also unwilling to receive or communicate with him, and he was equally unsuccessful when he visited Denmark; even his attempt to get the Vatican to impede the Federal recruitment of Irish and German Catholics was unsuccessful, though the pope received his request courteously. As a result, he seems to have spent much of his time contributing articles to English and Belgian newspapers and journals.

James Mason's ten years' experience as chairman of the Senate Foreign Relations Committee, and therefore presumably with some knowledge of European affairs, made him seem a better choice than his predecessors. But, like Yancey, he was also tainted by slavery, in his case as the author of the Fugitive Slave Act of 1850, and even someone as well disposed towards him as Mary Chesnut, who thought him "a manly old Virginian — straightforward, brave, truthful, clever," was appalled by his appointment:

> My wildest imagination will not picture Mr. Mason as a diplomat ... Well, this sending Mr. Mason to London is the maddest thing yet. Worse in some points of view than Yancey — and that was a catastrophe! ... You know it set all the world a-laughing when we sent Mr. Mason abroad as a *diplomat*! ... They say at the lordliest table Mr. Mason will turn round halfway in his chair and spit in the fire![16]

Further disparaging remarks came from Henry Adams, the son of Charles Francis Adams, and his unofficial private secretary, who in June 1862 wrote his brother, then serving with the Union Army: "I hear very little about our friend Mason ... He has little or no attention paid him except as a matter of curiosity, though occasionally we are told of his being at dinner somewhere or other."[17] Many years later, he expressed surprise that Jefferson Davis had chosen him: "The Confederacy had plenty of excellent men to send to London, but few who were less fitted than Mason. Possibly Mason had a certain amount of common sense, but he seemed to have nothing else, and in London society he counted merely as one eccentric more."[18] Benjamin Moran also thought Mason highly unsuitable, "the unfittest man they could have sent here ... an ignominious failure. His antecedents were bad, his associates were questionable, and his manners vulgar."[19]

Yet James Mason's mood at the start of his mission was remarkably optimistic. The day after his arrival, he wrote Secretary of State Robert M. T. Hunter: "Now with but a day's experience in London, my impressions decidedly are that, although the ministry may hang back in regard to the blockade and recognition ... the popular voice, through the House of Commons, will demand both."[20]

He lost no time in arranging an unofficial meeting with the foreign secretary, Lord John Russell. They met on February 10, but Lord Russell was not encouraging, and Mason concluded, wrongly as it happens, that his personal sympathies were not with the Confederates and that he was pursuing a policy of inaction; it was to be their only meeting. In the following months, he would liaise with purchasing agents, cooperate with propagandists, be involved in the raising of money for the Confederate cause, and correspond with the British government about the blockade, recognition and ironclads.

In addition, Mason greatly enjoyed the social life of the metropolis and cultivated the friendship of leading figures in the world of politics and commerce. His private memorandum book, in effect his diary, shows he dined with various members of the Southern lobby in Parliament, such as William H. Gregory, Sir James Fergusson, Sir Edward Kerrison and Lord Campbell; bankers like John S. Gilliat; John W. Cowell, "a retired gentleman of family," who had published a pro–Confederate pamphlet; and the veteran radical M.P. Richard Cobden, "decidedly Northern in his sympathies, but deploring the war." He met the Marquess of Bath, "an intelligent and accomplished young gentleman," whom he later visited at his seat at Longleat, in Wiltshire, attended a reception at Stafford House, the Duke of Sutherland's London residence, and had meetings with people as diverse as royal physician Sir Henry Holland, novelist Mrs. Caroline Norton and Prince Oscar of Sweden, who "expressed himself earnestly on the Southern side."[21]

He certainly did not lack for invitations, and on February 11, 1863, was a guest at the Lord Mayor's banquet at the Mansion House in London, where, in response to calls from the assembled gathering, he made an impromptu speech:

> I am a stranger in London — or, rather, I was a stranger; but I have learnt since I came to London that none of English blood from my own Southern land are strangers among you. (cheers) I speak this from my heart (cheers), for I have been by every circle in England and by every class of society a welcomed and honoured guest. (cheers) ... The day will come (great cheering) — and it is not far off— when the relationship between that Government which is now in its infant fortune and yours will be one of close and intimate alliance. (renewed cheers)[22]

A member of the audience wrote a friend the following day: "I was at the Mansion House last night and heard the Lord Mayor virtually recognize the South in the quietest and most inoffensive way that could be imagined. The *Times* gives a very good report of what Mr. Mason said, but no description can picture the effect of his calm and dignified delivery of these simple sentences."[23]

The home of Foreign Secretary Lord John Russell in Chesham Place, Belgravia. William Yancey, Pierre Rost and Dudley Mann visited him here in May 1861 and James Mason in February 1862. (Author's photograph)

At the beginning of March 1863 yet another Confederate commissioner arrived in London. He was Lucius Quintus Cincinnatus Lamar, who came from an old, established Georgia family. Born there in 1825, he moved to Mississippi after training as a lawyer and in the 1850s was elected to Congress. At the outbreak of the Civil War he served for a while in the Confederate Army until ill health forced his resignation in October 1862. The following month he was appointed commissioner to Russia. He was accompanied as secretary by John Fearn, who had previously worked with William Yancey in London and Pierre Rost in Madrid. Lamar and Fearn moved to Paris in April, but while there it was learned that their mission to Russia was unwelcome and it was terminated in June. For several months Lamar assisted with propaganda activities in London before returning to the Confederacy with Fearn towards the end of 1863.

Lucius Lamar seems to have been a more able and talented man than James Mason, and Henry Adams, who came to know him in the 1880s, concluded, "he would have done better in London, in place of Mason. London society would have delighted in him; his stories would have won success; his manners would have made him loved; his oratory would have swept every audience."[24]

A curious correspondence between James Mason and the Rev. Moncure Daniel Conway appeared in the *Times* in June 1863. Though he was the son of a Virginia slave-owner, Conway was an antislavery agitator and had arrived in England that year to lecture on behalf of Northern abolitionists. He proposed that, if the Confederate States would emancipate their slaves, "then the Abolitionists and Anti-slavery leaders of the Northern States shall immediately oppose the prosecution of the war ... and since they hold the balance of power, will certainly cause the war to cease by the immediate withdrawal of every kind of support from it."[25] Mason questioned Conway's authority for this sweeping claim, confirming that in any case the South would never negotiate with the North, and his unauthorized proposal also caused some embarrassment in abolitionist circles, from whom an overture of this kind would have been highly unlikely. Conway chose to remain in London, becoming pastor of South Place Chapel, Finsbury, a post he was to hold for more than twenty years.

In September 1863 James Mason informed Foreign Secretary Lord John Russell that he was "directed to withdraw at once from the country," the Confederate government having decided that their commissioner would never be recognized in London. "Mr. Mason has been very solemnly withdrawn from here on the grounds that Lord Russell treats him with hauteur," the U.S. minister wrote his soldier son that month.[26] On September 30 Mason left London for Paris, where he would now be based as a commissioner-at-large, or as he described it, "Commissioner on the Continent."

In Paris, his colleague, John Slidell, whose knowledge of the French language and customs had helped secure his appointment, had made a better impression than Pierre Rost. On his arrival in February 1862 he had been warmly welcomed by Confederate sympathizers, and had set up home in the Avenue d'Antin, with an office in the Rue de Marignan. He had two interviews with Napoleon III, at Vichy in July and at St. Cloud in October, though neither produced any material results, as the emperor was unwilling to act without Britain in recognizing the Confederacy. Slidell's proposal for a Franco-Confederate treaty came to nothing, and arrangements made in conjunction with naval purchasing agent James Bulloch in 1863 for the construction of two ironclads at Bordeaux and four wooden corvettes at Nantes were thwarted, following protests from the U.S. minister in Paris, William L. Dayton. He did, however, make an important contribution to the negotiations for the Confederate Cotton Loan earlier that year.

James Mason returned to London briefly about mid–October 1863 to clear up some outstanding matters, and he made a number of subsequent visits to London, during one of which, on July 14, 1864, there was an unofficial meeting with the prime minister, Lord Palmerston, at his residence, Cambridge House, Piccadilly. Towards the end of that month he embarked on a tour of Scotland and Ireland, stopping at Leamington Spa, Warwickshire, where a number of Confederate families were living, on the way back to London in September. The following month he paid a visit to the Confederate Bazaar held in St. George's Hall, Liverpool, in aid of the Southern Prisoners' Relief Fund.

News of the Confederate defeats at Franklin and Nashville reached London during December 1864, together with that of Sherman's occupation of Savannah. Even worse was to follow: on January 31, 1865, the *Times* reported the capture of Fort Fisher, at the mouth of the Cape Fear River in North Carolina, effectively closing Wilmington, the last major Confederate port, which surrendered within weeks.

When reports of the Hampton Roads Peace Conference were received in London in the middle of the following month, they caused consternation of a different kind:

> The public funds fell ... You would have thought that a great calamity had befallen the good people of England ... Happily for the distressed nerves of our friends, the next day brought them a little relief. A steamer had come with ... later news. It was not so bad as they had feared ... There would be no peace. Hurrah. The papers this morning are all congratulating the public that the war will go on indefinitely.[27]

The abandonment of Fort Sumter, where the war had started, and the evacuation of Charleston, reported on March 4, had an even more dramatic effect: "The news of the fall of Charleston has made a profound impression here. It is greater, perhaps, than any other event of the war," Charles Francis Adams wrote the secretary of state.[28]

As far back as the autumn of 1863 there had been rumors that the South was planning to arm and liberate some of its slaves for military and perhaps diplomatic reasons, while more recently similar ideas were being openly discussed in the Confederate press. "Richmond papers assert," stated the *Times* in January 1865, "that England and France would recognize the South upon conditions of negro emancipation, and urge that a proposition to that effect should be made to those Powers." Gladstone was no doubt expressing the feelings of many when, a few days after Appomattox, he wrote a friend that, had the Southerners been able to dissociate their cause from slavery by actually or virtually abolishing it, then his sympathies would have been with them.[29] The *Index*, previously a supporter of slavery, now prepared to support the proposal, arguing: "If it be necessary to convince the world that we are fighting for the self-government of the whites, that we should liberate the negroes, and if that liberation can be made to secure our independence, we believe that the people of these [Confederate] States would not hesitate to make the sacrifice."[30]

It was against this background that Duncan Farrar Kenner, a wealthy Louisiana sugar planter and horse breeder, and a member of the Confederate Congress, arrived in London at the end of February 1865. Traveling in disguise via New York, he had been sent as a special envoy by President Davis, and with him he carried the secret proposal to emancipate the slaves in return for diplomatic recognition.[31] Born in New Orleans in 1813, Kenner was himself a major slave-owner, but had long been convinced that European recognition was vital for Confederate success, and that it would only come if slavery was abolished.

Finding that James Mason was in Paris, Duncan Kenner proceeded there. Mason was initially reluctant to heed the instructions contained in Kenner's dispatch, in view of the deteriorating military situation, and the firm stand the British government had so far taken against recognition, but he eventually agreed to return to London. Here, Kenner and Mason obtained an interview with Lord Palmerston, who told them that their proposition could not be considered without the agreement of the emperor of the French. Kenner accordingly went back to Paris and secured an interview with the emperor; France, he was told, would do what England was willing to do in this matter, but would do nothing without her. By the time Kenner returned to London for a second meeting with Palmerston on March 14, news had arrived of Sherman's march through the Carolinas. The prime minister's reply was unequivocal: at no time had his government been convinced that Confederate independence could be achieved beyond all doubt, and now it was too late to grant recognition, whatever the terms might be.

Almost exactly a month later, on April 15, 1865, Benjamin Moran wrote in his diary: "Early this morning I got news of the capture of Richmond and Petersburg. This has staggered the English rebel sympathizers here. They give the rebels up now."[32] The *Times* purported to think otherwise, claiming: "The event has been anticipated not only in America, but in this country for some time past."[33] Three days later, in a letter to Secretary of State William H. Seward, Charles Francis Adams nevertheless confirmed: "The disappointment is undisguised. One of the daily journals correctly affirms of the higher circles that few expected, and still fewer desired the result."[34] In the early hours of April 23, 1865, a Reuter's telegram was received in London: General Lee had surrendered. "We this day received the grand news of Lee's surrender," noted Moran triumphantly in his journal.[35]

In what was to be his last dispatch as Confederate commissioner, James Mason wrote Secretary of State Judah Benjamin (a letter he was destined never to receive): "The evacuation of Richmond and surrender of Lee has produced the confident belief here, and throughout Europe generally, that further resistance is hopeless and that the war is at an end, to be followed on our part by passive submission to our fate. I need not say that I entertain no such impression and endeavor as far as I can to disabuse the public mind."[36] Writing many years after the war, James Bulloch echoed that view, observing: "Even in Europe it was not universally thought that the surrender of General Lee would immediately end the war," though he added that it was soon obvious to Confederates abroad who knew the real state of affairs in the South that the end had come; there could be no recovery.[37]

The Confederate government was unfortunate in the men it chose to represent it in London, but would it have made any difference, had it been a wiser choice? The answer is, probably not. Although for a brief period in the late summer of 1862, the British cabinet was indeed considering the possibility of extending diplomatic recognition to the Confederate States, the news of Antietam raised doubts in their minds and Lincoln's preliminary Emancipation Proclamation a few days later ended the possibility.

3

The Propaganda War

Few suspect, none know, the silent, unobtrusive agency through which it [the Index] has operated upon its contemporaries.
— Henry Hotze, August 27, 1863

Henry Hotze was to be the key figure in Confederate propaganda activities in London, and indeed in Europe, but books and pamphlets supporting the Confederacy were already being published before he appeared on the scene. One of the earliest and most important of these was James Spence's *The American Union* (1861). According to its author, a wealthy Liverpool tin and iron merchant, it was written in fourteen weeks, and it argued the right of the Southern states to secede, and the inevitability of secession, given the differences between North and South. It was seen as a major piece of Confederate propaganda, in spite of its condemnation of slavery. "It has attracted more attention and been more generally read both here and on the Continent than any production of like character of the many that have appeared," observed James Mason to Secretary of State Judah P. Benjamin.[1]

That was not an exaggeration, as favorable reviews in publications like the *Quarterly Review*, the *Athenaeum* and the *Times* demonstrated. On December 21, 1861, *All the Year Round*, the weekly magazine edited by Charles Dickens, commented: "Mr. Spence has assembled facts and authorities in support of his reasoning, and has grouped them with a temperate and logical clearness that cannot fail to convince. He writes with the discretion of a judge who has all the evidence before him, strong and honest in his own convictions." *The American Union* went through four editions in six months, and was translated into French and German.[2]

John W. Cowell's *Southern Secession: A Letter addressed to Captain M. F. Maury, Confederate Navy* (1862) attributed the war to Northern attempts to rob the South through protective tariffs, and described "the genuine Yankee nature" as "that amalgam of hypocrisy, cruelty, falsehood ... insensibility to the opinions of others, utter callousness to right, barbarous delight in wrong, and thoroughly moral ruffianism."[3] John Welsford Cowell, an economist who had served on both the Poor Law Commission and the Factory Commission, had been sent to the United States in 1837 as a representative of the Bank of England to collect money owed by American firms. He remained there until 1839, during which time he met many important Americans and came home convinced that Southern secession was inevitable.

Particularly influential was Alexander James Beresford Hope's *The American Disruption*, which also appeared in 1862. It contained the texts of three lectures — "A Popular View of the

American Civil War," "England, the North and the South" and "The Results of the American Disruption"—which had been published separately the previous year, the overriding theme of which was that Confederate independence was in Britain's best interests. Like James Spence, Beresford Hope was opposed to "the abominable institution of slavery," but this did not affect his support for the South. *The American Disruption* was a remarkably successful book, with no fewer than six editions in one year.

Alexander James Beresford Hope was an important figure in London Confederate circles. Born in 1820, he was a man of considerable wealth and culture and had commissioned the famous London church of All Saints', Margaret Street (built during 1850–1859 and designed by William Butterfield), as well as founding the influential *Saturday Review*. He was also the brother-in-law of Lord Robert Cecil, a leading member of the Southern lobby in the House of Commons. Beresford Hope himself had been an M.P. from 1841 through 1852 and again from 1857 through 1859, but he was not to return to Parliament until 1865 when the Civil War was over.

The steamer which brought Mason and Slidell to England on January 29, 1862, also carried Henry Hotze, the newly-appointed commercial agent for the Confederate States of America. Henry Hotze was born in Zurich, Switzerland, in 1834 and emigrated to the United States in early life, settling in Mobile, Alabama, where he became a naturalized citizen in 1856. After an appointment as secretary at the U.S., legation in Brussels in 1858–1859, he served as associate editor of the *Mobile Register* from 1859 to 1861. Following a short spell of service in the Confederate Army, as a member of the Mobile Cadets, which became part of the Third Alabama, he was sent to London in September 1861 by Secretary of War Leroy P. Walker to check on the purchase of arms and munitions; he also carried dispatches for William Yancey and Dudley Mann. The experience convinced him of the need for a Confederate propaganda offensive.

Alexander Beresford Hope, a Confederate supporter and early propagandist for the Southern cause. (*Cassell's Illustrated Family Paper*)

On his return to Richmond in November, he was appointed to the post of commercial agent, with a subsidiary role of organizing Southern propaganda. His instructions from Robert M. T. Hunter, the secretary of state, stated: "You will be diligent and earnest in your efforts to impress upon the public mind abroad the ability of the Confederate States to maintain their independence, and to this end you will publish whatever information you possess calculated to convey a just idea of their ample resources and vast military strength and to raise their character and Government in general estimation."[4] What Hotze regarded as his real mission was largely self-instigated; propaganda had not yet assumed a very high priority with his political masters, who probably had little understanding of what was required. It would be the greatest challenge of his career.

The need to counteract the "official," i.e., U.S., version of events in America, and so help promote the Confederate cause, had become considerably more pressing in the autumn of 1861, when Secretary of State William H. Seward had sent Thurlow Weed to Europe as a propaganda agent, and John Bigelow, who had been appointed U.S. consul general in Paris, had been given the job of coordinating Northern propaganda in Europe. Both were capable and experienced former journalists.

The prospect before Henry Hotze was daunting: "I confess that the nearer I approached the scene of my labors the more the difficulties of my position loomed up before me, and on arriving here as the advocate of our case through the most fastidious press in the world, a stranger with barely a few friends or introductory letters, with no extensive political or literary reputation to precede me and smooth my way, I felt almost disheartened," he wrote the secretary of state on 23 February 1862.[5] He took rooms initially in Bury Street, St. James's, before setting up his commercial agency in Savile Row.

Hotze lost no time in making contact with newspapers thought to be sympathetic to the Confederate cause and offering to write for them. His first contribution, on February 22, was a leader in the *Morning Post* (the mouthpiece of the Liberal prime minister, Lord Palmerston), describing the inauguration of Jefferson Davis as president of the Confederate States, a copy of which he sent to Richmond. It was published largely unaltered, "only one or two expressions being somewhat enfeebled," he observed, and "produced a deep impression in the clubs."[6] This was followed by others in the *Standard* and the *Morning Herald*, which represented the views of Lord Derby, leader of the Conservative opposition.

He was pleased with the result: "Now the most formidable obstacles are overcome. The columns of the journals to which I most desired access are open to me, and with this I have acquired the secret of the 'open sesame' of the others I may need." The next stage of his plan was to present his articles to professional "leader writers," the freelance journalists who wrote regularly for those papers, "thus conciliating friendly goodwill where otherwise annoying jealousies might arise."[7]

One of his earliest allies was Thomas Hamber, chief editor of the *Morning Herald* and the *Standard*, a colorful character who was known in Fleet Street as "Captain Hamber" or the "Swiss Captain." He was so called because he had been an officer in the British Swiss Legion, three regiments of light infantry which were raised as mercenaries to fight in the Crimean War (1854–1856). Having only got as far as the Turkish town of Smyrna (present-day Izmir) by the end of the war, he apparently did not see active service, though one of his foreign correspondents thought that he "looked every inch a fighting soldier."[8] He was a staunch supporter of the South, and during the Civil War the *Standard* became renowned for its "Manhattan Letters," written by the paper's New York correspondent, Joseph A. Scoville. So critical were they of the Federal government that at one stage their author was arrested and imprisoned. The effect of them in London was to increase the paper's circulation dramatically.

Addressing the new secretary of state, Judah P. Benjamin, on April 25, 1862, Hotze was able to write: "Two more newspapers, the *Herald* ... and the *Standard* ... have voluntarily placed themselves at my disposal. The editor-in-chief of both called on me and offered the use of

The offices of the Confederate States Commercial Agency in Savile Row, Mayfair. (Author's photograph)

the columns of both, including the editorial columns, of which offer I have, though guardedly, availed myself."⁹ Thereafter, the *Standard* was assured of a regular supply of news items about the Confederacy.

There was certainly no lack of demand for what Hotze had to offer. "All information concerning the South, and especially the material and organisation of our armies, is eagerly sought by the leader writers who find a profitable market for it in the journals and magazines with which they are connected. One writer usually writes for several publications, and I have thus the opportunity of multiplying myself, so to speak, to an almost unlimited extent."¹⁰

In spite of his success with his fellow journalists, Hotze felt that something more was needed to promote the Confederate cause. Accordingly, he wrote Judah Benjamin:

> I have now ... concluded to establish a newspaper wholly devoted to our interests, and which will be exclusively under my control, though my connection with it is known only to a few initiated and will not be suspected by the public at large ... The assistance of two personal friends, Mr H. O. Brewer of Mobile, and Mr A.P. Wetter of Savannah, together with my private resources, enabled me to overcome the pecuniary difficulties of the enterprise and to place its publication for at least three months ... beyond the possibility of failure.¹¹

The *Index*, "A Weekly Journal of Politics, Literature, and News devoted to the Exposition of the Mutual Interests, Political and Commercial, of Great Britain and the Confederate States of America," first appeared on Thursday, May 1, 1862, and in his first leader Hotze set out its aims:

> The manners and customs of the Confederate States, their resources and capabilities, and the real status of their people in the work of civilization, are still a sealed book to the intelligence of Europe ... If to this sealed book, which contains much worth studying, "The Index" can act that humble part which is intended to awake the interest of an indifferent reader, and induce him to turn over the pages, we shall have attained the highest reward of our labors...¹²

Each issue consisted of sixteen pages, containing events of the week, at home and abroad, the latest direct intelligence from the South, correspondence from Richmond, Charleston and New Orleans, leaders, extracts from Northern and Southern newspapers, cotton market news, Confederate state papers, book reviews and advertisements. Such topics as the Lancashire cotton famine, statistics on blockade-running, and the peace movement in the North were also featured from time to time. On May 15, Hotze sent copies of the first three issues to Judah Benjamin: "Nearly all of Southern talent available in Europe is rallied to its intellectual assistance," he wrote enthusiastically.¹³

While conveying the Confederate viewpoint, the *Index* was able to provide its readers with a much-needed Southern news service. As early as July 1861, Commissioner William Yancey, aware of the lack of information about events in the South, had suggested that files of the leading Richmond, Charleston and New Orleans papers should be kept and forwarded to the commission as opportunity allowed, and in April 1862 James Mason was told that this would be done "if possible." Some Southern newspapers were by then apparently available at Gun's American Agency and Reading Room in the Strand.

Henry Adams, the son of the U.S. minister, was inevitably unimpressed: "A Southern newspaper called the *Index* lately started here, contains numbers of Southern letters, all of which are so excruciatingly 'never conquer' in their tone, that one is forced to the belief that they think themselves very near that last ditch," he wrote his brother in June 1862.¹⁴

Index,

A Weekly Journal of Politics, Literature, and News devoted to the Exposition of the Mutual Interests Political and Commercial, of Great Britain and the Confederate States of America.

Published every Thursday Afternoon. Price 6d. Subscription 26s.

Office---13, Bouverie-street, Fleet-street, London, E. C.

The INDEX contains the Events of the Week at Home and Abroad. Latest Direct Intelligence from the South. Correspondence from New York. Correspondence from Richmond, Charleston, and New Orleans. Leaders on topics of Interest. Gleanings from the Northern and Southern Press. The Cotton and Dry Goods Market. Affairs, Financial and Commercial. Confederate State Papers. Reviews of Books. Magazine Articles. Southern Statistics, &c.

The INDEX enjoys an extensive and influential circulation in Great Britain, the Continent, the West Indies, and the Northern and Southern States of America. It goes into the hands of Shippers, Merchants, Members of both Houses of Parliament, &c. and all who, through business interests, political pursuits, or personal sympathy, are concerned in the great Transatlantic questions now in process of solution.

Money Orders to be made payable to J. B. Hopkins, 13, Bouverie-street, Fleet-street, E. C.

A contemporary description of the Index. (*Mitchell's Newspaper Press Directory*, 1864)

The *Index* was first published by William Freeman at 102 Fleet Street and printed by Henry F. Mackintosh in nearby Crane Court, but from October 30, 1862 it was issued from 13 Bouverie Street, where Mackintosh became both publisher and printer. On March 10, 1864 the journalist John Baker Hopkins, who had been engaged originally as the paper's business manager, became the publisher, with George A. Spottiswoode as the printer. Observing that "our offices in Bouverie Street [two rooms] have long been too confined for the transaction of our business," it moved later that year to 291 Strand, from where it was published from October 27, 1864 until it ceased publication the following year.

Although it claimed an extensive circulation in Great Britain, the Continent, the West Indies, and the Northern and Southern states of America, it was in fact fairly small — 2,250 copies at the end of 1864, according to the *Newspaper Press Directory* of that year, of which 400 were sent to the Northern states and 150 to France. This was approximately half that of other small-circulation London papers, like the *Morning Post* (4,500), the *Morning Star* (5,500) and the *Daily News* (6,000). (Newspapers like the the *Times* [70,000], the *Standard* [130,000] and the *Daily Telegraph* [150,000] were, of course, in a different league.)[15] The chief consideration was that the *Index* should reach the people who were thought to matter, and this seems to be borne out by the *Newspaper Press Directory*'s comment: "It goes into the hands of shippers, merchants, Members of both Houses of Parliament, etc, and all who ... are concerned in the great transatlantic questions now in process of solution."

From the outset, the *Index* went out of its way to emphasize the social, cultural and economic ties that were thought to exist between the Confederate States and Great Britain. The economic relationship received particular attention, and it was pointed out that the abolition of slavery would seriously curtail the production of cotton for the British market. The paper never set out to apologize for slavery, which was portrayed as being advantageous to both races; indeed, it was asserted, the South "had been the friend and benefactor of the negro race."[16] Late in the war, it accepted that arming some of the slaves, in conjunction with partial emancipation, might be required in order to secure Southern independence; total emancipation, as embodied in the Kenner mission, was seen as neither necessary nor desirable.

Following the usual journalistic practice of the time, none of the contributions to the *Index* was signed. Apart from those written by Henry Hotze himself, which included almost all those relating to slavery, some were presumably by John Hopkins, "my manager and assistant ... an Englishman who has zealously and successfully applied himself to the study of the great question involved in the independence of the South."[17] In addition, material came from a small group of American and English contributors in London, correspondents in Europe and America, private letters, and other newspapers, both English and foreign. "At least half the articles in the Index," wrote Hotze, "are written by Englishmen, who, only a few months ago, had but imperfect knowledge of and little active sympathy with the South."[18]

Among the American contributors were Robert B. Campbell, Albert T. Bledsoe, James Williams, Hiram Fuller and John L. O'Sullivan. Robert Blair Campbell, a South Carolinian and former congressman, had been U.S. consul in Havana, Cuba, from 1842 until 1850, and in London, from 1854 until 1861. When the administration changed, he was recalled, but returned to London to assist Henry Hotze. His death in July 1862, however, meant that his contribution to the propaganda war was short-lived.[19]

Albert Taylor Bledsoe was from Kentucky. A former college professor and lawyer, he had served in the Confederate War Department, first as Head of the Bureau of War, then as assistant secretary of war, before coming to London in October 1863. His mission there was to research and write the definitive justification of secession and he wrote President Davis: "After reading all the speeches in Congress, on both sides, I was profoundly ignorant of the transcendent merits of our cause ... No cause, in my humble opinion, so great and so glorious, has ever been so feebly advocated by the pen, or so nobly advocated by the sword."[20]

A native of Tennessee, James Williams had had experience of journalism as well as diplomacy, having founded and edited the *Knoxville Post* in the 1840s and served as U.S. minister to Turkey from 1858 through 1860. In 1861 he came to London, where he wrote influential articles about the slavery question for the *Times* and the *Standard*, as well as the *Index*. Some of Williams's essays, published in America in 1861 under the title *Letters on Slavery from the Old World*, were reissued the following year in an expanded English edition as *The South Vindicated*, with an introduction by John Hopkins, and were also translated into German. Benjamin Moran, who recorded seeing him with James Mason at the House of Commons one day in July 1863, described them both in distinctly unflattering terms as coarse, gross, ponderous, vulgar-looking men.

A New York newspaper editor from Massachusetts, Hiram Fuller's increasingly pro–Southern views made it advisable for him to leave America when the Civil War started. In London, in December 1861, he gave a lecture about secession and its causes at the St. James's Hall, Piccadilly, at the time of the *Trent* incident; it was published the following year as *The Causes and Consequences of the Civil War in America*. Between July 1862 and February 1863, under the pseudonym "A White Republican," he also contributed a series of articles to *Fraser's Magazine* which were reissued under the title *North and South* (1863).[21]

Like Hiram Fuller, John Louis O'Sullivan was a Northerner who identified with the Southern cause. He had been educated in France and England as well as America, and also had both journalistic and diplomatic experience. A founder and editor of the *United States Magazine and Democratic Review*, he is credited with the invention in 1845 of the famous phrase "manifest destiny," meaning the right of the United States to expand across the North American continent, and had also served as U.S. minister to Portugal in 1854–1858.

His *Union, Disunion and Reunion*, published in London in 1862 and favorably reviewed by the *Times* and the *Athenaeum*, set out what he saw as the main reasons for the breakup of the Union. It was intended to secure support in the North for the South's actions, but his efforts to get it published there were unsuccessful. The following year two more tracts appeared: *Peace the Sole Chance Now Left for Reunion* urged the Northern Democrats to end the war, because the North would never defeat the South, while *Recognition. A Letter to Lord Palmerston*, published to coincide with the parliamentary debate on Confederate recognition in July 1863, tried to persuade the British government to recognize the Confederacy. O'Sullivan's publications were subsidized by the Confederate propaganda fund; there is also a suggestion that he may have been on the Confederate secret service payroll. Certainly, in 1864, he began negotiations with a Copenhagen banker for the building of Confederate ironclads in Sweden, and though initially very promising, they ultimately proved fruitless.[22]

One of the first English contributors to the *Index* was James Spence, the author of *The American Union*, who was invited by Henry Hotze to write for his new paper. Though he declined any remuneration for this, he suggested to Commissioner James Mason that, as a businessman of many years' standing, with overseas experience, he might instead be considered for appointment as financial agent to the Confederate government.

It was Spence's uncompromising stance on slavery that was partly to blame for the rift with Hotze that occurred shortly after the *Index* began to appear. As he indeed became the

Confederacy's European financial agent, excuses were found, though it was already clear in October 1862 that there were problems. In a letter Hotze wrote to Judah Benjamin he commented: "Mr Spence, I regret to say, has of late rendered the idea of ultimate emancipation unduly conspicuous," adding that, while "Mr Spence is sincere to our cause ... at this juncture of affairs I almost dread the direction his friendship and devotion seem about to take." Not until a year later, when Spence was about to be replaced, was the real reason for the dispute made plain:

> I have differed from Mr Spence on almost all essential points relating to the manner and the means of recommending our cause to the public. For instance I was naturally prone to place perhaps an exaggerated estimate upon the value of *The Index*; he, after the third number, could scarcely bring himself to believe in its usefulness at all ... The fault then that I found with Mr Spence ... was that he assumed to occupy at one and the same time two opposite and irreconcilable positions — that of a high official [financial agent] of our government ... and that of a disinterested alien friend.[23]

It would not be the only time that James Spence would be criticized by prominent Confederates.

As well as writing for the *Index,* Spence also contributed a series of articles to the *Times*. Presented in the form of letters, under the heading, "American Affairs," and signed "S," they were a commentary on the war from a Southern viewpoint. Their author was undoubtedly well-informed about military events, though they contained some wishful thinking and wrongful prognostications. They appeared between February 1862 and January 1865 and were apparently commissioned by the paper. Spence also refused payment for his *Times* articles, but instead accepted a specially-bound set of the *Encyclopedia Britannica* when they were concluded.[24]

Another English contributor was the journalist and novelist Percy Greg, "one of the most talented leader writers of London, who, besides being a valuable contributor to the *Index*, is one of our most efficient supporters in the columns of the *Saturday Review* and other literary and political periodicals of high standing"; he also wrote for the *Standard* and the *Manchester Guardian*.[25] He, too, was to cause problems: after being turned down for the new post of assistant editor in 1864 because of ill health, he submitted a spate of increasingly spiteful and bitter articles which required drastic editing, resulting in even more acrimony.

These instances were not typical, however, and relations with other English contributors such as Thomas Colley Grattan, a travel writer and novelist, who had been British consul at Boston in 1839–1846, were much more harmonious. He was the author of *England and the Disrupted States of America* (1861), which suggested that England should prepare for war and encourage Spain to take the lead in recognizing the South. His work for the *Index* was terminated by his death in 1864.

In addition, there were those "professional leader writers" whom Hotze had been supplying with material for their London newspapers, who now also became contributors to the *Index*. "I have given partial employment by means of the *Index* up to the present time ... to seven writers on the daily London press," he wrote to Benjamin in March 1863. Four of them were "colleagues of one editorial corps" [possibly the *Standard*], and one of them, "the Chief Editor of one of the leading daily journals — for obvious reasons I omit the name."[26] It seems likely that this was Thomas Hamber. Among the others was Thornton Hunt, assistant editor of the *Daily Telegraph* and son of the famous Regency essayist Leigh Hunt. Hotze encouraged them with "little personal compliments such as boxes of cigars imported from Havana ... American Whiskey, and other articles which not being generally procurable, form acceptable presents."[27]

It was a cunning move: the ideas and information which they absorbed as writers on the *Index* would carry over into the articles they supplied to the other papers for which they wrote. The journalists employed by the *Index* were among the leading members of their profession, and through them Hotze was able to infiltrate the columns of some of the most influential publications in the country. His success in this was certainly helped by the fact that, before the *Index* began publication, or even before Hotze himself arrived in London, many journalists had already adopted a pro–Southern stance.

The *Index* received a subsidy from the Confederate government: from May through October 1862 it was $2,206, and from October 1862 through December 1863, $9,675.[28] It was not enough, however, and had to be supplemented by loans and donations from private individuals in Europe and America, and by Hotze himself. When he was first sent to London, he was given an annual contingency budget of only $750, an indication of how relatively unimportant his mission was then seen to be, though this was increased a number of times, and eventually reached $30,000.

Northerners in London also had a weekly newspaper called the *London American*. Established in May 1860, it was published by John Adams Knight and edited by George Haseltine and later by A.W. Bostwick. Each issue usually contained eight pages, and included U.S. and Canadian news, correspondence, details of American arrivals in London, literary notices, American inventions, commercial and shipping news and advertisements. It had not, of course, been founded for propaganda purposes, but with the outbreak of the Civil War it inevitably assumed that additional role with the introduction of a new feature, "Progress of the Great Rebellion." It was published on Wednesdays from a building in Fleet Street, where for some months in 1862 its close neighbor was the *Index*.

Unlike the *Index*, the *London American* received no government support, though it did get some financial assistance from the American George Train, who also made speeches in support of the North, and by October 1862 it was clearly in trouble. The following month, announcing itself as "the only American organ in Europe"— no doubt a dig at the *Index*, which it never actually deigned to mention by name — it appeared under new ownership, and published now from an address in the Strand.

Somewhat surprisingly, Benjamin Moran had a low opinion of it. At the end of January 1863 he noted in his diary that J.A. Knight and A.W. Bostwick, the publisher and editor, had called at the U.S. legation in an attempt to raise money to carry on their paper. It was, he thought, a hopeless scheme and, for all the good it did, their journal might as well cease to exist.[29] The *London American* did indeed die, ceasing publication with the issue of March 4, 1863.

Hotze drove himself hard, and admitted: "My physical as well as intellectual powers sometimes flag from sheer exhaustion from the unremitting strain upon them. My eyes have suffered most, and I am now unable to read small print or to write by artificial light, forced therefore to depend on the aid of a private secretary." In August 1862 he traveled to Germany "to consult oculists of eminence about my eyes, the condition of which from over-exertion had become alarming."[30] While there, he took advantage of the opportunity to arrange for the publication of a cheap edition of a German translation of "Mr Spence's celebrated book" (*The American Union*).

In his diary for July 30, 1862, William Ewart Gladstone, Chancellor of the Exchequer, recorded that he had dined at Lord Campbell's residence and had an interesting conversation with a "Mr Hotze, a Southern [sic] in office."[31] The talk was about the most suitable border between North and South, when Lincoln finally gave up his attempt to force the South back into the Union, and Gladstone sent a memorandum about it to Lord Palmerston; it was useful information for a government then considering mediation. The meeting took place at Stratheden House, Knightsbridge, and Hotze reported it to Secretary of State Benjamin:

> I met, a few days ago, by arrangement, Mr Gladstone, the Chancellor of the Exchequer, at a private dinner table, and had several hours' conversation with him. He is, of all the members of the cabinet, supposed to be the most friendly to us, and his manner and language certainly so impressed me ... The ... other salient feature of Mr Gladstone's conversation was an emphatic prediction that the war would speedily end in the acknowledged independence of the South.[32]

In the spring of 1862 a new propaganda agent appeared on the scene. Born in South Carolina in 1818, Edwin De Leon had been editor of several Southern newspapers before becoming U.S. consul general in Egypt in 1854. He resigned from this post in 1861 to offer his services to the Confederacy, and was appointed chief European propaganda agent by President Davis early the following year. The post carried with it a generous contingency allowance of $25,000, demonstrating the importance that was now being attached to propaganda. At this stage, neither Davis nor De Leon knew of the progress Henry Hotze was already making in this field.

When he reached London at the end of June 1862, De Leon had an interview with Lord Palmerston and also met with James Spence and Henry Hotze. His instructions were to base himself in Paris and conduct propaganda operations from there, with a view to influencing French public opinion, and although he collaborated with Hotze when necessary, the two men disagreed about policy, and criticized each other on a number of occasions. De Leon, like Spence, also thought the *Index* was a waste of time and advised Hotze to discontinue it.

Although De Leon did have some success in influencing the French press, contributed an article to the *Cornhill Magazine* about the ineffectiveness of the blockade, and wrote a pamphlet called *Three Letters from a South Carolinian Relating to Secession, Slavery and the Trent Case*, his contribution to the Confederate propaganda war was relatively short-lived. It came to an end when letters from him containing adverse comments about the French press, and Commissioner John Slidell, with whom he had a very acrimonious relationship, were intercepted on their way through the blockade in November 1863 and published in the *New York Daily Tribune*. His mission was terminated by Secretary of State Judah Benjamin the following month.

Henry Hotze's reponsibility increased considerably after this and now took on a European dimension. Through the Havas News Agency in Paris, he was able to control material about the war which appeared in French newspapers, and he supplied articles to the Italian and German press as well. "Some twenty newspapers in England, the Continent and the North are furnished through me with regular newspaper correspondence," he wrote Judah Benjamin in December 1864.[33]

His most spectacular propaganda initiative was the campaign he orchestrated in June 1863, prior to the debate in the House of Commons about diplomatic recognition of the Confederate States by Great Britain and the other European powers. Colored posters showing the new Confederate flag (the second national flag of 1863) in conjunction with the British flag, appeared in London and the principal towns and cities, as well as at railway stations throughout the country. "I have taken measures to placard every available space in the streets of London with representations of our newly adopted flag, conjoined to the British national ensign," he wrote.[34] In conjunction with the posters, the *Morning Herald* and the *Standard* were persuaded to print leading articles every other day between June 6 and July 1 in support of recognition; and all over London barrel organs could be heard playing the well-known Confederate tune, "The Bonnie Blue Flag." Efforts to combat his poster campaign, at least in the metropolis, were made by the London Emancipation Society and the Ladies' London Emancipation Society.

This was the high-water mark of Confederate hopes in London, and it was all in vain. The motion, introduced to the House of Commons on June 30, was withdrawn on July 13 without ever coming to a vote. Recognition would never again receive serious attention in Parliament, Hotze complained to the secretary of state.

In July 1864, the staff of the *Index* was augmented with the arrival in London of John R. Thompson, formerly the paper's Richmond correspondent, and the appointment in September of that year of John G. Witt as assistant editor. John George Witt, who had a legal background, is not thought to have had much influence on the way the paper was conducted, but John Reuben Thompson was to become its chief writer. He stayed at Haxell's Hotel in the Strand for a few days before moving to Savile Row on August 3, where the Confederate States Commercial Agency was located.

Before the war, Thompson, a Virginian, had been editor of the influential *Southern Literary Messenger*, and more recently of the short-lived *Southern Field and Fireside*, the *Richmond Record* and the *Southern Illustrated News*. He was considered a useful advocate for the Confederate cause, and his "gentlemanly presence, pleasant manners and intimacy with the Confederate leaders secured him entrance in both aristocratic and literary society."[35] On a previous visit to London in the 1850s he had been acquainted with such literary celebrities as Edward Bulwer-Lytton, William Makepeace Thackeray and Robert and Elizabeth Browning, and now he met well-known authors like Thomas Carlyle, Charles Dickens, Alfred Tennyson and Wilkie Collins, though not all of these were neccessarily sympathetic to his views.[36]

In March 1865, Hotze informed him that Confederate funds in Europe "were in a state of bankruptcy, and the *Index* would probably be discontinued in two or three months"; Thompson's connection with the paper ended in June.[37] The *Index* ceased publication on August 12, 1865 and in his final leader its founder concluded:

> To suppose that the continued publication of "The Index" has a political significance and that it must needs be hostile to the United States is natural, and almost inevitable. We have then no choice. We have sought to do the South good, and we cannot harm her to further our own views. We therefore suspend publication. "The Index" shall not be the excuse, the plausible excuse, for perpetuating a contest which can only aggravate the miseries of the conquered and disarmed.[38]

Henry Hotze was undoubtedly one of the most remarkable Confederates to be sent to Europe. Talented, able and hardworking, and in many ways ahead of his time, he employed the suave, subtle and silent methods of an experienced diplomat. Yet at the same time he had a blind spot: he never really understood the English dislike of slavery. He referred to the *Index* as "that little kingdom of mine," and as a source of Southern news it was certainly a success, though he probably exaggerated its influence; sympathy for the Southern cause already existed among journalists before the *Index* was established. And in spite of his best efforts, he ultimately failed in his mission to persuade England to recognize the Confederacy.

4

Supplies for the Confederate Army

I knew how dependent the South had been in almost everything upon the North. But little reflection was needed to present the whole matter clearly before my mind ... almost every article that can be mentioned, needed for the protection and comfort of an army, had to be obtained from a foreign source.
— Caleb Huse, July 3, 1862

These words were written by the Confederacy's principal army purchasing agent about a year after he first arrived in London. From the outset it had been apparent to the new Confederate government that, given the South's lack of resources and manufacturing capability, it would need to buy most of its armaments abroad. The most obvious source was Great Britain, then the world's leading industrial nation. The government acted remarkably quickly, and within weeks of the bombardment of Fort Sumter, Confederate purchasing agents began arriving in Britain. Many difficulties lay ahead: imprecise instructions, overlapping responsibilities, poor communications, problems with funds, competition with other agents and Federal surveillance of their activities. All these handicaps faced men representing a government not yet recognized abroad.

Captain Caleb Huse was the first to arrive. Born in Massachusetts in 1831, Huse was a graduate of the U.S. Military Academy at West Point, where he was an assistant professor of chemistry, mineralogy and geology in 1852–1859. He then took a year's leave of absence in 1859–1860 to travel abroad and study the European arms industry, experience which would prove to be of great value in the future. When the Civil War broke out, he was commandant of cadets at the University of Alabama.

Huse, who had a Southern wife, had chosen to serve the Confederacy, but his Northern background was to cause problems, and he was to be suspected of disloyalty, suffer from jealousy among his fellow agents and be accused of financial irregularities. In early April 1861, now a captain in the Confederate Army, he was sent to Europe by Colonel Josiah Gorgas, Head of the Ordnance Bureau, to buy arms and munitions.

He arrived at Liverpool on May 10, and recalled: "On arriving in London I went to what was then a favorite hotel for Americans — Morley's in Trafalgar Square ... My orders were to purchase 12,000 rifles and a battery of field artillery, and to procure one or two guns of large caliber as models."[1] His first visit was to the London Armory Company in Bermondsey, in south

London, where he encountered a Federal purchasing agent. Although the firm was under contract to the U.S. government, Huse persisted, and within a few days had succeeded in obtaining an agreement under which he was to have all the arms the company could manufacture after it had fulfilled its present obligations. "This company," he recalled, "during the remainder of the war, turned all its output of arms over to me for the Confederate Army."[2] He later expressed great satisfaction with the quality of their arms, commenting that the rifles manufactured by the company were far superior to those obtained from almost every other source.

For the moment, however, Huse found that the small arms market in England had been largely swept clean: "Everything has been taken by the agents from the Northern States, and the quantity they have secured is very small," he reported.[3] In spite of that, he succeeded in buying a substantial number of Enfield rifles. Later, Colonel Gorgas was to write: "He succeeded, with very little money, in buying a good supply, and in running my department in debt for nearly half a million sterling, the very best proof of his fitness for his place."[4]

Huse and the other purchasing agents made extensive use of commission merchants. One of them was Sinclair, Hamilton & Company, whose offices were in St. Helen's Place. Founded in the 1840s by Alexander Sinclair and Archibald Hamilton, by the time of the Civil War the firm was being run by Archibald Hamilton, who also happened to be a director of the London Armory Company.

Another was Isaac, Campbell & Company of Jermyn Street. This had been founded about 1852 by Samuel Isaac, an army contractor, who first appears in the London directories in 1848, and Alexander Campbell, an outfitter. Campbell had either retired or died by 1861 and the firm was then being operated by Samuel Isaac and his younger brother, Saul. Between 1852 and 1863 Isaac, Campbell are described as army contractors, but after that, simply as merchants. They had a far from unblemished reputation: there were scandals dating back to the time of the Crimean War (1854–1856), and in 1858 both brothers had been witnesses at an official enquiry concerning irregularities at the Army Stores and Clothing Depot at Weedon, Northamptonshire.[5] Huse, of course, knew nothing about this, and his close connection with the firm, which was later found to be overcharging the Confederate government, was to undermine his own position considerably.

The War Department had doubts about Huse's abilities, as well as his loyalties, and in June 1861 sent Major Edward Clifford Anderson to London. Born in 1815, Anderson was a Georgia businessman, planter and former officer in the U.S. Navy, and as well as buying weapons for the Confederate army he was to investigate Huse's trustworthiness and, if circumstances demanded it, take his place. Anderson met Huse in Liverpool on June 25 and the following day they traveled to London. Taking rooms at Hatchett's Hotel in Piccadilly, they called on Commissioner Yancey in Half Moon Street; Anderson met him again two days later, together with fellow commissioners Rost and Mann.

> My first duty on arrival in England," recorded Major Anderson in his diary, "was to comply with the instructions which I had received ... to scrutinize very closely the operations and sentiments of Capt. H[use]. To this end I conferred very fully with ... Capt. Bulloch, whose closer intimacy with H would enable him to afford me correct information ... I received the most satisfactory assurances of the fidelity and loyalty of Mr H. My own intercourse confirmed this, and I took the earliest opportunity to relieve the minds of the Confederate authorities....[6]

Though Anderson thought Huse lacked discretion and judgment, he clearly liked him and described him in his diary as honest, kind-hearted, and untiring in his duties, and the

The house in Clarendon Road, Notting Hill, where purchasing agent Major Caleb Huse lived in 1862–1863. (Author's photograph)

two men worked well together. Huse, for his part, apparently never suspected Anderson's real purpose, or the government's misgivings about his fidelity. The doubts about his loyalty now banished, Huse was given complete authority in July to purchase whatever he thought necessary for the Confederate war effort. At Colonel Gorgas's request, a special messenger was sent to London with new orders sewn between the layers of one of his boot soles. They informed Huse that he was to disregard all former instructions and act in accordance with his own judgment, based on the state of affairs indicated by the newspapers and other sources of information, and forward supplies and equipment as rapidly as possible.[7] In addition, "political agents of the Government" were to have no authority over him, something which would cause trouble later with Commissioner Mason.

On July 16, after returning from a visit to Liverpool, Major Anderson wrote in his diary: "Drove to 58 Jermyn Street where I found that Huse had secured me very comfortable quarters, consisting of a parlor, bedroom, bathroom, water closet &c, all on one floor."[8] Three weeks later he recorded: "We have a very pleasant mess composed of Huse, Bulloch, Fearn, George Jones and myself. Our rooms are on the second floor. Our sitting room is a large apartment, trenching on the yard and covered in overhead with glass so as to admit light and air."[9]

They had a number of visitors, including Charles Green, manager of the Savannah branch of a Liverpool firm who had been sent to London to help with purchasing operations; future propagandist Edwin de Leon, who would soon be on his way back to the Confederacy; James Kerr, of the London Armory Company; Mr Britton, "manufacturer of the Blakely shell"; and Major Charles J. Helm, on his way to Havana to take up his appointment as Confederate agent for the West Indies, who breakfasted with them one morning.[10]

There were many visits to London firms. From Isaac, Campbell, Major Anderson ordered 500 cavalry sabers, 10,000 muskets ("old army pattern"), a lot of Enfield rifles, and 11,000 English muskets. On another occasion he went with James Bulloch to Isaac, Campbell's packing establishment "to look after certain matters." At Sinclair, Hamilton's premises he inspected samples of Enfield rifles and pistols, and a storeroom which he referred to as "our warehouse," where Captain Huse proposed depositing future purchases of arms; from them he bought 12,000 Genoese muskets and gunpowder. While at the London Armory Company's works, he encountered Mr. C. McFarland, the Federal purchasing agent whom Captain Huse had met on his first visit to that firm. He also called on Curtis & Harvey, gunpowder manufacturers, in Lombard Street, and Alexander Ross & Company, the Bermondsey leather merchants and army accoutrement makers.

It was a busy time, with frequent trips to Liverpool, and others to places as far apart as Birmingham, Falmouth and Paris. Nevertheless, Major Anderson found time to visit the Royal Arsenal at Woolwich, "the largest in the world, covering more than 100 acres, and containing about 25,000 pieces of ordnance, besides other warlike stores ... everything that can attract the attention of military ... inquirers is abundant."[11] Admission was free on Tuesdays, by letter from the under secretary of war, or tickets from the master-general of Ordnance or "certain officers of artillery ... To be admitted through the interior, an order must be obtained from the Royal Board of Ordnance. Foreigners must apply for these orders through their respective ambassadors."[12]

Traveling down the Thames by steamer, in the company of naval purchasing agent James Bulloch, Anderson's first visit on July 9, was a failure, the two men arriving too late to be admitted. Two days later, accompanied this time by Captain Huse and John Fearn, as well as James Bulloch, he tried again. Although the party had a letter of introduction provided by

The London Armory Company supplied many weapons to the Confederates. (*Kelly's Post Office London Directory*)

one of the Isaac brothers, it proved insufficient to gain admittance, but they finally got in by a combination of bribery and subterfuge.

There was also a trip to Wimbledon Common on July 12 to see a grand review of 10,000 members of the Volunteer Force (the forerunner of the Territorial Army), which left Anderson unimpressed; an excursion with William Yancey and Samuel Isaac on September 17 to Greenhithe, Kent, where HMS *Warrior*, the Royal Navy's first ironclad warship and a vessel much admired by the Confederates, was at anchor in the Thames; and a visit to see the celebrated Crystal Palace at Sydenham in south London.

Major Anderson seems to have been fond of the theater, and while in London he paid a number of visits. At the Haymarket Theater on August 12, in company with James Bulloch and Charles Green, he saw a new comedy called *My Lord and My Lady; or It Might Have Been Worse*, by J.R. Planché, and paid a second visit there with Green about a month later to see another comedy, called *The Soft Sex*, by Charles Matthews. When he went to the Olympic Theater, Wych Street, on August 24, where the program included John Oxenford's drama, *The Porter's Knot*, and Henry Mayhew's farce, *The Wandering Minstrel*, starring the famous actor Frederick Robson, he found that Mr. Isaac had provided the tickets and obtained a stage box for them.

Samuel Isaac was undoubtedly generous; so was Archibald Hamilton. On September 15 Major Anderson was a guest at Mr. Hamilton's country house in Kent, to which he traveled by train from London Bridge station. "Our dinner was sumptuous, the costliest wines being lavished upon us ... his hospitality is princely," he noted.[13] Anderson remarked on the generous hospitality of some of the firms with whom he was doing business, particularly Isaac, Campbell and Sinclair, Hamilton. At the same time, he was under no illusions, observing, "Friend Isaac is a most useful man to us, but he never loses sight of his profits," while "Mr. Hamilton is the business man in the London Armoury Company contracts, and in trade haggles over a ha'penny [halfpenny]."[14]

Major Anderson's last few days in London were spent mainly in social activities. He dined at Richardson's Hotel in Covent Garden, an old-fashioned establishment, both dingy and dark, but where the major and his companions were served an excellent dinner, with copious amounts of good wine. This was followed by a visit to the Holborn Casino, a somewhat dubious establishment in High Holborn, where people went to dance and listen to the music. They remained there until quite late, enjoying the festivities and watching the dancers.[15] There was also time for the Zoological Gardens in Regent's Park and a final visit to the theater, this time to the Adelphi in the Strand to see Dion Boucicault's *The Colleen Bawn*. Unfortunately, on this occasion his visit was marred by the inability of one of his companions, Richard Meade, a former U.S. minister to Brazil, to understand the plot and his persistence in continually asking for explanations. On the way home they stopped for refreshment at one of the "gin houses" in the Haymarket, where Anderson realized that his brandy and soda had been drugged.

On October 2 Major Anderson left for Liverpool, on his way to Holyhead, to join the *Fingal*, the ship that would take him and James Bulloch and a cargo of much needed munitions and supplies back to the Confederacy. While in Liverpool Anderson met "a German [sic] gentleman by the name of [Henry] Hotze, sent over by the Govt. as a special bearer of dispatches, with instructions to return as soon as practicable."[16] Hotze would be returning to England the following January to undertake a much more demanding role.

The first shipment of arms bought by Huse left West Hartlepool in August 1861 in the steamer *Bermuda*, the first vessel to run the blockade. On board were field pieces, seacoast guns, rifles and cartridges, as well as large quantities of shoes and blankets. The steamer's safe arrival at Savannah in September was recorded in an angry note in Benjamin Moran's diary on October 17: "It appears the pirate *Bermuda* has actually run the blockade and safely landed all her warlike stores."[17] Another consignment, consisting of rifles and ammunition, blankets, surgical equipment and medicine, was in the *Gladiator*, which cleared London in November 1861, bound for Nassau. Confederate purchases made in London in January 1862 of Enfield rifles, percussion caps, blankets, shoes and other military equipment were sent in the blockade-runner *Economist*, which arrived at Charleston in March.[18] All three vessels belonged to Fraser, Trenholm & Company of Liverpool, who played a major role in shipping goods to the Confederacy.

Not all runs were so successful. One blockade-runner, carrying a shipment of goods sent by Huse and captured on its inward journey in May 1862, included a report from him to Colonel Josiah Gorgas, detailing the arms, munitions and military supplies he had dispatched. This reached the hands of the U.S. State Department, and was also published in a New York newspaper. Huse refers to this in a letter to William Yancey, written in July 1862. He also refers to allegations of financial misconduct, fueled no doubt by jealousy and resentment of his Northern background. These were to surface again.[19]

By the end of 1862 Huse had bought and shipped some 131,000 rifles and muskets, with another 23,000 in store in London awaiting shipment. To these must be added some 16,000 cavalry sabers, 139 pieces of heavy artillery, 484,000 pounds of gunpowder, 4 million cartridges, 10 million percussion caps, 1,000 hundredweight of saltpeter, and 100,000 pounds of lead. There were also sets of armorers', saddlers' and farriers' tools, knapsacks, greatcoats, boots, socks, trousers, shirts, and quantities of leather, cloth and flannel, some $5 million worth in all.[20] How much of this reached its destination is impossible to say.

Until then Huse, who had now been promoted to major, had acted on behalf of all War Department bureaus, but it had become apparent that additional agents were needed. One of them, Major James B. Ferguson, a Virginian, was sent to London in December 1862 by the Quartermaster's Bureau. Supplying the clothing needs of the armies of the Confederacy was a never-ending problem, and as late as September 1864 he was being instructed: "Purchase woollen cloths, or flannels or felt hats in lieu of socks, as we can manufacture the latter from cotton yarn. A cheap and serviceable felt hat would be very acceptable to the army. Also wanted, best quality of blankets, and gray cloths, with a fair proportion of trimmings."[21]

Earlier that year Ferguson was joined by his wife, Emma, who, together with their two children and a nursemaid, had run the blockade in the *Lynx*, another vessel belonging to Fraser, Trenholm. The passage from Wilmington to St. George's, Bermuda, was arranged by Major Benjamin Ficklin, "a government shipper of cotton," for whom Mrs. Ferguson carried dispatches for James Mason and John Slidell.[22] She also brought a letter from General Robert E. Lee, revealing that a box containing a uniform and blanket sent him by her husband had failed to get through the blockade.

In July 1864 Major Ferguson proposed to make another attempt, and Mrs. Irvine, "the wife of a Scotch manufacturer, and an ardent admirer of Gen. Lee," Lady Florence Eardley, the American-born wife of Sir Eardley Eardley, a Confederate sympathizer, and Mrs. Ferguson made up another box for Lee, with "a very fine uniform, cavalry boots, gauntlets, and the handsomest lieutenant general's scarf to be found in London." There was also cloth to make a uniform for General James Longstreet, whose measurements they did not have. It was sent from Liverpool in August and this time arrived safely at Wilmington. Lee expressed his thanks to Major Ferguson in a letter written from Petersburg in October, adding: "The army appreciates your zealous and self-sacrificing efforts in promoting their comfort, and hail with pleasure the arrival of every cargo you send. May you continue to be able to supply their wants!"[23]

Captain William Graves Crenshaw was a Richmond merchant who had formed an artillery company called Crenshaw's Battery. In the late autumn of 1862 he was sent to London to organize a blockade-running company and also supervise the purchase of commissary stores. When Huse returned from a visit to Paris in April 1863, he found that Crenshaw, in conjunction with Commissioner James Mason, had signed an agreement with Alexander Collie & Company, a firm of merchants, to buy and operate four blockade-runners for the War and Navy Departments, to be built by John & William Dudgeon at their yards at Cubitt Town, on the Thames. At a cost of £14,000 each, they were to be completed by July 1863.

Huse had already purchased several steamers for the Ordnance Bureau, and Crenshaw's demands that some of Huse's purchases should be carried in the Collie-Crenshaw steamers, and that he should also provide money to help pay for them, were refused. Friction over purchasing operations now reached a serious level, with Captain Crenshaw and Major Ferguson, supported by Commissioner Mason, pressing for Major Huse's recall on the grounds of lack of cooperation, as well as financial misconduct involving the firm of Isaac, Campbell.

News of this highly unsatisfactory situation reached John B. Jones, a clerk in the Confederate War Department in Richmond, who noted in his diary in August 1863:

> Letters from Mr. [W.G.] Crenshaw, in England, and the correspondence forwarded by him, might seem to implicate Major Caleb Huse, Colonel J. Gorgas's ordnance agent, in some very ugly operations. It appears that Major H. has contracted for 50,000 muskets at $4 above the current price, leaving $200,000 commission for whom? And that he really seems to be throwing obstacles in the way of Mr. C., who is endeavoring to procure commissary stores in England. Mr. C. has purchased £40,000 worth of bacon, but Major Huse, he apprehends, is endeavoring to prevent its shipment. Can this be so?[24]

The War Department, alarmed at this development, partly resolved the matter by making Huse responsible for medical and ordnance supplies only, while Crenshaw was to deal with quartermaster and commissary goods. At the same time, it was decided to examine Huse's accounts.

The man assigned to this task was Colin John McRae, the leading negotiator for the Seven Per Cent Cotton Loan (see chapter 7), who was now being sent back to Europe to manage it.[25] McRae was born in North Carolina in 1812, but subsequently moved to Mississippi and then to Alabama, where he settled in Mobile. He had become a highly successful businessman, with a wide range of interests which included coastal shipping, railroad promotion and real estate, and had already made a major contribution to the Confederate war effort with the establishment of the Selma Ordnance Works, the second largest ironworks in the South. In terms of what he achieved, he would prove to be one of the most important Confederates to come to London.

McRae reached Southampton on May 13, 1863, and after a visit to Paris, arrived in London at the beginning of June, staying at the Burlington Hotel in Cork Street. An assistant, M. Hildreth Bloodgood, was sent to help with the investigation of Huse's accounts and arrived at the end of August. A firm of accountants, Quilter, Ball, Jay & Company, was also employed to assist in the matter. No evidence of financial irregularities was found, and McRae concluded that although Huse "has made some very serious mistakes, I think there is no good reason to suspect his integrity, and that he has always sought what seemed the best interests of the government, and has with all his mistakes really been of great service and done great good."[26]

He soon had the measure of Isaac, Campbell, whom he suspected of fraudulent bookkeeping. His suspicions proved correct: it was found that the firm was keeping two sets of books, one showing the real price, and the other the price quoted to the Confederate government. As a result, all further dealings with them were terminated. They were almost certainly not the only ones guilty of unethical practice in dealings with the Confederacy.

Until the autumn of 1862, purchases of military supplies abroad had been made with coin shipped to Fraser, Trenholm in Liverpool, letters of credit and bills of exchange. As the volume of purchases increased, the Treasury Department then resorted to the issue of bonds, cotton certificates and warrants, backed by cotton stored in the Confederacy, as well as money from the Seven Per Cent Cotton Loan. To supplement these, the government also made a number of agreements with shipowners to purchase and deliver war materials, to be paid for with cotton at Confederate ports.[27]

These agreements often proved anything but satisfactory, with contractors competing with each other as well as with purchasing agents, and often supplying goods of inferior quality. Henry Hotze noted "the clashing interests, the rivalries and hostilities, sometimes the disgraceful public squabbles of contractors," as well as "the lax manner in which, in many instances, contracts appear to have been granted," in a letter to Richmond.[28]

In October 1863 Colin McRae suggested to Christopher Memminger, secretary of the treasury, that in order to rationalize these haphazard arrangements and restore Confederate credit abroad, all commission-based agreements with contractors should be canceled; that there should be one purchasing agent each for the War and Navy Departments; that one person should be put in overall charge of Confederate finances in Europe, with authority over government purchasing agents and their spending; and that the government should requisition all cotton and transport it to Liverpool, where it would be sold to finance the war effort.

James Spence, who had served as the Confederacy's financial agent in Europe since October 1862, was replaced in December 1863 by Colin McRae. Spence's antislavery views, which he had never attempted to hide, almost certainly influenced the decision to replace him. Though he was paid for his services, Spence had only acted in an advisory capacity, whereas McRae was an official of the Treasury Department and had authority over Confederate purchasing agents. The following February, his recommendations — what became known as the New Plan — were adopted by the Confederate government, bringing order into what had become a confused financial situation, centralizing purchasing operations, and largely ending the competition and friction between agents.

Not all Confederate purchasing agents came to buy arms and equipment. Major Norman Stewart Walker was a Virginian who had served in the Confederate Army before joining the Ordnance Bureau in 1862 and being appointed resident disbursing agent at Bermuda. Here his duties included the transshipment of goods to the Confederacy and the procurement of coal for Confederate vessels. He was sent to London in November 1862 with $2 million in Confederate bonds, partly to clear some of Major Huse's debts and partly to purchase steamers for the Bureau.

His business concluded, Major Walker was back in Bermuda by February 1863, but in August 1864, having moved his base to Halifax, Nova Scotia, because of a yellow fever outbreak, he returned to London. His wife and family were already there, having arrived the previous month in the blockade-runner *Index*. Conditions on board the vessel had been poor, with a shortage of sheets, towels, tablecloths and food, and a head steward whom Mrs. Georgiana Gholson Walker described as "the filthiest beast ... which it has ever been my misfortune to encounter." She was highly relieved when the voyage was over:

> On Monday afternoon about six, Capt. Horner raised the Confederate flag, & we entered one of the docks of London. Our party immediately took a boat & came on shore, determined not to spend another night on board ship. The baggage had to be left for the inspection of custom house officers — as if poor Confederates had any contraband goods![29]

Mrs. Walker had come to England to take her little daughter, Georgie, to see William Bowman, the leading ophthalmic surgeon in London, and "handsome apartments" had been found for her in Sackville Street, just off Piccadilly. Here, the first familiar face she saw was that of Mrs. Rose Greenhow, the Confederate spy and emissary, whom she had previously encountered in Bermuda, and who had rooms in the same house. Mrs. Walker was visited by James Mason, James McFarland, his secretary, and Major Huse, among others, before moving to Leamington Spa, where there was a small Confederate community. At the beginning of September the Walkers returned to London for a few hectic days — "Norman finds himself overrun with business engagements with the various officers of the Confederate

Government"—before leaving for Paris.[30] They went back to Leamington for a few weeks, but in October sailed from Liverpool for Halifax.

Captain John Moncure Robinson, former superintendent of the Seaboard and Roanoke Railroad, who was sent to England in February 1863 on behalf of the Engineer Bureau, was also authorized to act as a purchasing agent for five Virginia railroad companies, for whom he bought badly needed iron. A proposal that he should repeat the operation on behalf of the other railroads in the South, who were all in dire need, was rejected, the secretary of war refusing to become involved in what he regarded as private business matters.[31]

As well as Confederate purchasing agents, state agents were also sent to England. Major Anderson took on a dual role when he was informed, while on a visit to Liverpool in July 1861, that Governor Joseph E. Brown of Georgia had appointed him a state agent, with authorization to spend up to $100,000 acquiring arms and war material. "This will enable me to take up many muskets that are at this time being offered...," he remarked in a letter to Secretary of War Leroy P. Walker, "added to which is the advantage presented me of going continuously on with our purchases, without being compelled to stop for the arrival of additional means from Richmond."[32] In his diary in late September he noted that he had paid Sinclair, Hamilton in full for the Georgia muskets.[33]

Another state agent was Colonel John Lewis Peyton. Born near Staunton, Virginia, in 1824, Peyton was a former lawyer, and, though opposed to secession, had helped raise a regiment for Virginia, but was prevented by ill health from serving with it. Instead, he accepted an appointment by Governor Henry T. Clark as a state purchasing agent for North Carolina. Judah P. Benjamin, Leroy P. Walker's successor, asked Major Anderson and Captain Huse to assist Colonel Peyton in buying arms, but he warned them to give preference to government purchases; in the event, Anderson had departed before Peyton arrived. Accompanied by his wife, Peyton left Charleston in the CSS *Nashville* in October 1861, and arrived at Southampton in November. Proceeding to London, he spent a few days at a hotel near Charing Cross before moving to a suite of rooms in Jermyn Street, which cost three guineas a week, plus meals. "Nothing could exceed the snug and cosy character of my Jermyn Street abode, with its blazing coal fires, and its massive furniture, all selected with reference to convenience and comfort," he recalled.[34]

One of his first acts was to call on Messrs. Yancey and Mann in Half Moon Street, who were waiting for their replacements to arrive. He also wrote to the *Times*; his letter, headed "A Voice from the South," assured its readers that recent newspaper reports of disaffection towards the Confederate government in states like North Carolina were quite untrue.[35] While in London he was made an honorary member of the Reform Club in Pall Mall, and visited the House of Commons, as well as attending a soirée at Bath House, Piccadilly, the residence of Lord Ashburton.

He had only limited success with his purchasing mission, but was able to buy a consignment of 1,760 long Enfield rifles for the use of North Carolina troops, which left London in February 1862 on board the steamship *Southwick*, bound for Nassau. Though their safe arrival there was acknowledged, he was never informed whether they reached their final destination. Writing from Paris at the beginning of 1863, he complained about this to Governor Zebulon B. Vance, Henry Clark's successor, and reminded him that his services were still available if required: "A letter will always reach me addressed to the care of John Wilson Esq., 93 Great Russell Street, Bloomsbury, London."[36] He had had an unofficial interview with Lord Palmerston in May 1862 which had convinced him of Britain's determination to remain neutral and he reiterated this point in his letter to Vance.

In November 1862 Governor Vance appointed two more purchasing agents for North Carolina. They were John White and Thomas M. Crossan. John White, a Scotsman, was born in Fifeshire in 1814 and had emigrated to North Carolina in the late 1820s, where he had become a highly successful dry goods merchant at Warrenton; Thomas Morrow Crossan, also of Warrenton, was a former officer in the U.S. Navy and now a lieutenant in the Confederate Navy.

The two men left Charleston in November 1862 and reached London at the beginning of January 1863. With them they had $1.5 million in state cotton bonds, the proceeds from the sale of which were to purchase blankets, shoes, leather and clothing for North Carolina troops serving with the Confederate armies. The two men dealt with Alexander Collie, through whom they also acquired a steamer, the *Lord Clyde*, renamed the *Advance*, the only blockade-runner to be owned by an individual Confederate state. For its first few trips it was commanded by Lieutenant Crossan. A part interest in three other vessels was obtained, and during the rest of the war large quantities of supplies were purchased on behalf of North Carolina and taken through the blockade.[37]

Captain Crenshaw observed that John White had also been to see Isaac, Campbell: "Mr White ... sent here by the State of North Carolina, who has had some opportunity of seeing something of Isaac, Campbell & Co., informs me that he entertains of them the same opinion that I do; nor have I seen any man since my arrival here who would say a good word for them except Major Huse."[38]

Major Anderson had returned to Georgia at the end of 1861, but other purchasing agents from that state came to London to buy blankets, clothing and shoes for its troops, and early in 1864 Governor Joseph E. Brown chartered steamers to export cotton and import supplies.[39] Louisiana and Texas also sent agents to England, as apparently did Virginia, South Carolina and Alabama. Governor Thomas O. Moore of Louisiana appointed a Mr. Tilton as a state agent; Major Anderson encountered him in Piccadilly in August 1861 and seems to have formed a poor opinion of him, though his diary does not tell us why. The Texas State Military Board, set up to purchase supplies for Texas troops, sent John Swisher, an Austin merchant, to London in April 1862 to negotiate the sale of some 300 prewar U.S. bonds. Some were sold to George Peabody & Company, the well-known American banking house, but the result was far from satisfactory and ended in a lawsuit.

Nelson Clements, another Texas state agent, arrived in London at the end of March 1863 to buy supplies to be paid for with cotton. Dealing with Isaac, Campbell, he sent out rifles and muskets, blankets, flannel shirts, shoes and gray army cloth. He was also introduced to the firm of Sinclair, Hamilton by Edgar Stringer, a ship and insurance broker, and through them he purchased 7,000 long Enfield rifles, 1853 pattern, with bayonets, at a cost of £3 each, in May 1863.[40] For this service, Mr Stringer charged a commission of 5 percent, or £1,000.

Useful as it was, the work of the state agents was peripheral to that of the purchasing agents working for the Confederate government. Given the circumstances, theirs was a remarkable exercise in logistics, probably without precedent. It has been estimated that War Department agents spent more than $12 million, of which Caleb Huse alone accounted for at least $10 million. It was indeed a crucial role: for four years, their efforts helped the Confederacy maintain its armies in the field, and without them the South would almost certainly have been defeated much sooner.

5

Vessels Suitable for Our Purposes

I regard the possession of an iron-armoured ship as a matter of the first necessity. Such a vessel at this time could traverse the entire coast of the United States, prevent all blockades, and encounter, with a fair prospect of success, their entire Navy.
— Stephen R. Mallory, May 8, 1861

At its inception, the Confederate Navy had virtually no ships of any kind, ironclad or otherwise, and, as the secretary of the navy indicated, the purchase or construction of them was clearly of the utmost priority. At the beginning of the war, the Confederate government was offered the opportunity to purchase ten vessels belonging to the East India Company, then in the process of disposing of its assets, following the transfer of authority to the British crown. The ships, iron-hulled steamers of recent construction, capable of being fitted with guns, were available for £2 million, and the company was willing to accept Confederate government bonds in payment, backed by 40,000 bales of cotton. This proposition was put to the government by influential businessman George A. Trenholm, but it was turned down, partly because the ships were thought unsuitable for most Southern harbors.[1]

Although approximately twenty ironclads were built and launched in the South during the war, these were for coastal and river defense; they were not oceangoing vessels. These, it was very quickly realized, would have to be obtained abroad, and in May 1861 James D. Bulloch was sent to England as a purchasing agent for the Confederate Navy Department. His mission was threefold: to initiate the construction of ironclads; to buy or have built cruisers or commerce raiders to prey on enemy merchantmen; and to purchase weapons and equipment for the Navy and Marine Corps.

James Dunwody Bulloch was born near Savannah, Georgia, in 1823 and, after serving in the U.S. Navy from 1839 until 1853, resigned to work for a New York shipping company operating between there and New Orleans.[2] When the Civil War broke out, he was captain of the steamer *Bienville*, which he felt morally bound to return to her owners before offering his services to the Confederate government at Montgomery, Alabama.

To avoid the blockade, he traveled by train to Detroit and Montreal, where he took passage in the steamer *North America*, and arrived at Liverpool on June 4. Here he called on Fraser, Trenholm & Company, who were to be the Confederacy's overseas financial agents, then proceeded to London to see the Confederate commissioners. Though he was to be based in Liverpool, James Bulloch's work inevitably involved many visits to London, including liaison with his army counterparts, with whom at times he shared accommodations. In August 1861 he was able to report to Secretary of the Navy Mallory: "Major Anderson, Captain Huse and myself consult freely together upon our duties and are now engaged in sending forward a quantity of munitions."[3]

Like his army counterparts, Bulloch did not find his task an easy one. "There were at that date," he recalled, "numerous agents of the United States in England, who seemed in no way desirous to conceal their operations. They went about their business with the air of men who were sure of their position, and who neither anticipated nor feared interference or opposition. They were well provided with money, or satisfactory bank-credits, and they rapidly swept the gun market of well-nigh every weapon, whether good or bad."[4] Confederate agents, on the other hand, were often embarrassed by lack of funds.

By the end of June 1861 a contract had been signed at Liverpool with William C. Miller & Sons and Fawcett, Preston & Company for a ship to be called the *Oreto*, supposedly destined for the Italian government. Though Thomas H. Dudley, the U.S. consul at Liverpool, was highly suspicious, and conveyed those suspicions to U.S. minister Charles Francis Adams and Foreign Secretary Lord John Russell in London, searches of the vessel found nothing to prove she was intended for Confederate service. James Bulloch had found a loophole in the Foreign Enlistment Act by making sure that when his commerce raiders put to sea they were not yet equipped for war.

The *Oreto* was ready to be launched by January 1862, and on March 22 she sailed for Nassau, where she was joined by her new captain, Lieutenant John N. Maffitt, and a cargo of arms brought out separately in the steamer *Bahama*. In August the *Oreto* was commissioned as the CSS *Florida*. After capturing or sinking thirty-seven U.S. merchant ships, her career as a commerce raider came to an end in October 1864 when she was rammed and captured in the Brazilian port of Bahia by the USS *Wachusett*.

Work on a second commerce raider began in August 1861 at John Laird & Sons' shipyard across the Mersey at Birkenhead. She was the No. 290, destined to be the largest of the Confederate cruisers, and her construction was watched closely by Federal spies, and the Foreign Office in London kept abreast of developments.

When launched on May 15, 1862 she was named the *Enrica* to foster the impression that she was being built for the Spanish government. Informed privately in late July that she was about to be impounded by the British government, Bulloch arranged for her to sail from the Mersey, on the pretext of a trial run, on July 29.[5] Successfully eluding the USS *Tuscarora*, which was lying in wait, she set course for the Azores. Here the bark *Agrippina*, purchased in London in May as her tender, and loaded with ordnance, ammunition, stores and coal, joined her, and armed and provisioned, she was commissioned as the CSS *Alabama* in August 1862, under the command of Captain Raphael Semmes. She had captured or destroyed sixty-five merchant ships by the time she was sunk off Cherbourg by the USS *Kearsarge* in June 1864.

Both these cruisers or commerce raiders were wooden vessels, but in July 1862, the month that the *Alabama* sailed, Bulloch signed another contract with John Laird, this time to build two ironclads. They were powerful vessels, 230 feet long, with twin revolving turrets and capable of speeds of up to ten knots. Designed by Captain Cowper Coles, R.N., a leading naval architect who was related to the Laird family, they were fitted with underwater rams which could stave in the hull of any wooden ship, and might be used to break the blockade or threaten cities like New York and Washington. Ostensibly for the pasha of Egypt, and known at one stage as *El Tousson* and *El Mounassir*, they were to be ready by the spring of 1863. The Laird rams were to prove the most contentious of all the Confederate ships built in Britain.

As their true purpose could not be disguised, Bulloch, all too aware that the British government might try to prevent their departure, transferred ownership to a French citizen. The Foreign Office, informed of developments, at first refused to act for lack of hard evidence, but U.S. minister Charles Francis Adams, knowing that at least one of the rams was ready for sea, was determined to prevent a repetition of the escape of the *Florida* and *Alabama*. On September 5, 1863, he indicated to Foreign Secretary Lord John Russell, in the strongest terms, that it would be superfluous of him to point out that allowing them to sail would mean war with the United States. His letter had the desired effect, and on September 8 it was reported that the rams were being detained. Impounded by the British government, they were later purchased for use by the Royal Navy.

As well as the vessels built on Merseyside, Bulloch also contracted late in the war for a number of gunboats for the Confederate Navy. Four of these were to be built in Scotland, at Denny & Company's yards at Dumbarton, on the Clyde, and two more in London, by John & William Dudgeon at Cubitt Town, on the Thames; all were to be iron-hulled, twin-propeller steamers. Only one of Denny's vessels, the *Ajax*, was completed in time to go into service, but, unable to reach the South, it returned to Liverpool in June 1865. Another, the *Hercules,* attracted unwelcome attention from the authorities, but they found nothing to connect her with the Confederates.[6]

The two vessels built by Dudgeons were the *Louisa Ann Fanny* and the *Mary Augusta*. These appear to have been named after the wives of John Gilliat, head of J.K. Gilliat & Company, and his younger brother, Algernon, perhaps because the firm was financially involved in their construction or in recognition of previous services rendered to the Confederacy. The *Louisa Ann Fanny* was completed on January 18, 1865. The Federals were well-informed about her, the Dudgeons' foreman, Mr Cooper, having obligingly supplied one of their agents with a detailed description. When she made her trial trip down the Thames, from Gravesend to Maplin Sands later that month, under the command of her nominal master, William Pinchon, a *Times* correspondent who was on board had this to say:

> The engines are amply protected by the arrangements of the coal bunkers from shot if the ship in her future career should ever come within range of hostile guns. The *Louisa Ann Fanny* has been built for purely commercial purposes, but as she may not improbably some day cross Wilmington bar, this protection afforded to her machinery by the arrangement of her coal bunkers is a very necessary precaution.[7]

Commanded now by Lieutenant William F. Carter, the *Louisa Ann Fanny* left Victoria Docks on February 9, 1865, with seven passengers, and delivered dispatches to the CSS *Stonewall* at Lisbon before departing for Bermuda. From there, in March 1865, she took Major Norman Walker to Nassau and Havana. She never ran the blockade, and in May brought the major and his family back to England.

The war was nearing its end when the *Mary Augusta* embarked on her sea trial on March 14, 1865. It consisted of a race from Dover to Calais with the London, Chatham & Dover Railway Company's new mail steamer *La France*, which was described by the *Times* as "the most exciting and interesting contest that has ever yet occurred since steam was first applied for the propulsion of ships."[8] The *Mary Augusta* emerged as the winner, but the

Confederates never took delivery of her. She was laid up in Victoria Docks, and at the beginning of May 1865 was reported for sale, to be joined later that month by the *Louisa Ann Fanny*.

The *Sea King*, which Commander Bulloch purchased in September 1864 as a replacement for the *Alabama*, was a merchant ship, built on the Clyde in 1863 by Alexander Stephen and Sons and constructed of wood and iron. She would become the CSS *Shenandoah*, the last Confederate raider. Lieutenant William Conway Whittle, Jr., her future executive officer, was in Liverpool when he received his orders from Commander Bulloch, written in an uncharacteristic, cloak-and-dagger style:

> You will proceed to London by the 5 o'clock train this afternoon and go to Wood's Hotel, Furnival's Inn, High Holborn ... It has been arranged for you to be in the coffee room of the hotel at 11 o'clock a.m. precisely tomorrow, and that you will sit in a prominent position, with a white pocket handkerchief ... through a buttonhole of your coat, and a newspaper in your hand ... you will be recognized by Mr. Richard Wright, who will ... ask you if your name is Brown. You may say yes, and ask his name; he will give it, and you will then retire with him to your room, hand him the enclosed letter of introduction, and then ... discuss freely the business in hand....[9]

Richard Wright, the father-in-law of Charles K. Prioleau, the head of Fraser, Trenholm, had inspected the *Sea King* prior to its purchase and was her nominal owner. He would introduce Lieutenant Whittle to Captain Peter Corbett, who was to sail the *Sea King* to Madeira. Corbett was later arrested for attempting to enlist men to serve on the CSS *Shenandoah* and tried under the Foreign Enlistment Act, but was acquitted.

The *Sea King*, which sailed from London in October 1864 to become the CSS *Shenandoah*, the last Confederate raider. (*Illustrated London News*)

On October 8, 1864, the *Sea King* left the Port of London with Lieutenant Whittle, and early on the following day the steamer *Laurel* left Liverpool. The *Sea King's* departure was noted by Federal spies and reported to Washington by U.S. consul Freeman Morse together with details of her history and previous and present owners. At Madeira she rendezvoused with the *Laurel*, and was fitted out and commissioned as the CSS *Shenandoah*. Her captain was Lieutenant Commander James Iredell Waddell, who, together with his officers and the ship's guns and ammunition, had traveled out in the *Laurel*. She would remain at sea long after the surrender of all Confederate land forces, capturing or destroying no fewer than thirty-eight ships, and not finally returning to Liverpool until November 1865.

Another purchasing agent to be sent to Europe by the Confederate Navy Department in the spring of 1861 was Lieutenant James Heyward North, C.S.N. Born in 1813 into a seafaring family in Charleston, North had spent many years in the U.S. Navy before the secession crisis forced him to resign. His orders were to buy, or have constructed, an ironclad in England or France, of which he would then take command. In addition, he was to consult with naval experts like Captain Cowper Coles, R.N., and also assist and collaborate with James Bulloch in any way he could.

Together with his wife and daughter, Lieutenant North left Savannah for Liverpool on May 25, 1861, in the *Camilla* (the former racing yacht *America*, which had won the first cup race against England in 1851 and had now been acquired by the Confederate government). It proved to be a trying voyage — the *Camilla* rolled excessively and most of those on board were ill. Among the other passengers was Major Anderson, on his way to buy munitions for the Confederate Army and investigate Captain Huse's progress.

Exactly a month later, on June 25, 1861, they finally reached their destination.[10] There, North met James Bulloch, then in company with Major Anderson and Captain Huse, who happened to be visiting Liverpool, he took the train to London the next day. He had important papers for Commissioners Yancey and Mann, with whom he had a long talk before returning to Liverpool.

On this first visit to London, James North stayed at Hatchett's Hotel in Piccadilly, but when he returned with his family on July 16, they lodged in less expensive accommodations in nearby Jermyn Street, found for them by Major Anderson. Over the following weeks, North had several more meetings with the commissioners, made two trips to inspect the exterior of HMS *Warrior*, the new British ironclad nearing completion on the Thames, and had a talk with a Mr. Pritchard, of the firm of Henry S. Pitcher, wood and iron shipbuilders, of Tokenhouse Yard.

Much of his time, however, was spent in sightseeing: St. James's Palace, the Houses of Parliament, Westminster Abbey, Hyde Park, Madame Tussaud's waxworks, the Tower of London, St. Paul's Cathedral, Covent Garden, Regent Street and Oxford Street, and, further afield, the Crystal Palace at Sydenham and the Botanical Gardens at Kew. In his diary he expressed some concern at this inactivity: "I have been so much worried at the news from America that it has almost made me sick, especially when I think how little I am doing for my poor country. The only consolation that I have is, that the fault is *not* mine, and I am ready and willing to do any thing in the world for her." Nevertheless, he left London at the beginning of August for Cowes, and after a fortnight spent in the yacht *Camilla*, off the Isle of Wight, proceeded to Paris, where sightseeing again seemed to be a principal occupation.[11]

North's stay in Paris was interrupted by a hasty trip to Liverpool in early October, when he learned that Bulloch and Anderson were about to return to the Confederacy in the blockade-runner *Fingal*. This was a fast, iron-framed steamer which had been purchased jointly by the army and navy in September to transport war supplies back to the Confederacy. The *Colletis*, a Thames freighter, was hired to carry some of the supplies from warehouses in London up to Greenock, in Scotland, where the *Fingal* was waiting; the rest went by train. The cargo consisted of rifles, cartridges, percussion caps, revolvers, cavalry sabers, four pieces of naval ordnance, lead shot and shells, gunpowder, medicines, blankets, clothing and leather; because the *Colletis* was delayed in the Thames by fog, Anderson arranged for Sinclair, Hamilton to put an additional amount of gunpowder onboard.[12] It would be the largest consignment of war materials ever sent to the Confederacy. On October 15, Bulloch, and Anderson, whose task in England was now complete, joined the *Fingal* at Holyhead, for her voyage to Savannah; Bulloch returned to England the following March in the blockade-runner *Annie Childs*.

North's requests, both verbal and written, that as a precautionary measure, Bulloch should hand over all drawings, contracts and specifications to him, as "the only agent of the Navy Dept. left out here," were refused. "It is nothing more than I expected," he concluded. "Sorry! but so much for sending a naval officer and civilian on the same duty."[13] This encounter marked the beginning of the animosity which was to mar their relationship for the rest of the war.

In January 1862, while he was still in the Confederacy, James Bulloch was commissioned a commander in the Confederate States Navy. Officers who had resigned from the U.S. Navy to join the Confederate Navy had usually done so in their original rank. Bulloch had left the U.S. Navy in 1853 after fifteen years' service, but with less than a year in the rank of lieutenant, and realized that such a senior appointment might not be well received in Confederate naval circles. An astute man, he was all too aware of the trouble it might bring.

The trouble was not long in coming. James North, who had served in the U.S. Navy for thirty-three years, more than twice as long as Bulloch, including twelve years in the rank of lieutenant, was incensed by it, and took it as a personal slight. "I am not aware of anything that I have done to merit such treatment from the department," he complained to Secretary of the Navy Stephen Mallory in March 1862. "Rank to a military man is everything and that rank has been taken from me."[14] His own promotion to the rank of commander in May 1862, news of which unfortunately did not reach him until August, did little to pacify him, and he then insisted that Secretary Mallory should inform him who was now the ranking officer. The matter of rank, he was told, was of no great importance among agents serving abroad, but in fact Commander Bulloch was the senior officer. The fact that, as a result of confusion, North did not get command of either of the cruisers Bulloch was having built on Merseyside — the *Florida* and the *Alabama*— caused even more resentment.

James North was really not suited for the admittedly difficult job he had been sent to do. Lacking initiative and persistance, rather dilatory, with limited imagination and short on tact, he was also inflexible and stubborn. His complaints and inactivity soon irritated the secretary of the navy, who several times considered recalling him, and their correspondence was often acrimonious and aggravated by the problem of poor communications.

In September 1861, North reported to the Navy Department that he had not yet made any progress in acquiring an ironclad in France. This news was not well received by Secretary Mallory, and North was ordered to remain in England to investigate the purchase or building of an ironclad there. The Norths returned to London in mid–November and were soon installed in lodgings in Russell Square, Bloomsbury.

The following spring, North was introduced to Glasgow shipbuilders James & George Thomson by Edgar Pinchback Stringer, a member of the firm of William S. Lindsay & Company, shipowners and insurance brokers. In spite of Bulloch's reservations about its suitability, North signed a contract with the Thomsons on May 21, 1862, for an armored frigate, which he hoped to command, and on June 7 he reported to the Navy Department that work had now commenced on his ironclad. Negotiations were then started with Joseph Whitworth & Company in Manchester for cannon, gun carriages and ammunition.

The Confederate Navy, however, was to receive no benefit from his belated efforts. Fears that the ship might be seized led to the contract for "Number 61" or "Lieutenant North's ironclad" being terminated in December 1863 and its subsequent sale to the Royal Danish Navy. "It has been a sad, sad disappointment to me after so many months of labor to find it was necessary to part with so noble a ship when I felt confident she would have done us most valuable service," he wrote to Mallory.[15] After that, North moved to France, where he hoped to take command of one of the ironclads which Bulloch was having built there.

In the spring of 1863, the Federal government, greatly concerned about Confederate shipbuilding in England, sent two agents, John Murray Forbes and William H. Aspinwall, with instructions to buy any ships which were thought to be potentially dangerous in order to keep them out of Southern hands. When they arrived, they not only found that the newly launched Cotton Loan had seriously reduced the likelihood of their being able to purchase ships from cash-starved Confederates, but also that their "secret" mission was already public knowledge, with a report in the *Times* describing the large sums they had at their disposal to buy up "the gunboats now building in England for the rebels."[16] Forbes and Aspinwall liaised with Freeman Morse and Thomas Dudley, the U.S. consuls in London and Liverpool, from whom they obtained lists of suspicious vessels, and decided to concentrate on those rather than the ones being constructed for the Confederates. In the end, they found that their mission of purchasing ironclads or potential commerce raiders was not feasible and it was terminated at the end of June 1863.

It is difficult to believe that they were unaware of the large commerce raider then being built on the Clyde, in Scotland, for Lieutenant George T. Sinclair. Born in Norfolk, Virginia, George Terry Sinclair also came from a family with a long naval tradition; six of his relatives were officers in the Confederate Navy and like James North, of whom he was an old friend, he had served in the U.S. Navy for many years. Major Anderson formed a poor opinion of him, though he was apparently well regarded by Secretary of the Navy Mallory. Sent to England in May 1862 as a naval purchasing agent, Sinclair's instructions were to consult Commander Bulloch about the design, as well as the funding, of a commerce raider, of which, when complete, he was to take command. Bulloch gave him details of the *Alabama*, but as he had no spare funds at that time, Sinclair was obliged to look elsewhere. With the help of Confederate commissioner James Mason, finance was arranged with William S. Lindsay, who agreed to accept cotton certificates worth £51,000 for the ship, also to be built by J. & G. Thomson. The contract was again arranged by Edgar Stringer and signed in August 1862.[17]

While their respective vessels were being built, Sinclair lodged with North near Glasgow, but in February 1863, while on a visit to London, he stayed at a house in Buckland Crescent, Belsize Park, belonging to the Rev. Francis W. Tremlett, a well-known Southern sympathizer. He wrote to North: "We have a grand dinner party here today, to all the Confederates. Chapman and Evans are here." Bulloch was also present on that occasion.[18]

Though it was completed, his ship, known as the *Canton* or *Pampero,* never reached the

Confederates. In November 1863, its seizure becoming ever more likely, Sinclair, who had also now been promoted to commander, was advised to leave the Glasgow area; the vessel was impounded by government officials the following month.[19] After being ordered to Paris to join Flag Officer Barron's staff, Sinclair traveled to Cherbourg in June 1864, where the engagement between the CSS *Alabama* and the USS *Kearsarge* was imminent, but his request to be allowed to join the *Alabama* for the battle was refused. Both he and North were ordered back to the Confederacy early in 1865.

Most of the Confederates who came to London during the Civil War were quite unknown. One exception was Commander Raphael Semmes, who arrived in April 1862 after relinquishing command of the CSS *Sumter*. The most famous Confederate naval officer of the war, Raphael Semmes was born in 1809 in Maryland, and joined the U.S. Navy in 1826. As well as serving in the Mexican War, he also found time during long leaves of absence to study law, and had reached the rank of commander by the time he resigned from the U.S. Navy in 1861 to offer his services to the Confederacy. After being sent north to buy naval supplies, he was given command of the *Sumter*, the Confederate Navy's first commerce raider.

Semmes was accompanied by Lieutenant John McIntosh Kell. Born at Darien, Georgia, in 1823, Kell, a graduate of the Naval Academy at Annapolis, had joined the U.S. Navy in 1841 and like Semmes had seen service in the Mexican War; he had also taken part in Commodore Perry's expedition to Japan in 1852–1854.

The two men now found rooms in Euston Square, "our windows looking out, even at this early season, upon well-grown and fragrant grasses, trees in leaf, and flowers in bloom." Semmes lost no time in calling on Commissioner James Mason, whom he found "a great favorite with everybody. In his company I saw much of the society of the English capital, and soon became satisfied that Mr Davis could not have intrusted the affairs of the Confederacy to better hands. English hearts had warmed towards him and his name was the sesame to open all English doors."[20] He learned from Mason that the *Florida* had sailed the previous month and that the *Alabama* would soon be launched, and subsequently had discussions with Bulloch and North. Semmes and Kell returned to the Confederacy in the latter part of May on board the *Melita*, one of Isaac, Campbell's steamers.

On his second visit in June 1864, after the loss of the CSS *Alabama*, Semmes, by now a captain, and accompanied as before by Lieutenant Kell, found himself a considerable celebrity. A group of naval officers at the Junior United Service Club in Charles II Street presented him with "a magnificent sword, which was manufactured to their order in the City of London," to replace the one lost when the *Alabama* was sunk. "To keep company with this sword, a noble English lady presented me with a mammoth Confederate flag, wrought with her own hands from the richest silk," he wrote.[21] He was also offered a public dinner by the Army & Navy Club in Pall Mall, an honor he declined. Kell went back to the Confederacy in early July, and Semmes, after a recuperative tour in Europe, began his own journey back to the Confederate States in October.

Another Confederate who was extremely well-known was Commander Matthew Fontaine Maury. Born near Fredericksburg, Virginia, in 1806, Matthew Maury had joined the U.S. Navy in 1825 and taken part in three long cruises, including that of the USS *Vincennes* on her famous four-year voyage around the world. After being crippled in a stagecoach accident in 1839, he had been restricted to shore duties and was subsequently appointed superintendent of what became the U.S. Naval Observatory and Hydrographic Office in Washington, D.C. He had already begun to make his name as a scientific author with his *New Theoretical and Practical Treatise on Navigation* (1836), but it was as the founder of the new science of oceanography that he secured an international reputation, becoming the recipient of many foreign honors and awards. His *Physical Geography of the Sea* (1855), one of the most famous scientific textbooks of the nineteenth century, went through many editions and was translated into a number of languages. His great knowledge of the sea also helped in planning the laying of the first transatlantic cable.

At the start of the Civil War, as a commander in the Confederate States Navy, Maury was given responsibility for Virginia's harbor and river defenses. He had divided his time between superintending the construction of small wooden gunboats and experimenting with electric torpedoes (floating mines) before being ordered to England in September 1862 on special service, partly as a spokesman for the Confederate cause.[22] It was also, recalled James Bulloch, "to investigate the subject of submarine defences, and he gave much time to researches into electricity, the manufacture and use of gun-cotton, torpedoes, magnetic explosives and insulated wire. In addition, he had general authority to buy and despatch a vessel to cruise against the commerce of the United States whenever he thought the attempt practicable."[23]

It was October 9 before Commander Maury finally left for England, accompanied by his son, 13-year-old Matthew, Jr., and Midshipman James Morris Morgan, who had been at the U.S. Naval Academy at Annapolis when the war broke out. From Charleston, they traveled via Bermuda and Halifax, Nova Scotia, and finally reached Liverpool in the steamer *Arabia* on November 23, 1862. After several days, during which he met Commander Bulloch, who was to pay his salary and expenses, Commander Maury, his son and Midshipman Morgan proceeded to London.

"When we reached London I found that a house in Sackville Street had already been engaged for the commodore, who kindly invited me to be his guest," recalled Midshipman Morgan.[24] The rooms in Sackville Street cost about £10 a week and Matthew, Jr., in a letter to his mother and sisters, later described their maid, somewhat unkindly: "Pa calls her the donkey engine because she is so small and darts about so quick and like a little engine."[25]

Maury had been to London several times before — most recently in 1860 — and he conferred with Commissioner Mason about Confederate recognition and purchasing activities. In addition, there were visits from friends like Lord Wrottesley, a former president of the Royal Astronomical Society, Rear Admiral Robert Fitzroy, the inventor of the Fitzroy barometer, Sir Henry Holland, the eminent physician, and Captain Marin H. Jansen, of the Royal Netherlands Navy. Maury, it seemed, was more appreciated in Europe than he was in America: "All day long there would be in front of the house a string of carriages with coronets on their doors, while their owners were paying their respects to the celebrated Lieutenant Maury."[26]

At the beginning of February 1863 Lieutenant William Lowndes Maury, a distant cousin of Commander Maury, arrived in London with $1.5 million in cotton certificates, and authorization to buy and equip a commerce raider. The *Japan*, an iron-propeller steamer being built in Scotland, had already been selected on Commander Maury's behalf by Captain Jansen; in March 1863 she was purchased for him by Thomas Bold, another cousin, in conjunction with the banking firm of J. Henry Schroder. The outfitting of the ship was supervised at great personal risk by Captain Jansen, who was a serving Dutch naval officer, and in April 1863, off the coast of France, the vessel was commissioned as the CSS *Georgia*.

After brief spells of duty in Liverpool and Paris, Midshipman Morgan was ordered to return to London and await instructions at the Westminster Palace Hotel. "On the 4th of April, 1863," he recalled, "I received an order to go to a house in Little St James's Street and

Premises in New Bond Street where Maury lodged in 1863. (Author's photograph)

inquire for a 'Mr. Grigson,' who would give me further instructions. When I found the house the door was opened by a pleasant-faced, middle-aged woman who seemed much amused when I asked for 'Mr. Grigson.' She replied, laughing, 'You will find them in there,' pointing to a door. From her language I inferred that the mysterious Mr. Grigson was not so singular a man after all; evidently there must be more than one of him."[27]

Among the assembled naval officers, Morgan found Lieutenants Robert T. Chapman and William E. Evans, who had both served on the CSS *Sumter*. They had arrived in London the previous August, lodging in Bury Street, but following the murder of an acting midshipman in the *Sumter* in October 1862, Chapman had been ordered back to Gibraltar to take temporary command of the ship.

Morgan was instructed to go back to his hotel, get his belongings and return to Little St. James's Street. Then, in company with his fellow officers, he took the train "for a little seaport about an hour's ride from London" (Newhaven, Sussex), to meet his future captain, Lieutenant William L. Maury, and join the steamer *Alar*, which would rendezvous with the *Georgia*.[28] Although she remained at sea for seven months and captured or destroyed a number of American merchant ships, lack of sail power and the consequent need for frequent recoaling rendered the *Georgia* unsuitable as a cruiser and in May 1864 she was taken to Liverpool, decommissioned and sold.

Meanwhile, the search for ships went on. In May 1863 Commander Maury went to France to negotiate for a twin-turreted ironclad, but it was decided not to proceed with this, and in July he ordered Lieutenant William F. Carter "to visit the ship yards on

Maury's first ship, the CSS *Georgia*, which proved unsatisfactory as a commerce raider. (*Illustrated London News*)

the Thames, examine the vessels there for sale, and report such as may be suitable for our purposes."[29]

In November 1863, as a replacement for the *Georgia*, Maury arranged to buy an ex–Royal Navy wooden gunboat called HMS *Victor*. The purchase, also with cotton certificates, was made by the firm of Gordon Coleman & Company, acting as agents for Thomas Bold, but the vessel was to prove even less successful than the *Georgia*. After an initial refit at Sheerness Dockyard, where she was known as the *Scylla*, she quietly departed on November 24, towed by a tug, and headed for Calais for further necessary repairs. At sea she was commissioned as the CSS *Rappahannock*, under the command of Lieutenant William P.A. Campbell and later of Lieutenant Charles M. Fauntleroy. After she had arrived at Calais, the French authorities refused to let her leave, and she was obliged to remain there as a depot ship; to her officers she became known as the "Confederate White Elephant." Her crew was discharged and her officers detached at the end of March 1865 and she was sold four months later.

One of the officers assigned to the *Rappahannock* was Assistant Paymaster Douglas French Forrest. The son of Captain French Forrest, Head of the Bureau of Orders and Detail in the Navy Department, he was born in Baltimore in 1837 and had spent a year in the Confederate Army before transferring to the Navy and receiving his commission. In May 1863 he was sent abroad, and arrived in London at the end of July in company with several other naval officers. He spent the first two nights at the Berners Hotel in Berners Street, "a very quiet house, staid & respectable ... Very nice room, regularly English — no gilt, all solid, substantial, pure bed linens ... & the never failing bed-curtains."[30] In his first couple of days in

The CSS *Rappahannock*, Maury's second ship, which got no further than Calais. (*Illustrated London News*)

London, Forrest made several calls, including one on Commissioner Mason, who "rec[eive]d us kindly & gave us every aid & offer of aid." He also found time to visit Madame Tussaud's Waxworks on Baker Street, and the Princess's Theater on Oxford Street for a performance of *Romeo and Juliet*, which failed to impress — "indifferent theatre, very moderate acting" — though he was amused by the women who came around selling soda water, lemonade, bottled ale and stout during the intermissions.

Following a brief visit to Liverpool, Forrest spent a further ten days in London in the early part of August. After three nights, again probably at the Berners Hotel, he and his companions moved to lodgings in New Bond Street, premises occupied at street level by a tailor. "I've a small room in the upper story but it's neat & pleasant & our mess, consisting of the Senacs, Graves, Morris & myself have a nice sitting room for our company. Our first dinner was plain but substantial," he recorded.[31]

While awaiting orders, much of his time was spent in sightseeing: the Zoological Gardens, the Old Bailey, the Monument, Westminster Abbey, the Burlington Arcade and several of the London parks. One of his acquaintances, Lieutenant Charles L. Hobson, who had come to London with Captain Crenshaw earlier that year, and was now involved in blockade-running, accompanied him on a visit to the Bank of England, "a rare privilege."[32] Another novelty was a ride on the underground Metropolitan Railway, which had opened at the beginning of that year. He also saw something of the nightlife of the metropolis, with visits to two music halls — the London Pavilion, on Tichborne Street, which he entered only after being persuaded that it was "perfectly respectable," and Evans' Music-and-Supper Rooms in King Street, Covent Garden, where he tried to have "Dixie" sung, to annoy a Federal naval officer who was present, and Cremorne Gardens at Chelsea. On August 12 Douglas Forrest departed for Scotland.

By late November 1863 he was in Calais awaiting the arrival of the *Rappahannock*. No sooner had it arrived than he was sent back to London "to see Mr. Maury & get money etc." On this occasion he stayed at the Grosvenor Hotel, by Victoria Station, "one of the finest in London." Commander Maury, he found, was out of town, but he called on Major Huse at Isaac, Campbell's offices in Jermyn Street, and Zachariah Pearson, "who is largely concerned in the fitting out of our ship," and who was lodging in Hereford Road, Bayswater. On subsequent visits to London, in February and April 1864, he stayed at the Tavistock Hotel in Covent Garden, "a miserable concern for all its reputation," and at Morley's Hotel in Trafalgar Square.

The *Rappahannock*, which had already been the subject of news reports when the British authorities failed to prevent her leaving Sheerness, was to become even better known to the public as the focus of two trials involving the attempted recruitment of men to serve in her.[33] The first involved John Seymour, a shipping agent and roominghouse keeper, of Wellclose Square, Whitechapel, who was known to his associates as "John the Greek." On July 14, 1864, he pleaded guilty at the Central Criminal Court, Old Bailey, to a violation of the Foreign Enlistment Act, by attempting to recruit a number of seamen and firemen "for a ship in Calais" (the *Rappahannock*). Probably because he was acting on instructions from the shipping broker Gordon Coleman, Seymour was discharged, on condition that he refrain from repeating the offense.

Seymour was not the only boardinghouse keeper engaged in this activity. According to his deposition made on December 2, 1863, William Wynn, of Lower Berners Street, Stepney, procured eleven seamen for "a ship to run the blockade." The seamen went to London Bridge

Station to meet a man calling himself "Captain Brown," where tickets for Calais were purchased for them and about twenty-eight others. After an overnight stay at Dover, the seamen crossed to Calais, where they went onboard "a ship then called the *Rappahannock*," where they were told by the captain: "You are now going privateering, the same as the *Alabama* and the *Florida*. You men are going to fight for money, and I am going to fight for glory." Within three days, unhappy at the arrangements, twenty-one of the men had been allowed to leave and were sent back to London.[34] The remainder were discharged in August 1864.

The case against William Rumble, the chief inspector of machinery afloat at Sheerness Dockyard, who was an Admiralty official, was rather more serious. Not only had he been involved in the refit of the *Rappahannock*, both there and at Calais, he had also engaged in recruiting activities. Indeed, it was viewed so seriously by the U.S. minister that he made a representation to the British government about it.

The preliminary hearing took place at the Court of Queen's Bench, Westminster, on April 25, 1864, and resumed on December 5, 1864, and February 1, 3, and 4, 1865. During the proceedings it appeared that, although the registered owner was Gordon Coleman, the real owner was actually Zachariah Pearson of Hull, "the partner of Coleman (and a bankrupt to the amount of some £600,000 during the past summer)" as a result of his involvement in blockade-running. "Mr. Pearson who does not deny that he has sent the Confederates ships — of what kind he does not specify — complains piteously that while the Federals robbed him of the ships, the Confederates refused to pay for them."[35]

At the beginning of the trial, Charles Francis Adams made a remarkably accurate prediction of the outcome: "It is ... rather doubtful whether Mr. Rumble, though unquestionably guilty of all and more than all that is charged, will be convicted."[36] William Rumble was seen by the court as "the tool of others" and was indeed acquitted. As a result of this trial, Adams felt that the United States could expect no justice from British courts for prosecutions brought under the Foreign Enlistment Act. "Their rebel sympathies got the better of their oaths," Benjamin Moran noted disgustedly in his journal. Though acquitted, Rumble was placed on half pay, "as an officer in whom [their lordships] can no longer place any confidence."

In April 1863 a volunteer navy — a modified version of privateering — was authorized by the Confederate Congress. The man behind this idea was Bernard Janin Sage, who came from Connecticut, but had later settled in New Orleans, where he studied law and also became the owner of a sugar plantation. He now set about finding investors in Richmond to form the Virginia Volunteer Navy Company, then in 1864, now a master in the Confederate Navy assigned to special duty, traveled to England in a fruitless attempt to raise enough money to purchase a ship for the company. He was still in London in September of that year, when he wrote to Commander Maury about the misfortunes of another volunteer navy company in Tennessee.

The Virginia Volunteer Navy Company, meanwhile, had chosen its own purchasing agent in the person of Lieutenant Edward C. Stiles, C.S.N., who was commissioned a commander and given leave-of-absence to go to Europe to buy a steamer. The vessel chosen, the *Hawk*, "one of the finest steamers of her class to be found in England, perfectly strengthened and thoroughly fitted in every respect, for immediate advance against the enemy," had been built on the Clyde in 1863, and was owned by Thomas Begbie.[37] After changing hands, she was modified, with strengthened decking, increased storage for coal, and additional living quarters, and sailed from Glasgow to London in April 1864. The Federals were very aware of her presence in Victoria Docks, and there is a note of exasperation in the dispatch about her which

Freeman Morse sent to Charles Francis Adams in June: "Owing to the extreme prudence and reticence of those who direct and execute rebel operations in this country, and the skill in evading the laws which three years' experience has taught them, I have found it quite impossible to procure such legal evidence as is here required for her detention."[38] By the time that was written, the *Hawk* had left for Bermuda, under the command of Lieutenant Knox.

The *Hawk* was bought partly on credit, and until the debt was discharged, Commander Stiles and a colleague, Assistant Paymaster Daniel Talley, agreed to remain in England. As no funds had arrived from Richmond by the autumn of 1864, Stiles turned for assistance to Commissioner Mason and Commander Bulloch, but none was available from those quarters. After several months lying idle in Bermuda, the *Hawk* returned to London about the end of 1864, by which time Commander Robert B. Pegram, C.S.N., former captain of the CSS *Nashville*, had also arrived there. On his instructions, the ship was put up for auction in January 1865 and sold. His debts settled, Commander Stiles and his fellow officers returned to the Confederacy, only to be captured when they attempted to land on the Louisiana coast. Commander Pegram abandoned any attempt to buy another steamer.

Many of the vessels offered to the Confederate Navy Department during the war were referred to Commander Bulloch for further investigation. Some of the offers came from speculators looking for a quick profit, while others were from "honest men, really desirous to do the South a service, but having no technical knowledge of ships, and no faculty for estimating the essential requirements of a Confederate cruiser."[39] The latter included two large, outdated and overpriced paddle steamers from the Indian navy, a number of redundant steamers belonging to the banking house of Overend, Gurney & Company laid up in the London docks, which would have been very costly to operate, and vessels from foreign navies, which turned out to be defective or otherwise unsuitable. There was an offer from a firm of English shipbuilders to build another *Alabama*, which was subsequently withdrawn, as well as another from a foreign banker to buy an ironclad frigate and deliver her at sea to anyone appointed by Bulloch to receive her; this was also withdrawn, perhaps because of the financial conditions attached.[40]

The most senior Confederate officer to visit London during the Civil War was Samuel Barron. Born in Hampton, Virginia, in 1809, he had had more than forty years' service in the U.S. Navy. After secession he had been placed in charge of the naval defenses of Virginia and North Carolina, and then been a prisoner-of-war for eleven months before being exchanged. His substantive rank was captain, but with the temporary one of commodore, and the impressive-sounding title of Flag Officer Commanding Confederate States Naval Forces in Europe, he was now being sent to take command of the ships being built for the Confederacy in Britain and France. Accompanied by Lieutenant William C. Whittle, Jr., he left Richmond at the end of August 1863 and from Wilmington traveled to Bermuda, where there was a wait of ten days before he could join the British steamer *Florida*. Both the weather and the food onboard were bad, and the "unpleasant passage" to England took more than three weeks. Barron finally reached Liverpool on October 12, and following a visit to Glasgow to inspect the two Confederate ships under construction on the Clyde, arrived in London four days later. After a week, during which he stayed at the Burlington Hotel in Cork Street, he left for Paris and set up his headquarters in the Rue Drouot, where he was to remain until the early part of 1865.

Flag Officer Barron's assignment to Europe, however, was to prove an empty one. The ships which he was to command were all seized or sold, and even the rams built at Bordeaux for Commander Bulloch were acquired by foreign navies. One of these, however, was repurchased from Denmark, to become, in January 1865, the CSS *Stonewall*. It was to be commanded by Captain Thomas Jefferson Page, a Virginian who had originally been sent to Europe to command one of the Laird rams, then to relieve Captain Semmes on the *Alabama*, though in the event he had done neither. A London-built blockade-runner, the *City of Richmond*, belonging to Captain Crenshaw, was lent to Commander Bulloch to carry the crew, who were from the *Rappahannock* and the *Florida*, to a rendezvous with the *Stonewall* off the French coast.[41] The *City of Richmond*, commanded by Lieutenant Hunter Davidson, left Greenhithe, on the Thames, on January 11, 1865, and met the *Stonewall* thirteen days later. The only Confederate ironclad ever to put to sea, the war had ended by the time it finally reached Cuba in early May.

On February 28, 1865, Flag Officer Barron relinquished his command as senior Confederate naval officer in Europe, and on April 3, together with Commanders North, Sinclair, Pegram and Barney (the former captain of the *Florida*), Lieutenant Holcombe, Assistant Paymaster Forrest and Midshipman Dyke from the *Rappahannock*, he left Southampton in the steamer *Tasmanian*, en route for Havana and the Confederacy.

Commander Maury, who had latterly concentrated chiefly on his torpedo experiments, both in London and at Bowdon, near Manchester, where his son was in school, sending torpedo supplies and equipment back to Richmond in August and October 1864, also attempted to return to the Confederacy in the closing weeks of the war. He was probably not sorry to be leaving; he had regarded his wartime duties in England as a form of banishment by enemies in high places, in particular Jefferson Davis and Stephen Mallory, to keep him from any further role in Confederate affairs at home.

Before his departure, a dinner in his honor was planned, and a circular dated March 30, 1865, was issued by the honorary secretary of the testimonial fund.[42] The dinner was to be held on April 26. Six days later, on May 2, 1865, together with his son, he left for Havana. When he arrived on May 22 he found the war was over; waiting there was the CSS *Stonewall*, which had surrendered to the Spanish authorities, and Commodore Barron and his party, who had arrived a month previously, officers in a navy which no longer existed. Dispatching his son to New York, Maury departed for Mexico.

The Confederacy's attempts to procure ships in Britain had only limited success, and most of that was attributable to one man, the resourceful Commander Bulloch. The commerce raiders built or purchased by him — the *Florida*, the *Alabama* and the *Shenandoah* — did at least put to sea to do the job for which they were intended, and the vessels he had constructed in London — the *Louisa Ann Fanny* and the *Mary Augusta* — were completed, though the Confederates never took delivery of the latter; given the political implications, the seizure of the Laird rams built at Birkenhead was a foregone conclusion. The ironclads constructed on the Clyde for Commanders North and Sinclair were sold abroad or impounded, while the two vessels acquired by Commander Maury as commerce raiders — the *Georgia* and the *Rappahannock* — proved unsuitable or downright disastrous.[43]

6

The Spying Game

A system of espionage of the most extensive and searching character has been for some time going on in England, and every move of a warlike character has been immediately reported to the Government of the United States.
—*Morning Chronicle*, December 1861

The activities of Confederates, in both London and elsewhere, were already under observation by the middle of 1861. Henry Shelton Sanford, the newly appointed U.S. minister to Belgium, who had been made responsible for the Federal secret service in Europe, was soon writing to Secretary of State William H. Seward, asking for more agents to be sent to "aid in routing up this nest of secessionists ... London & Paris are the keys of the position & ... I do hope you will provide sufficient secret service funds when Congress meets."[1] Every Confederate purchasing agent, he thought, should be shadowed night and day by one or more Federal agents.

In June 1861, with the assistance of Freeman H. Morse, the United States consul in London, Sanford engaged the services of Ignatius Paul Pollaky, who had a "private continental inquiry office" near the Mansion House in London. Though Pollaky seemed to be "just the man," Morse admitted that he knew nothing about Pollaky, "& there may be some risk in dealing with him. But it is a 'risky business' anyway & I think we had better engage him at once."[2]

According to his own newspaper advertisements, Pollaky had been employed for some years by Charles Frederick Field, usually known as "Inspector Field of the Detective Force," during which time he had been entrusted with "the most delicate and confidential inquiries in this country and abroad."[3] Field, who had joined the Metropolitan Police when it was established in 1829, was the most famous British police officer of his day, chiefly because of his appearance in Charles Dickens' magazine *Household Words*, and when he left the force in 1852 he set up his own private inquiry office.[4]

Once engaged, Pollaky lost no time in setting up a surveillance system, which he claimed, would "leave no room for any further improvement." Known Confederates were pointed out to his agents; the rendezvous of Confederates in London were watched, and daily reports made of their comings and goings; warehouses, where goods waiting to be shipped through the blockade might be stored, were placed under observation; postmen were bribed to supply details of postmarks on letters delivered to Confederates, with a view to identifying ports where ships might be preparing to run the blockade; and the telegraph offices were watched.

PRIVATE INQUIRY OFFICE, established 1852,

20, Devereux-court, Temple, under the direction of CHARLES FREDERICK FIELD (late chief Inspector of the Detective Police of the Metropolis). Confidential inquiries made for noblemen, gentlemen, solicitors, railway and insurance companies. Evidence collected in divorce and other cases. This office is unconnected with the police.

PRIVATE CONTINENTAL INQUIRY OFFICE.

--- Mr. POLLAKY, formerly superintendent of the foreign department in Mr. Field's office, and who has been entrusted during the last 12 years with the most delicate and confidential inquiries in this country and abroad, has OPENED the above ESTABLISHMENT with the view of protecting the interests of the British public in its social, legal, and commercial relations with foreigners. Inquiries of every description, which do not come within the province of the regular police authorities can be made through this office on any part of the continent. Offices at 14, George-street, Mansion-house, E. C.

Ignatius P. Pollaky, who was engaged in 1861 to spy on the Confederates, learned his craft with the famous "Inspector Field of the Detective Force." (*Times*, 23 January 1862)

In addition, one of the clerks in Isaac, Campbell's office was paid to provide details of contracts with the Confederate government.

In September the resourceful and zealous Sanford suggested an even more ambitious surveillance operation to Seward: officials of the steamship companies and clerks of the main business houses might be bribed to provide details of transactions with the Confederates, and a contact at Lloyd's marine insurance office could supply useful information about ships sailing to Confederate ports. They might then either be seized, or delayed by court action; if that proved impossible, details could at least be sent to the Federal blockading squadrons, so they might be intercepted. It was even proposed that an entire blockade-runner loaded with war materials could be purchased from its owner, thus depriving the Confederates of a quantity of arms and ammunition. It would all cost a great deal of money.

Early in October Pollaky's men traced crates of guns from warehouses in London to the Scottish port of Greenock. Large amounts of arms, ammunition and military equipment had been transported there by freighter, and were being loaded on board the steamer *Fingal*. "I fortunately observed *the cases*. There is no mistake about them as in addition to the marks ... they also have a card on each *Isaac, Campbell & Co*.... depend upon it, I will keep a bright look out on them," reported one of the detectives.[5] It proved impossible, however, to detain the *Fingal*, and she sailed from Greenock on October 9, bound for Savannah.

The following month Sanford was annoyed to discover that Charles Francis Adams and Freeman Morse had in the meantime set up their own surveillance operation and complained about this to William H. Seward.⁶ Adams, who considered Sanford a meddler who was encroaching on his domain, also protested to Washington about the unsatisfactory double system that now prevailed. As a result, it was decided that Sanford's responsibilities should be restricted to mainland Europe, and by January 1862 his arrangements with Pollaky had been terminated. At the end of that month, Benjamin Moran, who appears to have had little faith in Ignatius Pollaky, referring to him dismissively as "a German Jew ... who is acting as a detective, and whom S[anford] was so silly as to employ," nonetheless met with him and was presented with his bill for work done for both Henry Sanford and also Freeman Morse.⁷

From then on, operations in London were under the day-to-day control of Freeman Morse, who had taken over as U.S. consul in London in May 1861. Freeman Harlow Morse, a former congressman from Maine, was to play an increasingly important part in Federal espionage activities in London. As the war progressed, his workload at the consulate in Gracechurch Street increased so much that he found it necesssary to ask for the appointment of a deputy consul to assist him; his chief clerk, Joshua Nunn, was recommended for the post and appointed in April 1863.

Federal surveillance work was also considerably enhanced about this time as a result of the visit of John M. Forbes and William H. Aspinwall, who had been sent to England to attempt to buy up Confederate ironclads and commerce raiders. They recommended that for espionage purposes Morse and his Liverpool counterpart, Thomas H. Dudley, should divide the country between them, Morse having overall responsibility for the South of England and the Midlands, and Dudley for the North and Scotland, and also made additional money available for surveillance work from their own funds.⁸

There was an enormous amount of correspondence with the State Department in Washington, much of it concerned with ships thought to be carrying war supplies for the Confederates. "The iron screw steamer *Gladiator* has been purchased by the Confederates and is now in the Thames loading with arms and ammunition, and those who control her here say she *can and will run the blockade*...," Morse reported to Secretary of State Seward on November 1, 1861.⁹ The following day he went to have a look at the ship: "I have just returned from a short trip down the river to see the Confederate steamer *Gladiator* ... She will take out a large quantity of Enfield rifles, besides ammunition, clothing, &c."¹⁰ The *Gladiator* sailed on November 10 with a cargo which included more than 22,000 Enfield rifles.

Towards the end of January 1862, intelligence concerning another vessel was sent to Washington:

> The steamer *Economist* is now loading with Enfield rifles, blankets, socks, army cloths, made-up clothing etc ... She is loading in ... the Thames, a few miles below London Bridge ... The *Economist* is managed here by I[saac], Campbell & Co. This house has acted as agents for the rebels in most of their transactions here ... I do not think there is a question about her cargo being destined for the South and as she is perhaps the largest steamer yet sent out by the insurgents and their friends here it must be valuable, but especially so to the rebels.¹¹

The *Economist* left London on January 30, 1862, and within a few days of her departure Morse was informed that yet another steamer, the *Southwick*, was in the Thames, loading with a similar cargo. The information came from a man called Thomas H. Chase, whom Morse occasionally refers to as "my chief agent." He was also sometimes called Captain Chase, and his familiarity with nautical matters — he was adept at supplying details and sketches of ships under investigation — suggests he was probably a former merchant seaman. With an assistant

The U.S. legation, Upper Portland Place (now Portland Place), where Minister Charles Francis Adams received many reports of Confederate activity in London. (Author's photograph)

he traveled down the river and through the docks every day and made frequent visits to the shipyards.

There were to be reports on many more ships. In March 1862, for instance, 200 cases of Enfield rifles were reported as "shipped on board the *Minna* within the last three days," while "the side-wheel steamer *Pacific* continues taking in cargo of a similar description to that going into the steamer *Minna*. I learn that 5,000 Enfield rifles are expected to be shipped on her."[12] The *Minna*, it was discovered, carried tea, coffee, blankets, leather, boots and shoes, swords, knapsacks, gunpowder, saltpeter and revolvers, as well as at least 8,580 rifles.

The *Princess Royal,* which cleared London on December 8, 1862, carried quantities of semimilitary equipment supplied by William S. Lindsay & Company, it was reported, but she was captured while trying to enter Charleston harbor the following month. The *Harriet Pinckney,* destined for Bermuda, was observed in May 1863 loading in the Thames with rifles, artillery and carbines; when she returned to England the following September she carried a number of passengers, among them the Confederate spy and emissary, Mrs. Rose Greenhow.

In a report on ships loading in the Thames in June 1863, Chase observed that "the clothing is coming up from more directions than usual — Manchester, Leeds, Dewsbury, York, etc and by different routes, viz, Great Northern Railway, North Western, and also by the old-fashioned canal boats direct from Manchester."[13]

Occasionally Chase reported on matters unconnected with shipping, such as the public meeting held near Fitzroy Square in November 1862 which was attended by some four hundred people, all of them seemingly respectable. At it, the conduct of the press, especially the *Times,* was condemned, and hopes were expressed that the U.S. government would prevail.[14]

He was one of several men whose services were paid for out of the Federal secret service account and who reported to Consul Morse. There was also J.G. Bunting, who spent a considerable amount of time in Calais observing the *Rappahannock*, and the man who usually signed himself "G" (C.W. Geddes), who enjoyed the confidence of Confederates in both London and Paris. "He is still considered by most or all of them who know him as one of their number and they speak as unreservedly to him about their doings as they do to each other," Morse observed in a note accompanying a report from him in July 1864.[15] "I ... get an occasional *inside view*," he had commented in an earlier letter, and it is evident from other remarks in the consular dispatches that more than one confidant of leading Confederates in London was passing information to the U.S. consulate, presumably in return for money. No wonder Commander North remarked to "G", during a visit to Paris in July 1864: "We have almost given up in despair ever being able to do anything in England, the Federals have so many spies and they are so active that it is impossible to do anything, no matter how secret we may act, or how few we have engaged in it."[16] For once, it was a realistic assessment of the situation.

Information came to the Federals from other sources, too, though it was not always very reliable. Occasionally it was from firms who had dealings with the Confederates, such as Bennett & Wake, ship and insurance brokers, who sent details to the U.S. consulate in late 1862, though some doubts were expressed as to the authenticity of the letter.[17] There was also the inevitable defector, or supposed defector, and as Benjamin Moran found, there was no shortage of people willing to sell information, both genuine and bogus.

One such was John Magoffin, supposedly a captain in the Confederate Army, who in July 1864 came to the U.S. consulate to take the oath of allegiance and give information about rebel sympathizers in the United States. This turned out to be of dubious value, and its bearer was later thought to have reverted to his original allegiance. Dealings with W.F. Gray, a Virginian long resident in Texas, and a Union sympathizer, proved equally unsatisfactory for the Federals. He claimed to have the confidence of many Confederate agents, and on the strength of that obtained money from the London consulate in January 1864; he was later found to have done the same thing at U.S. consulates in France, Germany and Italy.

Particularly notorious was "the infamous traitor," Clarence R. Yonge, who had been dismissed from his post of assistant paymaster on the CSS *Alabama*. In April 1863, having arrived in London, he gave information to the U.S. minister about his previous duties as private secretary to Commander Bulloch, as well as providing details about the two Laird rams and the *Alexandra*, a ship being built for Fraser, Trenholm as a present for the Confederate government. As a crown witness in the trial in June 1863, at the Court of Exchequer, Westminster, which followed the seizure of the *Alexandra*, Yonge was completely discredited, being referred to on one occasion as "this specimen of humanity," and the court found in favor of the defendants.

Morse received many reports about a warehouse at St. Bride's Wharf, Wapping, where goods supplied by Sinclair, Hamilton were believed to be stored. These were eventually removed by Pickford's vans and taken by barge to the *Hawk*, a steamer owned by Thomas Begbie, and thought to be intended as a privateer. She had come from Glasgow, where she had been under observation, and after arriving near the mouth of the Thames about April 19, 1864, had remained there for some three weeks before proceeding to Victoria Docks. However, Morse admitted, in a letter to Charles Francis Adams, "owing to the extreme prudence and reticence of those who direct and execute rebel operations in this country, and the skill in evading the laws which three years' experience has taught them, I have found it quite impossible to procure such legal evidence as is here required for her detention."[18]

Various alterations had been made to the vessel before she left the Clyde. "These alterations and her equipment and fittings," reported Morse, "were done by the direction of Captain Bulloch, of the so-called Confederate Navy. This Captain Bulloch visited her several times while in the process of completion and ... made a thorough examination of her and directed various alterations to be made ... Bulloch was undoubtedly the chief superintendent and director in the purchase and fitting out of the *Hawk* ... yet she stands registered in Mr Begbie's name ... until she can be placed safely in Confederate hands."[19]

As a result of Morse's intelligence, Adams registered a complaint with the British Foreign Office, and the *Hawk* was examined by customs officers, but nothing unusual was found. The "officers had no difficulty in going over every part of the ship, and ... in so doing, they saw nothing whatever to arouse any suspicion of the vessel; she appeared to be a very fast merchant ship ... not fitted for war purposes, her iron plates being so thin and light," Adams was told.[20] Her cargo consisted of iron, bar steel and "divers articles of merchandise." In spite of this, Morse concluded, "I am satisfied that she belongs to the so-called Confederate government, and that said government intends to use her for purposes of war, or for committing depredations against the commerce of the United States."[21] The *Hawk* left Victoria Docks on June 13, 1864 and, after anchoring in the Thames off Woolwich, sailed for Bermuda two days later.

As early as July 1862 Morse had reported to Washington: "Rifles in considerable quantities have been sent this week from here to Liverpool. Three hundred cases, with 20 in each case, have gone down within three days." A week later he added: "About 700 cases of Enfield rifles containing 20 in each case have gone from the London Armoury and Barnett's establishment within a week or ten days past to Liverpool to be shipped from there for the Confederates."[22] This may have been the beginning of a trend, because in September 1864 he remarked: "For the last two or three months the rebels seem nearly to have abandoned this port as a place from whence to forward supplies. Even the rifles manufactured here for them have lately been sent to Liverpool to forward from that port."[23]

The Federals took a keen interest in arrivals from the Confederacy. One Confederate who was singled out for special attention was James Bulloch, whose supposedly secret mission was known about almost before he arrived at Liverpool. He was astonished to discover that full details of his assignment had appeared in a New York newspaper which had now reached England, and he found himself under surveillance from the outset. "This man is here and his movements are observed," Consul Morse reported to Secretary of State Seward on July 19, 1861.[24] Seward was told by Henry Sanford that he had "doubled the force upon Bulloch's surveillance ... He is the most dangerous man the South have here and fully up to his business. I am disbursing at the rate of £150 a month on this one man which will give you an idea of the importance I attach to his movements."[25] Adams thought, quite correctly, that Bulloch was one of the most efficient agents the Confederacy had in Europe.

It was not just in Liverpool that Bulloch was a marked man. On one occasion, towards the end of the war, he remarked that he thought it best not to go to London, "as I am so well known there." In his memoirs he recalled: "The consular agents of the United States had already begun to practise an inquisitive system of espionage, and it was soon manifest that the movements of those who were supposed to be agents of the Confederate Government were closely and vigilantly watched."[26]

Bulloch commented on this several times in letters to the Confederate Navy Department, remarking, for instance, in November 1863:

> The extent to which the system of bribery and spying has been and continues to be practised by the agents of the United States in Europe is scarcely credible. The servants of gentlemen supposed to have Southern sympathies are tampered with, confidential clerks, and even the messengers from telegraph offices, are bribed to betray their trust, and I have lately been informed that the English and French Post Offices, hitherto considered immaculate, are now scarcely safe modes of communication...[27]

He returned to this theme the following February:

> The spies of the United States are numerous, active and unscrupulous. They invade the privacy of families, tamper with the confidential clerks of merchants, and have succeeded in converting a portion of the police of this country into secret agents of the United States, who have practised a prying watchfulness over the movements and business of individuals ... which has excited the disgust and openly expressed indignation of many prominent Englishmen...[28]

Sanford's description of Bulloch as "the most dangerous man the South have here" was not an exaggeration. His strategically placed agents included a "mole" in the Foreign Office, thought to have been a certain Victor Buckley. Adams had seen a note from Buckley to Caleb Huse, warning him of danger to his "protégé" (the *Alabama*) when there was a likelihood of its being impounded by the British authorities, and in his diary Adams noted: "This Victor Buckley is a clerk in the Foreign Office."[29]

Another Confederate agent who was "closely and vigilantly watched" was Major Edward Anderson. For some time he had no idea he was under surveillance, until one morning one of the Isaac brothers came over to his lodgings and asked him if he knew he was being watched. Through the window Mr. Isaac then pointed out a rough-looking man standing on the corner of the street; he was one of the detectives employed by Charles Francis Adams, the U.S. minister. "These men are indefatigable in their attentions," Anderson noted in his diary, "following me specially wherever I go, even into the shops in cases where I have purchases of the most trivial kind to make."[30]

Anderson went out into Jermyn Street to take a closer look

Naval purchasing agent Cdr. James D. Bulloch was singled out for special attention by the Federals and eventually became reluctant to come to London because he was so well-known there. (*Battles and Leaders of the Civil War*)

at his "shadow," "a plain, countrified-looking man, roughly clad & by no means bearing about him the appearance of a detective officer."[31] He was to see him again many times during his stay in London, in many different disguises. "I never failed however to recognize my shadow. Assisting him were one or two others, employed in like manner in the pay of the American minister."[32]

Later, Anderson discovered that "a well dressed man" (one of Adams' detectives) had made an unsuccessful attempt to obtain a copy of a telegram he had recently sent from the telegraph office in St. James's Street, and that he had offered a telegraph boy a bribe to open one addressed to him. Although Anderson instructed the boy to accept the bribe and employed a plainclothes policeman to watch the telegram being handed over, his ploy failed, the Federal detective probably recognizing the plainclothes police officer.[33]

When he left his lodgings in Jermyn Street for the last time on October 2 to catch the Liverpool train, Anderson was followed to Euston station. As soon as his luggage had been put on board his hansom cab and he got in, he saw his shadow run to the corner of St. James's Street and jump into another one which he had ready waiting for him. As he passed out of Jermyn Street into St. James's Street, Anderson saw his shadow seated in his cab, which trailed him as far as the railway station, then carried on past it, suggesting that the detective had merely satisfied himself that he was leaving for Liverpool. However, inside Euston station, as Anderson was counting his change after buying his railway ticket, he happened to turn around and who should be there, standing within a foot of him, but "my friend of Jermyn St." That was to be his final encounter with this particular shadow, but another detective followed him onto the train, to watch him during his remaining days in Liverpool before he joined the *Fingal* at Holyhead.[34]

Even on the Continent, Confederate agents were not free from the attentions of the Federals. When Captain Huse went to Hamburg to superintend the loading of ten batteries of field artillery purchased in Vienna, onboard the *Bahama*, a steamer belonging to Fraser, Trenholm, he found he was being watched by "spies sent from London by the United States minister, as well as by the United States consulate in Hamburg."[35] That, coupled with the fact that the ship was not large enough to accommodate all the batteries, and that it also seemed likely that it would be seized, caused him, after taking legal advice, to decide to abort that particular mission. He was fortunate in finding a ready buyer for his artillery in the person of Captain Alexander Blakely of the Blakely Cannon Company.

It was not just leading figures like Commander Bulloch, Major Anderson and Major Huse who were under observation; minor players were also being watched, and Morse reported on two of these in March 1864:

> A Mr. Archer from Virginia is ... here. He is an engineer in the rebel navy and has come to look into the construction of ships of war ... and to purchase machinery for the Tredegar iron works at Richmond. He has gone to Sheffield to examine the machinery for rolling armor plates. A man by the name of Talley who is connected with the Tredegar works is with him.[36]

Archer and Talley were to cause Consul Morse further annoyance a year later when it was discovered that they, along with Lieutenant John McGill of the Virginia Volunteer Navy, had obtained British passports in order to return to the United States.

Federal surveillance of Confederate activities in London — whether of ships loading with war supplies, vessels being built in the shipyards, or the movements of Southern agents — was thorough and well-organized, though it had no dramatic results as it did at Liverpool, with the seizure of the Laird rams and the *Alexandra*. The Federals were unable to prevent the departure of the *Sea King* (the future CSS *Shenandoah*) or the *Louisa Ann Fanny*, but much information about cargoes intended for the South was sent to Washington and passed to the blockading squadrons. At the same time, Confederate agents involved in procurement and purchasing activities found their work increasingly hampered by the attentions of Federal spies.

7

The Cotton Loan

The loan is attracting much attention, and it is certain that it will be readily placed.
—*Economist,* March 21, 1863

To raise more money to pay for the arms and supplies being purchased in Europe by the Confederate government, a twenty-year foreign loan, based on cotton, was proposed in the autumn of 1862. The proposal is believed to have originated with a man called Felix Carteret, a former French civil servant with Confederate connections, who put the idea to Emile Erlanger, the German-born head of a Paris banking house, with branches in Frankfort and Amsterdam, and he in turn discussed it with John Slidell, the Confederate commissioner in Paris.

Erlanger was a confidant of Napoleon III, and Slidell thought that political as well as financial advantages might result from such a loan. He wrote about it to his colleague James Mason in London, pointing out that Erlangers' was "one of the richest ... banking houses in Europe, having extensive business relations throughout France and free access to some very important men about the Court. They will ... exert themselves in our favor and enlist ... persons who will be politically useful."[1]

Mason was not so enthusiastic; he had been considering another scheme for a loan from William S. Lindsay & Company, shipowners and insurance brokers, which appeared to offer more favorable terms.[2] In the event, however, the matter was referred to Secretary of State Judah P. Benjamin in December 1862, and after intense discussions in Richmond, London and Paris, agreement was reached, and the Seven Per Cent Cotton Loan, or Erlanger Loan, was authorized by secret act of Congress on January 29, 1863.

Bonds to the value of £3 million would be issued.[3] They would carry 7 percent interest, payable half-yearly, but the real attraction for investors was that they could also be exchanged for cotton at a fixed price of sixpence per pound, at sixty days' notice, at any time up to six months after a treaty of peace between the belligerents had been concluded. Every six months, starting on March 1, 1864, one-fortieth of the bonds would be drawn by lot and redeemed at face value, by means of a sinking fund, with the intention of extinguishing the loan in twenty years. Investors would pay for the bonds in eight installments, and Erlanger would pay the money raised to the Confederate government in the same way.

John K. Gilliat & Company had been asked to act as English agents for the loan, but had declined to do so, and J. Henry Schroder & Company, one of the leading merchant banks in London, was appointed instead. Schroder's was an Anglo-German concern, originally founded in 1818 as the London branch of a Hamburg firm of merchants; there was also a Liverpool branch, established in 1840 to provide finance for the cotton trade. Acting for Erlanger was the old established firm of Freshfields & Newman, who had been solicitors to the Bank of England since 1743, while Crowder, Maynard, Son & Lawford represented Schroder's. Negotiations were conducted chiefly by John Slidell and Treasury Department agent, Colin McRae; others involved included James Mason, Henry Hotze and the firm of Fraser, Trenholm.

James Spence, who had been the Confederacy's financial agent in Europe since October 1862, and who would later be replaced by McRae, was not involved in the negotiations. He had been unimpressed by the conditions of the loan, which he thought a very hard bargain, and that far better terms might have been procured from "an old-established banking house"—perhaps a reference to John K. Gilliat or William S. Lindsay.[4] His criticisms and suggested amendments to the terms of the loan were not appreciated by Erlanger or Slidell, who both resented his interference.

Rumors about the Confederate Cotton Loan began to circulate in London financial circles in February 1863, though the exact details were not yet known. When they were, they caused a sensation. On March 19, 1863, the bonds went on sale in London, Amsterdam, Paris, Frankfurt and Liverpool, and subscriptions were open for three days. In London and Amsterdam they were handled by Schroder's, in Paris and Frankfurt by Erlanger, and in Liverpool by Fraser, Trenholm. Working in conjunction with Schroder's in London were the bankers Jones, Loyd & Company and the brokers Laurence, Son & Pearce.

The loan proved to be heavily oversubscribed; many of the buyers and would-be buyers had London addresses. "The Confederate Loan has constituted the sole topic of conversation today in the Stock Exchange," commented the *Times* on the first day of trading.[5] Some others, however, were less enthusiastic. The Stock Exchange had declined to give it official recognition, and a member of the London banking house of Rothschild, writing to their agent in New York, commented: "The Confederate Loan was of so speculative a nature that it was very likely to attract all wild speculators ... It was brought out by foreigners, and we do not hear of any respectable people having anything to do with it ... We ourselves have been quite neutral and have had nothing to do with it."[6]

"It may appear somewhat startling that the Confederates should be able to borrow money in Europe, while the Federal Government has been unable to obtain a shilling from that usually liberal and enterprising quarter," observed the *Economist*. "But the terms of the loan are peculiar, and at first look attractive, as proposals involving a gambling element often do; and they merit full consideration." It assured its readers that the Confederate States would have enough cotton to pay all the subscribers, should they so demand, but was unwilling to offer an opinion on the chances of getting the cotton across the Atlantic while the war was still in progress, and thought the likelihood of the South being defeated "so slight that, of itself, it need not deter any man," just as it considered the possibility of it repudiating the debt and evading payment, after the establishment of its independence, most unlikely.[7]

Noting that the legality of the loan had been questioned, the *Economist* reminded its readers that the Corporation of the City of London had lent money to the Greek insurgents at the time of their War of Independence (1821–1827), and concluded: "If the greatest Corporation in England may subscribe in aid of rebellion, unquestionably mere individuals may be so bold as to lend to rebels."[8] Fears that the loan would have an unfavorable effect on the

A bond-holder's certificate for the Seven Per Cent Cotton Loan. (C. Narbeth, R. Hendy & C. Stocker, *Collecting Paper Money and Bonds*)

money market, with a drain on bullion, were also thought to be unfounded: "It is probable that most of the loan will be spent here in paying outstanding debts, and in purchasing new warlike stores and arms for the Confederate States."[9]

"Last night Mason ... and Erlanger had a great carnival at Morley's Hotel, at the expense of the English dupes who have taken up the Loan," wrote Benjamin Moran caustically in his journal on March 26.[10] His comment was to prove remarkably prophetic, as events were soon to demonstrate.

By early April the price of the bonds had fallen, and to sustain the confidence of investors, as well as the credibility of the loan, it was agreed that Erlanger should buy back some of the bonds, using loan money. As a result of this rescue operation, prices recovered somewhat, but fell dramatically when news of Lee's defeat at Gettysburg and the surrender of Vicksburg reached Europe in the second half of July 1863. "If the battle of Gettysburg had been won by the Confederates," remarked the *Times*, "the loan ... would probably have experienced a rise nearly as great as the fall now witnessed ... Those who now suffer, therefore, are not to be reproached for want of sagacity, however much they may have exhibited a want of caution. The example furnished is simply a confirmation of the fearful uncertainties that must beset all investments that depend upon military successes or reverses ... the sudden retreat of Lee and the simultaneous fall of Vicksburg ... constituting an accumulation of disaster rarely paralleled."[11]

After this, the value of the bonds fluctuated considerably, reaching one of their lowest points in December 1863, when reports of the Confederate defeat at Chattanooga arrived.[12] Prices remained depressed until the spring of 1864, though hopes for Confederate independence were still high among English investors. The market had recovered by the summer, and was strengthened in August by rumors that peace negotiations were a probability, and further reinforced in September by news that General George B. McClellan had been chosen as the Democratic Party's presidential candidate on a peace ticket. At the beginning of that month the *Times* reported that nearly one-sixth of the entire loan had already been redeemed—£340,800 by cotton and £137,800 by the sinking fund.

Though prices fell back in October, they remained fairly steady until the beginning of March 1865, when optimism among bondholders received a serious blow with reports that Charleston had been evacuated. Then, on April 15, came news of the fall of Petersburg and Richmond: "The Confederate Loan during the earlier hours was totally unmarketable," reported the *Times*, though a low price was eventually established, but there were further falls in its value on successive days. The market was further affected when President Lincoln's assassination was reported in the *Times* on April 27. The last payment of interest and redemption of bonds was made on March 1, 1865, but they continued to be quoted on the London market at nominal prices as late as November.

Post-war attempts by subscribers to the Cotton Loan to recover some of their investments were to prove unsuccessful. Of the £3 million worth of bonds originally issued, some £581,000 had been exchanged for cotton certificates or redeemed by the sinking fund before the war ended, leaving approximately £2,419,000 in circulation. Erlanger and Schroder indicated that there was no money to pay any more interest, but the bondholders, encouraged by a decision of the vice-chancellor, Sir W. Page Wood, clung to the hope that sooner or later the U.S. government, or some of the former states of the Confederacy, would redeem the loan.[13] This was in spite of a statement by Secretary of State William H. Seward that there was no likelihood that any of the debt would be assumed or recognized by his government.[14]

Meanwhile, the situation was further clouded by the publication, in various American and English newspapers, of a list of alleged bondholders. On September 30, 1865, the *Times* announced that a list of some of the English holders of the Confederate Cotton Loan had been published in the New York papers. That same day, copies of the *New York Times* containing the list reached London, and it was not long before it was being reprinted in the English press. The *Morning Star*, not noted for its Southern sympathies, published it on October 3:

The Rebel Loan
List of the English Victims

The New York papers of the 19th September have the following dispatch:

Many of the holders of the Confederate Cotton Loan in England avoided the recent meeting in London, evidently for fear of an exposure of their individual complicity in the ridiculous transaction. As the London journals therefore seem at a loss to know who the happy speculators are, they will be enlightened by the following list of some of the British subjects who have thus invested, with an estimate of the losses sustained by them respectively.

The list which followed contained some well-known names, including Isaac, Campbell & Company (£150,000), the Marquess of Bath (£50,000), John Laird, M.P. (£20,000), Alexander Collie & Partners (£20,000), Lord Wharncliffe (£5,000) and owner of the *Morning Post,* W.J. Rideout (£4,000). The most astonishing name was that of Chancellor of the Exchequer William E. Gladstone (£2,000), who telegraphed the *Morning Star*, stating that his name had been included in error and asking to have it removed. Gladstone said nothing further to the press about it, and though John Morley, his biographer, later considered it to be a malicious misrepresentation, contemporary observers like Dudley Mann and Lord Houghton both thought that he was indeed a subscriber.[15]

The paper included a long, incredulous editorial and followed it with a scathing attack on John T. Delane (£10,000), the editor of the *Times,* and M.B. Sampson (£15,000), its city editor, whose names were also on the list. It singled out "Mr. James Spence, the Liverpool correspondent and prophet ... What a charming arrangement it was! The prophet with £50,000 opposite his name in the

Chancellor of the Exchequer William E. Gladstone may also have been a subscriber to the Confederate Cotton Loan. (Author's collection)

books of the Loan, wrote letters from Liverpool depicting the hopes of the Confederacy in the most glowing colours." Other known Confederate supporters on the list who came in for abuse were Alexander Beresford Hope (£40,000), William S. Lindsay, M.P. (£20,000), William H. Gregory, M.P. (£4,000) and Lord Campbell (£1,000).[16]

Apart from the *Morning Star*, the attitude of the London papers was generally skeptical. The *Times* was suspicious from the start and declined to publish it, calling it "The Lying List," and even journals like the *Spectator*, which had supported the North, dismissed it as a forgery which had been planted on the Federal government, probably by a Confederate wanting to earn a reward and provoke W.H. Seward. The list had been passed to the New York press by the State Department and this had inevitably given it official status. "Yet," commented the *Daily News*, another pro–Northern paper:

> No American journal assumed any responsibility for its accuracy. None of them pretended to have spent any pains in verifying it. The New York journals did not even know what it was—whether it was a list of the original subscribers to the loan or of actual holders. Some of them wrote upon the latter supposition, though how the names of the holders of a stock that was frequently changing hands could be ascertained has never been suggested.[17]

The *Saturday Review* admitted: "Most likely it does include the names of some capitalists who have invested, and of course lost, in the Confederate Loan; but the principal persons concerned ... have denied that they ever held a shilling of the loan."[18] People whose names appeared on the list were indeed writing to the newspapers, denying all connection with it. Between October 4, 1865 and January 17, 1866, twenty-one individuals wrote to the *Times* to protest; the only one to admit having invested in the loan was William Lindsay, who commented (October 7, 1865) that "the small [£20,000!] investment I held in the Confederate Loan was made long after the loan was issued, and years after my opinion in regard to the War in America had been expressed in and out of Parliament." This gave the *Morning Star* ammunition for another attack:

Wealthy shipowner, Member of Parliament and Confederate supporter William S. Lindsay was one of the investors in the Cotton Loan. (*Cassell's Illustrated Family Paper*)

Why, some of the men who are now as indignant when accused of having subscribed to the Confederate Loan as if they had been accused of ... burglary or murder — some of these very men used to rave and rhapsodise about the glory of the Confederate cause and invincibility of the Confederate arms only one little year ago ... It would have been accepted as a graceful compliment a twelvemonth back if a man ... were alluded to as a subscriber to the Southern loan — and now hint that such a man did such a thing and he foams over in the indignation of his denial.[19]

On December 9 the New York papers printed a second list of English subscribers to the loan, "some doubt having been expressed as to the authenticity of the list previously published," showing the number of bonds held, and whether their owners had received any interest on their investments. This was a very long list of approximately three hundred names, of whom some two-thirds turned out to have London addresses, and included titled persons, Members of Parliament, naval and military men, clergymen and a number of firms; about forty were known Confederate sympathizers. It was followed by "Personal Sketches of Some of the Rebel Bondholders," containing various biographical details.[20] Though the publication of this second "Lying List" was reported in the *Times*, it attracted less attention than its predecessor and seemingly went unnoticed by papers like the *Morning Star*.[21]

By this time some information about the origins of the list had started to come to light, via the *Times'* New York correspondent. According to William H. Seward, it had been obtained from Confederate agents in Paris: "The Confederates are poor now, and are willing to sell all their secrets. Besides ... we are entitled to their papers." Shown the list, "foolscap sheets, fastened together by a piece of blue riband in the corner," the correspondent recognized the handwriting of John Bigelow, the U.S. minister in Paris. "Of this ... there is not the slightest doubt ... I think it right to add that, in my belief, Mr Seward was as much deceived as anyone by the imposture, and that Mr Bigelow is the person chiefly responsible for putting it in circulation."[22]

John Bigelow had been U.S. consul general in Paris during the war, involved in planning Federal surveillance and counterespionage activities, and U.S. minister in 1865–1866. In 1905 he published a book called *Lest We Forget. Gladstone, Morley and the Confederate Loan of 1863*, which still maintained that the "Lying List" was genuine, but presented a somewhat different version of the story. Some months after the war, Bigelow maintained, he was approached by a man called Dugald Forbes Campbell, who was a holder of Confederate bonds. Campbell, who was acting as attorney for the firm of Isaac, Campbell in the *Springbok* affair, offered to supply Bigelow with lists of the principal subscribers to the Confederate Loan, as well as the members of the Southern Independence Association of London. His offer was taken up, but the responsibility for giving the list of subscribers to the loan to the public, Bigelow wrote, was destined not to devolve upon him. Before he could forward the list to Washington, another copy of it had been obtained and published by the New York papers, and subsequently reached London.[23]

The commencement in 1866 of negotiations by the U.S. government for compensation for the damage done to her merchant shipping by the *Alabama* resulted in a counterclaim by Confederate bondholders, which the *Morning Star* described as "certainly the most wonderful step ever yet adopted by those unfortunate gentlemen."[24] The fact that the cotton stockpiled in connection with the loan had been forcibly seized by the Federal government seemed to reinforce their case, which was supported by the opinion of no less a person than Sir Robert Collier, the former solicitor-general, though there seem to have been no further developments.

The unfortunate bondholders were to be sadly disappointed, though their efforts to obtain compensation were to continue, on and off, for many years. As Judah Benjamin observed in a letter to a correspondent in New York as late as 1881: "If anything can ever be recovered by the bondholders, it can only be done through government action in the United States, and you can judge better than I if there is the remotest hope of any such action."[25]

Various attempts have been made to calculate how much money the Confederate government actually received from the Cotton Loan. One estimate, based on surviving records, is £1,759,894 or $8,535,486.[26] Whatever the final amount, the real losers were not the Confederate States but the speculators who invested in the loan and found that, on the defeat of the South, their bonds were just worthless bits of paper. The extent of Emile Erlanger's profits seems uncertain, though it is generally agreed that they were considerable. According to a report in the *Richmond Sentinel* in 1864, they amounted to 13.5 million francs (about £540,000).[27] J. Henry Schroder made a more modest, but still handsome, profit of £37,637.

Was the Confederate Cotton Loan a success? Writing to Secretary of the Treasury Christopher Memminger, less than three months after it was launched, Fraser, Trenholm were already of the opinion that it was "more successful as a political demonstration than as a source of revenue"; some forty years later John C. Schwab (1901) also thought that, while the loan itself was perhaps unsuccessful as a source of revenue, it had political significance, "a moral recognition of the Confederacy by the commercial world"; while more recently Judith F. Gentry (1970) has stated that "the Erlanger loan must be considered a success."[28]

8

Business with the Southern States

There is a numerous class of enterprising mercantile men and speculators here who are always on the watch for trading and money making. They are energetic, have great wealth at their command and are not at all particular as to the kind of trade they engage in [provided] that it bring a handsome return. They appear to think it is an Englishman's right to trade where and with whom they please, whatever may be the state of the countries with which they desire to trade.

— Freeman Morse, April 24, 1863

British businessmen were not slow to see the opportunities which the American Civil War presented. The Proclamation of Neutrality issued in May 1861, after the establishment of the Federal blockade of Southern ports, recognized both the United States and the Confederate States as belligerents. Though there was a warning against assisting either side, British firms soon found they could deal with them with impunity. It was the Confederacy which had most need of British manufactured goods and there was no shortage of people willing to supply them. Not all were entirely honest and substandard goods at inflated prices were not unknown.

At the beginning of the war, the Confederacy's prime need was for armaments. The South's manufacturing capability was limited: it was able to produce a certain amount of gunpowder, but a great deal of it had to be imported and, though some small arms were made there, most came from abroad. London was an important center of gun making, and housed such firms as John E. Barnett & Sons, the London Armory Company, Benjamin Beasley, Robert Adams, Thomas Bissell and Charles W. Lancaster, all of whom supplied weapons to the Confederates.

One of the most important of these was the London Armory Company in Bermondsey, on the south bank of the Thames. Founded in 1856 to supplement the output of the Royal Small Arms Factory at Enfield, Middlesex, the London Armory Company had imported "costly and elaborate machinery ... direct from America." They were, proclaimed their advertisements, "wholesale manufacturers of firearms and contractors to Her Majesty's War Department," and, in particular, "sole manufacturers of Adams' Patent Revolvers, which have obtained a world-wide celebrity," and which, two years later, they were producing at the rate of three hundred a week. Robert Adams, who had been a partner in the firm of Deane, Adams &

Deane, had first patented his five-chamber, self-cocking, percussion revolver in 1851, and when that firm was dissolved in 1856, Adams sold his patents to the London Armory Company and became their first manager. They also manufactured Enfield rifles, as well as Kerr rifles and revolvers, designed by James Kerr, who was foreman of the gun factory.[1] Through their contacts with Captain Huse, the London Armory Company was to become the leading supplier of small arms to the Confederacy.

Robert Adams left the London Armory Company in 1858, and taking over Deane, Adams & Deane's former premises in King William Street, he set up on his own as a gun, rifle and pistol manufacturer. One of "Adams' Revolving Pistols, made and sold by the patentee only," was presented to General Thomas J. "Stonewall" Jackson and another to General Robert E. Lee; a letter of thanks from Lee, dated October 30, 1863, was brought to London by Colonel Josiah Gorgas, head of the Ordnance Bureau, in January 1864.[2] When the London Armory Company moved to Victoria Park Mills in Hackney in 1863, Robert Adams took over their Bermondsey factory, but went bankrupt two years later.

Another London manufacturer was Charles W. Lancaster, who had a shop and factory in Mayfair. Between 1850 and 1869 he registered a number of firearms patents, including ones for an oval-bored barrel, and was also patentee of the British Lancaster short rifle. In the 1860s he claimed to be the "inventor and maker of the first central fire breech-loading gun."[3]

A number of firms whose factories were in the North of England also had offices in London. They included the rival firms of Whitworth & Company of Manchester and Armstrong & Company of Newcastle-upon-Tyne, as well as Greenwood & Batley of Leeds. Joseph Whitworth, engineer and machine tool manufacturer, had spent some years working in London before setting up on his own in Manchester in 1833 as a toolmaker. In the 1850s, he began to conduct experiments for the War Office and produced successful designs for both rifles and cannon, which he started making in 1858. By the time of the Civil War, the firm was famous for its long-range rifles equipped with telescopic sights, and in July 1861 two of these were bought by Major Anderson as samples and sent to Colonel Gorgas in Richmond for his consideration. As a result, in the autumn of 1861, Major Anderson and Captain Huse were instructed to place an order for a consignment of them. Whitworths was equally renowned for its field guns, which included both breechloaders and muzzle-loaders.

In 1847 William George Armstrong had founded a company at Newcastle to produce hydraulic machinery, but in 1855, at the time of the Crimean War, he developed a superior field gun. Armstrong's breechloading gun was accepted by the War Office in 1858, and the following year its designer was appointed superintendent of the Royal Gun Factory at Woolwich Arsenal, as well as being knighted. A separate ordnance company, set up to manufacture both breechloaders and muzzle-loaders for the British government, as well as for export, was merged with the original engineering firm in 1863. Armstrong guns were not cheap, ranging in price from £120 for a six-pounder to £650 for a 100-pounder. A number of them were imported by the Confederates.

Greenwood & Batley, "constructors of special tools for making rifles, rifled artillery and ammunition," had been established in 1856 by Thomas Greenwood and John Batley, two former partners of Peter Fairbairn, a Leeds manufacturer of heavy machine tools. Among their earliest customers were the Royal Small Arms factory at Enfield, Middlesex, and the Birmingham Small Arms Company, and they soon acquired an excellent reputation, going on to supply many arsenals in Europe and beyond. In June 1863 they were visited by James Henry Burton, superintendent of armories in the Confederacy. Before the war, Burton had spent some years at the Harpers Ferry Armory, then worked at Enfield as the chief engineer. He had been instrumental in the building of the Macon Armory, Georgia, in 1862, and was now authorized by Colonel Gorgas to return to England to buy much-needed machinery for it. On his arrival there, he conferred with James Mason and Major Huse, who was in Paris, before visiting Greenwood & Batley, with whom he placed an order for machinery for the manufacture of a rifle-musket.[4] There were problems with the funding of this order, but Fraser, Trenholm came to the rescue, and Burton was able to return to the Confederacy at the beginning of September.

The *Trent* incident resulted in a ban on the export of armaments, and within days the *Times* was bemoaning the "injurious effect" on ordnance manufacturers. Captain Alexander T. Blakely, formerly of the Royal Artillery, and manufacturer at his Southwark works of the highly regarded, muzzle-loading Blakely gun, "for which he had orders from different foreign governments," was particularly singled out, "in view of the many guns of large calibre ... nearly ready for delivery ... besides numerous smaller guns ... just the thing for a merchant ship to be armed with."[5] Before 1864, when Captain Blakely was able to expand his operation, his guns were also made under license by other manufacturers as well as by the original patentee. Captain Huse is known to have bought at least nine of them.

The ban on exports, in fact, proved to be short-lived and, with the resolution of the crisis surrounding the *Trent* incident, it was lifted within seven weeks. "The revocation of the order prohibiting the exportation of arms and munitions of war ... will probably renew the activity of the Confederate emissaries in forwarding supplies to the insurgents," wrote U.S. minister Charles Francis Adams towards the end of January 1862.[6] As if to confirm this, Secretary of State William H. Seward, writing to him in June of that year, referred to a captured report by Caleb Huse which listed "purchases of arms, munitions of war, and military supplies which have been shipped by him in England," and "the real abuses of neutrality which have been committed in Great Britain in the very face of Her Majesty's government."[7] "The Blakely Cannon Co. pretend they have some cannon for Peru and Hayti, and ... want a licence for their exemption from seizure by our cruisers," noted Benjamin Moran in his journal in November 1862. "This is a trick ... these guns are for the rebels. They have furnished them more ordnance than any other concern in England...."[8] Two giant, muzzle-loading Blakely guns, each weighing twenty-seven tons and costing more than £11,000, were imported by the state of South Carolina in 1863 for the defense of Charleston, but were not very successful, one of them bursting when fired for the first time.

Fort Fisher, at the mouth of the Cape Fear River in North Carolina, was defended by Blakely guns, as well as a 150-pounder Armstrong and a battery of six Whitworths presented by British merchants. They were not the only things found when the fort was finally captured by Federal forces in January 1865. There were also some Abel fuses, named after their inventor, Professor Frederick Abel, who was director of ordnance at Woolwich Arsenal in London and the chief official authority on explosives. Abel fuses were used for exploding charges of gunpowder and their discovery caused a furor: they had, alleged U.S. consul Freeman Morse, been "bought through English agents directly from the government arsenal at Woolwich" for rebel agents.[9] Their appearance at Fort Fisher seemed to be a particularly blatant breach of neutrality, and the matter was deemed so important it was referred to General Ulysses S. Grant himself, and by him to the secretary of state, who wrote the U.S. minister in London, asking him to take it up with the British foreign secretary.

In his report Professor Abel firmly denied that any of the fuses had come from Woolwich

Arsenal. He went on to explain that William Ladd, a man who was to play an important part in the practical application of electricity in the 1860s, had been authorized to manufacture and sell the fuses, but that none had knowingly been sold to the Confederates. However, he admitted, "I need hardly point out that it would be impossible for Mr Ladd to guard against supplying Confederate agents at second or third hand with my fuses, as is proved by the discovery in Fort Fisher of some of these, which, from their nature, must have been manufactured about two years and a half ago."[10]

Later it transpired that behind the whole affair was a man called Taliaffero P. Shaffner, an American inventor known to both Freeman Morse and Benjamin Moran. The latter, who referred to him disparagingly as a "scamp" and a "trickster," noted in his diary in May 1865 that Shaffner had accused Professor Abel of selling his fuses to the rebels as an act of revenge, after he had failed to obtain the formula for the fuses to sell to the Federal government.[11]

The firm of Thomas & Charles Hood of Blackfriars, "contractors for iron ordnance and munitions of war," sold cannon to the Confederate Navy. In July and August 1863 they were corresponding with Commander North about gunsights, shells and fuses, and in June 1864 he sent them an order which included: "10 x 68-pounder guns; 1,680 x 8" naval shells; 400 shell boxes; 50 spare fuses; 18 rammers and staffs; 14 patent sponges and staffs; 12 gunners' shoulder belts and haversacks; 30 ships' hatchets; 84 rounds 8" grapeshot; 84 shrapnel shells, 8"; and 10 sliding carriages for 68-pounders."[12]

In May 1864 the prize medal-winning firm of Negretti & Zambra supplied equipment to the Signal Bureau, which had been established in 1862 as part of the Confederate War Department. Insulated wire, made by the firm of Stephen W. Silver & Company and originally intended for the electric telegraph, could be adapted for use with torpedoes (electrically discharged floating mines). Commander Maury had a particular interest in this, and a report was sent to Washington in November 1864 by Consul Morse:

> Silver, at his works at Silvertown, has already manufactured and delivered to Fraser, Trenholm & Co from 300 to 400 miles of wire insulated by india rubber, and has an order from them for more. A manufacturer has also made and delivered to them 12 electric batteries and a great many fuses to go with the same. The batteries were delivered between three and four weeks ago, and he has *six* more that will be ready for delivery in about two weeks. Maury has contracted directly with the same man for 20,000 fuses.[13]

In August 1862, in a paragraph headed "English Cannon in the South," the *London American* quoted a report in the *Richmond Enquirer* that twenty-two pieces of Russian artillery, captured in the Crimean War, had been presented to the Confederate government by a group of British merchants and taken over in the CSS *Nashville*. Their arrival at Macon, Georgia, was reported in the paper, which went on to say that thirty-eight more pieces were expected at the same place.[14]

This remarkably generous act was perhaps intended to foster business relations between Britain and the Confederacy. As a further move in that direction, the London Confederate States Commercial League was formed in September 1863. Meetings were to be held every Wednesday in St. Mildred's Court, Poultry; perhaps significantly, the honorary secretary, James Yeomans, was a member of a firm of wholesale small arms and sword manufacturers.[15] There were long advertisements for it in the *Index* between October and December 1863, but no further mention after that, suggesting it failed from lack of support.

There was also the proposal, about the same time, to establish the Confederate States Exchange Rooms:

> The want of some rallying point at which the friends of the Confederate cause and those interested in business with the Southern States might meet, exchange views, and discuss matters of common concern, has been long and severely felt in this metropolis. It is proposed to supply this want by opening in some central and convenient locality a set of rooms, to be called "The Confederate States Exchange Rooms" ... Arrangements will be made to ensure a regular supply of late Southern papers ... The principal American journals will be kept on hand...[16]

John Hopkins at the *Index* office in Bouverie Street was to be the temporary secretary, but again nothing more was heard of the project after the initial announcement in October 1863.

Confederate army and naval officers who visited London could order uniforms from firms like Goody & Jones, who advertised in the *Index*:

> **GOODY & JONES, MILITARY AND NAVAL OUTFITTERS AND ACCOUTREMENT MANUFACTURERS, 40 PALL MALL**
> Begs to inform officers of both Services, and Gentlemen, that theirs is the only Establishment at which the Confederate Grey Cloth can be obtained, having already made a great number of outfits according to the Regulations issued by the War Department of the Confederate States.[17]

Although some buttons were made in the South, particularly in Richmond, large numbers were imported from England. One of the leading London makers was Firmin & Sons, "wholesale army and navy button manufacturers," whose origins went back to 1677. Assistant Paymaster Forrest recorded a visit to their offices and showroom in the Strand in April 1864.[18] Infantry and cavalry buttons were also supplied by Isaac, Campbell & Company.

In February 1864 Turner Bros, Hyde & Company, a London firm which had taken over Isaac, Campbell's old factory at Northampton, were advertising their boots and shoes in "American shapes and styles" in the *Index*, while as late as January 1865 William Wilson & Sons, "export boot merchants," were announcing "boots manufactured as worn in the Confederate States of America."[19]

In the early months of the war Confederate postage stamps were being printed by the Richmond firm of Hoyer & Ludwig, but the results, though acceptable, were not outstanding. Consequently, in October 1861, Postmaster General John H. Reagan asked Major Benjamin F. Ficklin, in London on Treasury Department business, to find a source of stamps, stamp-making equipment and materials. He approached Thomas De La Rue & Company, of Bunhill Row, Finsbury, printers of playing cards, visiting cards, railway tickets and, more recently, banknotes and stamps for the British and foreign governments. The firm had been established in 1837 and though it had suffered financial setbacks in its early days, was now highly successful. Its founder had retired in 1859, and it was now being run by his two sons, Warren and William Frederick De La Rue.

An order was placed with them for a one-cent orange stamp, showing the Southern statesman, John C. Calhoun, and a five-cent blue, bearing a portrait of President Jefferson Davis; both stamps were designed by the French-born artist, Jean Ferdinand Joubert de la Ferté, and were supplied unperforated and ungummed.[20]

In February 1862 the first consignment from De La Rue, consisting of 5 million five-cent blue stamps, together with a supply of glazed postage paper and printing ink and a

The former premises in Pall Mall of Goody & Jones, military and naval outfitters, allegedly "the only Establishment at which the Confederate Grey Cloth [could] be obtained." (Author's photograph)

perforating machine, was dispatched in the blockade-runner *Bermuda*, whose cargo also included tea, coffee, drugs, surgical instruments, saddlery, cutlery engraved "Jeff Davis, Our First President, the Right Man in the Right Place," artillery pieces, shells, small arms and saltpeter. Additional postal stationery was sent in the CSS *Nashville*, which left Southampton the same month. The *Bermuda*, which had successfully transported Major Huse's first arms shipment the previous year, was to be unlucky this time: it was captured by the USS *Mercedita* off the Bahamas in April 1862, while en route for Nassau, and those stamps not thrown overboard were pulped by the Federals.

In spite of this initial setback, large quantities of stamps, as well as printing plates, presses, ink and paper were subsequently supplied by De La Rue and brought through the blockade. Not everything went smoothly: in June 1863 the firm recorded that a printing press obtained in March 1862 and probably sent out in the blockade-runner *Giraffe* in November, had been "accepted and subsequently declined" by the Confederate Post Office Department, "so that this item of value in 1862 becomes a loss in 1863." Major Ficklin, it was noted, was "to sell it for our account."[21]

In March 1863 Major Ficklin was joined in London by another Confederate agent, Major J.A. Weston, and both men seem to have enjoyed a close, and at times unusual, business relationship with De La Rue. For Ficklin, for instance, the firm obtained twelve copies of James Spence's *American Union* in February 1862, and the following month purchased, through their Paris agents, 180 pairs of ladies' kid gloves (presumably a private business speculation), and their account books show that they also lent him money on occasion, in various amounts from £5 upwards. For Weston, they supplied whiskey and copies of the *Index*. They also purchased a canteen of cutlery for General Pierre G.T. Beauregard, though whether as a present or on request is not clear.

There was also a need for skilled engravers, lithographers and printers for the Confederate treasury note printing works at Charleston. These were recruited by Major Ficklin from Samuel Straker & Sons of Bishopsgate, a firm of printers, lithographers and stationers which had been established about 1820. The terms offered were generous: $20 a week in gold and between £40 and £60 to cover the expenses of the journey.[22]

Major Ficklin's dealings with Samuel Straker seem to have been rather less happy than those with De La Rue. Mr. Straker complained bitterly to the Confederate government about the major, who "served me very shabbily and ungentlemanlike. I had many interviews with him and gave him all necessary information; furnished him with a list of requirements, compromising myself with several workmen and put myself to many inconveniences. He admitted my price being proper and correct and led me to believe that he would give me his order, but having got out of me all he could, he then entrusted the order with another house" (De La Rue).[23] Straker's letter was being carried in the *Bermuda* when she was captured, and so never reached the eyes of the Confederate government.

By the beginning of 1863, even the most common, everyday necessities were in short supply in the Confederacy. They included ink, candles, matches, pins and needles, cutlery and soap, as well as basic foodstuffs such as tea, coffee, bacon, canned meat, biscuits and salt, which were all brought in through the blockade, while medicines and medical equipment were in constant demand.

Bibles, which before the war had been printed mostly in the North, were among the more unexpected imports. In August 1862 the Rev. Moses D. Hoge, who had been a volunteer chaplain to Confederate soldiers in Richmond, ran the blockade from Charleston with a letter from the Bible Society of the Confederate States, requesting help from the British and Foreign Bible Society in London. As a result, 10,000 Bibles, 50,000 New Testaments and a large quantity of miscellaneous religious books were eventually supplied, the first consignment on interest-free credit. They were forwarded via Fraser, Trenholm in Liverpool for transshipment to the Confederate States and distribution among Southern soldiers. This was particularly important in the light of the religious revivals which swept the armies of the Confederacy in 1863 and 1864.[24]

The Great Seal of the Confederacy was authorized by Congress in April 1863 and the following month Secretary of State Judah Benjamin instructed Commissioner James Mason to have it made in London. Accordingly, he asked Dublin-born John H. Foley, a leading sculptor, and Joseph S. Wyon, "Chief Engraver of Her Majesty's Seals," to design and produce it. Made of silver with an ivory handle, it shows the equestrian statue of George Washington, which stands in Richmond, encircled by a wreath of the main agricultural products of the Confederacy; the Latin motto, *Deo Vindice*, means "God our Defender," and the date, 22 February 1862, is that of Jefferson Davis's inauguration, as well as being Washington's birthday.

The Great Seal, together with the iron press for making impressions, and a supply of wax and other necessary materials, was carried from London to Richmond by Lieutenant Robert T. Chapman, C.S.N., in August 1864. He traveled in a blockade-runner via Halifax, Nova Scotia, and Bermuda, where the iron press had to be left because of its weight, and where it apparently still remains. After Richmond was evacuated in April 1865, the Great Seal passed through several hands, until in 1912 it was presented to the Museum of the Confederacy, where it now resides.

In April 1863 James Mason sent the secretary of state "a box containing the model of a railroad with its appropriate car," together with "all the explanatory papers connected with it, which I hope will make its structure and use sufficiently intelligible." The inventor of this new type of railroad, which used guide wheels and wooden rails, was William Prosser, who had not only registered several patents in connection with it, but in 1845 had built a full-scale trial version on Wimbledon Common, at a cost of "some six or seven thousand pounds." On the two occasions he had attempted to construct an actual working line, in England and Ireland, however, he had been bought off by rival interests. Mason met Mr. Prosser, "a very intelligent man ... thoroughly versed in mechanics," and clearly felt his invention was worth a trial. Although the railroads in the South were in a sorry state, partly because of the desperate shortage of iron, nothing further was heard of "Prosser's patent railway guide wheels" and their wooden rails.[25]

Fraser, Trenholm & Company, a branch of a wealthy Charleston importing and exporting firm, had been established in Liverpool since at least 1853. During the Civil War they acted as the Confederacy's overseas bankers or depositories, but remained Liverpool-based, apparently never finding it necessary to have a London office. Another financial institution with Confederate links was John K. Gilliat & Company of Crosby Square, an old London firm with pre-war connections in the Southern states. James Mason referred to them as "my bankers," and at one stage they advanced the Confederate government £150,000, with cotton bonds as collateral.

Several firms in London traded in Confederate and state bonds. They included M. Kramer ("Dealer in Confederate securities"); Thomas Bensusan ("The 6, 7, and 8 per cent bonds purchased or sold"); Joseph Buckley ("Goods purchased payable in Confederate bonds"); and J.

H. Ashbridge & Company, a Liverpool firm with a London office, which dealt in bonds issued by South Carolina, Alabama, Tennessee and Georgia.[26] Joseph Buckley's advertisement, in November 1864, suggests that few in England at that time realized how close to collapse the Confederacy really was.

Forged Confederate bonds also made their appearance. In June 1864 the *Times* reported that a large quantity of $100 bonds had been sent from New York to London and put into circulation, and that samples shown to an engraver of genuine ones were pronounced to be counterfeit.[27]

As well as dabbling in blockade-running themselves, the banking house of Overend, Gurney & Company, in Lombard Street, lent money to shipbuilder James Ash to enable him to build more blockade-runners, and sold several vessels on credit to shipowner Zachariah Pearson, who also became heavily involved in blockade-running, though in his case with disastrous consequences.[28]

There were at least two proposals for a Confederate bank in Europe. In 1863 it was reported that "Mr Soutter of Virginia ... who is engaged in blockade-running ... intends (it is said) to establish a Confederate Bank with branches in [the] States of [the] Confederacy." In June of the following year a similar scheme, with a capital of £10 million was proposed by a group of English and French bankers and sent to Christopher Memminger, the secretary of the treasury. Memminger's successor, George A. Trenholm, was sent further details in December 1864.[29] Plans to raise a further foreign loan of £15 million, based on this proposal, were overtaken by events in the early part of 1865.

As a result of the Confederate Cotton Loan, several companies were formed to bring out cotton through the blockade. These included the Albion Trading Company, the European Trading Company, the Mercantile Trading Company and the Universal Trading Company. The Albion Trading Company owned the *Ivanhoe*, the *Lady Sterling*, the *Marmion* and the *Talisman*, the first two of which were operated for them by Thomas Stirling Begbie. The European Trading Company was established in October 1863 by J. Henry Schroder, Emile Erlanger and H. O. Brewer, a Mobile businessman who had helped Henry Hotze establish the *Index*; their steamers included the *Denbigh*, which made a large number of runs between Mobile and Havana. The Mercantile Trading Company, formed by Edgar Stringer and Edward Pembroke, of the firm of William S. Lindsay & Company, owned the *Atalanta*, the *Charlotte* and the *Juno*. Of these, the *Atalanta* was the most successful; the careers of the other two were brief. The Universal Trading Company owned the *Helen* and the *North Heath*, which were also operated by Thomas Begbie.

In addition, there was the Atlantic Trading Company, "formed for the purchase of first-class paddle-wheel steamers, of light draught, great speed, and an average capacity of 800 bales of cotton, which forms the basis of the *business to be transacted*" (blockade-running), with a capital of £200,000 in £100 shares, with power of increasing to £500,000. The promoters were Isaac, Campbell, and T. & J. Johnston and George Wigg, both of Liverpool. Wigg, formerly of Nassau, was an experienced blockade-running agent who had been a cotton merchant in New Orleans before the war, and had worked with both the Albion Trading Company and the European Trading Company. Arrangements were put in hand with Colin McRae "to carry in merchandise, and to bring out on the return journey full cargoes of cotton." The company planned to have five steamers in operation, starting in April 1864, and a copy of its prospectus, which came into the hands of U.S. minister Charles Francis Adams, indicated the remarkable profits that might be expected — perhaps as much as £750,000 for five trips.[30]

The offices in Lombard Street of Overend, Gurney & Company, who lent money to London shipbuilders for the construction of blockade-runners and were themselves involved in the traffic. (*Illustrated Times*)

Though many of the blockade-runners were built in Scotland and the North of England, some were constructed in London, where shipbuilding was still an important industry. Writing in 1862, Charles Capper, who was manager of the Victoria Docks, commented:

> There are a considerable number of building yards upon the Thames, at which first-class vessels are built; and the trade of shipbuilding has been increasing of late years in consequence of iron

vessels having come more and more into use, and the skilled labour always to be obtained in London making the Thames very available for the construction of these vessels. At the present time there are more iron than wooden vessels constructed on the river...[31]

John & William Dudgeon, engineers and boilermakers, had begun making marine machinery at the Sun Ironworks at Millwall, but between 1859 and 1862 they also established a shipyard at Cubitt Town, where they eventually employed a workforce of some 1,500 men. Here, according to their own account, written just after the war, they constructed twelve twin-screw steamers as blockade-runners between 1862 and 1865. Some of their steamers made a dozen runs, though the average was five.[32] One of them, the *Flora*, built in 1862, caused a sensation at her trials, being described by the *Illustrated London News* as "the fastest screw steam-ship afloat," being capable of fourteen knots. She was highly successful and made the Dudgeons' reputation; her twin screws made her highly maneuverable and she was soon snapped up by Alexander Collie for blockade-running.

Another vessel, the *Edith*, launched in March 1864, was built for Alexander Collie. Sold to the Confederate Navy in September 1864, she was commissioned as the CSS *Chickamauga*, commanded by Lieutenant John Wilkinson. As a commerce raider, she accounted for seven U.S. merchantmen, but was burnt by her crew in the Cape Fear River in February 1865, after the fall of Wilmington.

The *Atalanta*, designed by Captain T.E. Symonds, R.N., for the London, Chatham & Dover Railway and launched at the same time, was purchased by Edgar Stringer and Edward Pembroke as a blockade-runner for their Mercantile Trading Company. In July 1864 she was sold to the Confederate Navy for conversion into a commerce raider and commissioned as

The *Flora*, built in London by John & William Dudgeon, was snapped up by Alexander Collie for use as a blockade-runner. (*Illustrated London News*)

the CSS *Tallahassee*. The *Illustrated London News* described the ship as "a most efficient instrument of maritime warfare" and in August 1864, in the space of ten days, it captured or destroyed no fewer than thirty-three U.S. merchant ships. Renamed the CSS *Olustee*, she destroyed another six ships in November, before being converted back into a blockade-runner called the *Chameleon*. She was seized on her return to Liverpool in April 1865 and subsequently turned over to the U.S. government.

In 1862, James Ash, who had been a naval architect for the important shipbuilding firms of C.J. Mare and the Thames Ironworks, also established an extensive yard at Cubitt Town. It had the most impressive set of offices and works of any of the Thames shipyards, and here he built vessels for the P. & O. Company, as well as a sumptuous yacht for its chairman. A blockade-runner he built for Edgar Stringer was called the *Nutfield*, and, when she was launched in September 1863, it was alleged that "this splendid iron screw steam-vessel" was intended for use as a passenger steamer in Australia, though it is unlikely that many actually believed this.[33] In the event, her career was brief, and she was destroyed on her first attempt to run the blockade in February 1864.

The *Lady Sterling* was built by John Scott Russell at Blackwall in 1864; she was captured on her second attempt to run the blockade in October of that year.[34] The firm also had a shipyard at Northfleet, some twenty-five miles downriver, where vessels could be repaired away from prying eyes. The *Index*, built at Deptford for Alexander Collie in 1863, possibly by Charles Lungley, proved to be too slow, and was retired from blockade-running after only six trips.[35] On the other hand, the *Syren*, built at Greenwich in the same year, ran the blockade no fewer than thirty-three times before being captured early in 1865, a record apparently unmatched by any other vessel.

The purpose for which these vessels were being built was an open secret, and there was no lack of people eager to supply information to the Federals in return for a reward. Benjamin Moran recorded one such instance in January 1863, when "a half-frantic Irishman

The CSS *Tallahassee*, which started life as the London-built blockade-runner *Atalanta*. (*Illustrated London News*)

in shabby clothes came in in a hurried manner and for a consideration wanted to supply the particulars of a blockade breaker fitting out in the West India Docks."[36]

To bring out government cotton under the terms of the New Plan, Colin McRae needed to acquire a number of steamers, and in April 1864 he began negotiations with the Mercantile Trading Company. These proved fruitless, and in July Fraser, Trenholm agreed to provide eight vessels, to be built on Merseyside. In addition, the banking firm of John K. Gilliat undertook to have six more steamers built for the Confederate government, also on Merseyside. They were to be delivered by December 1864, though in the event the war had ended before they were finished.

Until the Fraser, Trenholm and John K. Gilliat vessels were ready, McRae arranged for Alexander Collie to supply four steamers. The ones chosen, the *Condor*, *Falcon*, *Flamingo* and *Ptarmigan*, were large and powerful sidewheelers, recently built on the River Clyde and thought to be the best blockade-runners afloat.

Alexander Collie & Company were one of the largest owners of blockade-runners. Originally based in Manchester, the firm soon found Liverpool to be a more convenient location once blockade-running started; they also had a London office in Austin Friars and later in Leadenhall Street. At one time or another they owned, or had an interest in, more than twenty vessels, some of which were operated for them by other firms. Huge profits could be made out of blockade-running, and in 1864 Alexander Collie himself bought a house in Kensington Palace Gardens, then as now a private road lined with opulent mansions, and once known as "Millionaires' Row." Collie paid £25,000 for it, which was a bargain as it had originally cost between £45,000 and £50,000 when it was built twenty years before. In addition, its new owner spent several thousand pounds on alterations which were carried out by the celebrated architect Matthew Digby Wyatt, including a new breakfast room and a billiard room decorated in the "Moorish" taste.[37]

Like Alexander Collie, Isaac, Campbell & Company were also major operators of blockade-runners. In the summer of 1862 one of their representatives arrived at Nassau with the stated intention of taking over the blockade-running business there, boasting that they had been responsible for all the Confederates' successes to date. One of Isaac, Campbell's steamers was the *Melita*. She sailed for Nassau in May 1862, with a cargo which included rifles, gunpowder, knapsacks, cavalry swords, shoes, bayonet scabbards and saddles, destined for transshipment to the Confederacy; also on board were Commander Raphael Semmes and Lieutenant John Kell, formerly of the CSS *Sumter*.

The firm also owned the cargo in the *Springbok*, a small sailing ship belonging to a man called Thomas May, which was under charter to Thomas Begbie. This included army blankets and clothing, army and navy footwear, buttons, samples of cavalry swords and rifle bayonets, and saltpeter. The ship left London for Nassau in December 1862, but the following February was captured some 150 to 200 miles east of there. Whether her cargo was intended for sale at Nassau or for transshipment to a Confederate port was a matter of opinion. The ship was impounded for the duration, but after the war the seizure of the vessel, but not the cargo, was ruled illegal, and she was returned to her owner.[38]

In addition to this misfortune, Thomas Begbie lost five of his own vessels when they were captured in 1862 and 1863. However, his steamer, the *Harriet Pinckney*, named after the wife of Caleb Huse, did make a successful run from London to Bermuda in 1862 with a cargo which included rifles, cannon and torpedoes; it was sold the following year to Samuel Isaac, of Isaac, Campbell.

Zachariah C. Pearson & Company of Hull and London, whose owner was a highly successful merchant, shipowner and prominent local citizen — he had twice been mayor of Hull — also found blockade-running could be a far from profitable undertaking. Between May and August 1862, no fewer than six of Pearson's steamers — three of which had been bought on credit — were captured by the Federals, and a seventh, the *Modern Greece*, ran aground off the North Carolina coast and was destroyed. He had already lost two vessels in the Baltic the previous year, and another ship, the *Indian Empire*, was destroyed by fire in the Thames when being moved from one dock to another. In August 1862 he stopped payment, and the following month was declared bankrupt, with debts and liabilities of more than £600,000.

Bankruptcy proceedings, which began in July 1863 and continued until April 1864, were reported in the *Times*, and included a list of people and firms with whom Pearson was involved.[39] One of them was the Hull shipbuilder Martin Samuelson, who was owed some £25,000. In February 1864, Samuelson, who is known to have built at least one blockade-runner, and was described during the hearings as having "a 'little interest' in the consignments," nevertheless wrote an indignant letter to the *Times*, denying his involvement in blockade-running or any other Confederate speculation.[40] Among Pearson's assets was the steamer *Merrimac*, which had been purchased by the Ordnance Bureau, but for which he had never received payment from the Confederate government, and which was subsequently sold by the mortgagees, Overend, Gurney.

Pile, Spence & Company of West Hartlepool were part owners, as well as builders, of the steamer *Lloyd* (later the *Sea Queen*), which left London in April 1862 with a cargo later said to have been worth £1 million, and was successfully run into Charleston. They also purchased the *Peterhoff* from Zachariah Pearson. In February 1863 this steamer became the focus of a diplomatic row when it was captured off St. Thomas in the West Indies, on suspicion of being a blockade-runner, while en route for Matamoras, in Mexico. Whether she was or not, she was also carrying mail, and her seizure caused a considerable furor; the situation was defused when the mail bags were returned, unopened, to the British consul in New York.

Given the money to be made out of trade with the Confederacy, it was almost inevitable that there should be rivalry and animosity between some of the firms involved. Alexander Collie complained that the Isaac brothers treated his clerks with disdain; at the same time, there was no love lost between him and Edgar Stringer. "As for Mr Stringer," he remarked to Lord Wharncliffe, writing to him after the war, "I heeded him as little as the buzz of a mosquito. He meant mischief, but had neither power nor influence to effect it."[41]

Firms who dealt with the Confederacy did so in the belief that, in the unlikely event of the South being defeated, the Federal government would take over any outstanding debts; they were to be sadly disappointed. The Fourteenth Amendment to the American Constitution, passed in June 1866, repudiated any debts or liabilities "contracted for the purpose of supporting the insurrection or rebellion against the United States."

Commission merchants like Isaac, Campbell, who had latterly been willing to accept payment in Confederate bonds, were largely ruined as a result, while shipbuilders like James Ash, who had borrowed heavily from the banking house of Overend, Gurney in order to expand, was forced to close down when the latter failed in 1866. Even the canny Alexander Collie, who had been a major operator of blockade-runners, had to sell his remaining steamers at a heavy loss.

Once the Confederacy was defeated, firms which had once been only too happy to supply it with whatever it required, and had made handsome profits in the process, hastened to deny all connections with it. Merchants like Charles W. & Wentworth Gray wanted readers of the *Times* to know that they "were never interested to the extent of one shilling either as owners of blockade-runners or as shippers of goods for the South."[42]

Though London was not the main port for blockade-running, which has been called "the lifeline of the Confederacy," the leading firms engaged in it had offices there, and many of the weapons and supplies the Confederates so desperately needed were either made or obtained there. And as a leading financial center, it provided the infrastructure for the launch of the Cotton Loan, which was vital for the continuation of purchasing operations in Britain.

9

Artistic Reflections, Literary Echoes

The name of America five years ago called up to the ordinary English mind nothing but a vague cluster of associations, compounded of Mrs Trollope, "Martin Chuzzlewit" and "Uncle Tom's Cabin."

—Leslie Stephen, *The Times on the American War* (1865)

Leslie Stephen's statement is somewhat exaggerated. The writings of popular authors like Frances Trollope (*Domestic Manners of the Americans*) and Charles Dickens (*American Notes* and *Martin Chuzzlewit*) had already helped make the British public more aware of America, but the Civil War focused additional attention on it, and, sheet music, magazine articles, books and particularly in London, plays, panoramas, exhibitions of paintings and photographs all reflect this.

In addition, plays like Tom Taylor's *Our American Cousin* and the many dramatized versions of Harriet Beecher Stowe's *Uncle Tom's Cabin* were already familiar to British audiences, and events across the Atlantic undoubtedly increased the appeal of ones with an American theme. It was not unusual for new plays to refer to current events, and several were written and produced in the early 1860s as a result of the Civil War. They were usually part of a double or triple bill, and one or two of them ran for four or five weeks, a fairly long time by the standards of the day.

One of the earliest examples was a one-act farce called *A Southerner Just Arrived*, by the actor-dramatist Horace Wigan, which was performed at the Olympic Theatre, Wych Street, from November 3 through December 6, 1862. Though the war is there in the background—"Great news, most encouraging intelligence ... the Federal General something or other ... I can't read his name ... has gloriously defeated the Confederate General ... something else ... I can't read his name either"—it is peripheral to the absurd plot, which concerns a planter from South Carolina (Jabez Julep, the "Southerner" of the title, played by Horace Wigan) who arrives at the home of a gullible Manchester abolitionist in pursuit of a runaway slave. An example of situation comedy, involving mistaken identities, it included a specially written song, beginning:

> I was born in Carolina, that's a long way off you know,
> And there I suffered all you've read in Mrs Beecher Stowe.

The Alabama: A Nautical Extravaganza, apparently a reworking of an earlier piece called *Her Majesty's Sloop Spitfire*, was produced at the Theater Royal, Drury Lane (March 7–19, 1864); then, coupled with Shakespeare's *Henry IV, part I*, it returned for a further five-day run (March 28–April 1). It was written by John Maddison Morton, a prolific playwright who was famous as the author of *Box and Cox* (once described as "the most popular play ever written"), and used the ship as a backdrop for a one-act romantic comedy. Its three scenes are set in the Confederate Arms, Havana, in a cabin, and on the quarterdeck of the CSS *Alabama*. Scene three concludes with a "spectacle"— an engagement with the "Fighting *Philadelphia*, a Federal war steamer"— a curious premonition of the *Alabama*'s own encounter with the *Kearsarge* later that year. A well-known burlesque actress called Lydia Thompson played the female lead of Phoebe, "in which character," it was announced, "she will dance her celebrated sailor's hornpipe." While the audience was watching Mr. Morton's extravaganza, the real *Alabama* was still at sea; less than three months later, she would be lying on the seabed off Cherbourg.

Colin Henry Hazlewood's two-act drama, *The Confederate's Daughter; or, the Tyrant of New Orleans*, was the only one of these three plays to portray actual historical figures and events. Set in and around New Orleans in 1862, at the time of Major General Benjamin Butler's military governorship, it concerns the adventures of Frances Herbert, "the Confederate's daughter" (whose father has been executed by General Butler), Lieutenant Travers, C.S.A., her sweetheart, and Pompey, "a faithful black." It ends with Butler being relieved of his command at the end of that year, while the heroine's closing speech, on being told of plans to go to England —"And when you do, bear this in mind, that the flag of liberty which was first raised there still waves triumphant in Albion's Isle, ever ready to shelter within its folds an African's son or a Confederate's daughter"— no doubt brought rousing cheers from the audience at the Britannia Theater, Hoxton, where it ran from August 7 through September 9, 1865. Confederate journalist John R. Thompson went to see it during its third week and noted in his diary: "The villain, as General Butler, was almost as great a scoundrel as the original."[1]

Other plays which reflected increased public interest in life and events across the Atlantic included *Down South; or, Life in the Cotton Fields*, a farce by an unknown author, "in which the Alabama Minstrels will appear," which had a successful run at the Royal Victoria Theater, Waterloo Road (the Old Vic), from June 19 through July 15, 1865; and *Cora; or, The Slaves of the South*, a three-act drama by George Augustus Conquest, which was first performed at the Grecian Theater, City Road, on June 26, 1865.

On March 11, 1863, a new entertainment called *Federals and Confederates* opened at the Polygraphic Hall, King William Street, Strand, and ran until May 6. Presented every evening (except Saturdays) at 8:0, and Wednesdays and Saturdays at 3:0, it played to "crowded houses" and was described as a "highly instructive narrative of the present state of affairs in America, with pictorial and musical illustrations." It was advertised in both the *London American* and the *Index*. Its author was Henri Drayton, an American opera singer and minor dramatist, who before the war had sung in England and on the Continent. Some of the songs were by Henry Russell, one of the best-known singers and songwriters of his time, and included "Sunny Days Will Come Again," with lyrics by Edwin Ransford, though many were composed and written by Drayton himself, who also provided sketches to illustrate the show.[2]

Although the *Times* was impressed with the production, describing it as "exceedingly well put together," *Federals and Confederates* did not present an impartial view of the war, and the reviewer left his readers in no doubt about where its sympathies lay:

HENRI DRAYTON. ----- Polygraphic-hall, King William-street, Strand. --- HENRI DRAYTON has the honour to announce his PICTORIAL and MUSICAL ENTERTAINMENT entitled "Federals and Confederates," at the above Hall, THIS and EVERY EVENING (Saturday excepted), at 8; and Wednesday and Saturday, at 3. Tickets of Cramer and Co.'s, Regent-street; Chappell's, New Bond-street; and at the Hall. Admission 1s., 2s., and 3s.

> Mr Henri Drayton ... gives an "entertainment," in the strict sense of the word, ... narrating by means of song, anecdote, piano and picture, his recent experiences in America. Of his predilections he makes no secret, and the serious object of *Federals and Confederates* ... is to prove that the Confederates are all right and the Federals are all wrong ... "Dixie's Land" with the proper Secession words, honoured with an encore ... seems to indicate that the audience are not only pleased with the tune itself and the execution of the vocalist, but also with the sentiment embodied...[3]

Was Mr. Drayton merely giving the audience what he thought it wanted, or was his show, as the *Times* seems to suggest, actually a form of Confederate propaganda, presented as entertainment? There is no evidence to connect it with propagandists like Henry Hotze, but its possibilities would certainly not have escaped him.

Madame Tussaud's waxworks, located on Baker Street since 1835, was one of the sights of London. It had had "a full-length portrait model of Mr Lincoln" since November 1861, and in January 1862 the proprietors announced that they had recently added "the effigies of ... the notorious 'ambassadors,' Mason and Slidell." These were joined in August 1863 by "a model of [Major] General McClellan, in military uniform, late Commander-in-Chief of the Federal Army."[4] Assistant Paymaster Douglas Forrest records an amusing incident concerning a colleague, Lieutenant Charles King, Jr., who visited Madame Tussaud's in naval uniform. While intently examining a wax figure in the Chamber of Horrors, he was mistaken for one of them by a lady visitor, who looked in vain for his number; "King was a *very* hard-looking figure in his Confederate rig," he adds.[5] In June 1865 Tussaud's introduced "a full-length portrait model of John Wilkes Booth, the Assassin, taken from a likeness presented by himself to Mrs. Stratton, the wife of General Tom Thumb," and added "the late Presidents Lincoln and Davis" the following month. The figure of Lincoln was presumably an updated version from that of 1861.[6]

Panoramas had been a popular form of entertainment for many years, but by the early 1860s they had lost much of their appeal for London audiences, partly as a result of the growth of illustrated weekly magazines, with their topical engravings. Nevertheless, in March 1863, readers of the *Illustrated London News* were told that "M. Gompertz's New Panorama of the War in America, printed principally from his own sketches, will shortly be submitted to the public."[7]

Later that year another Civil War panorama was presented at the St. James's Hall, Piccadilly. "Civil War in America — Church's Historical Panorama" opened on November 9, and with "descriptive lecture and music" could be seen every evening at 8:0 and on Saturdays at 3:0. "This magnificent work of art," claimed its presenters, "portrays with life-like fidelity (from original sketches and photographs taken on the spot) the principal battles, sieges and naval engagements, illustrating historically and impartially the Civil War."[8]

> CIVIL WAR in AMERICA. --- CHURCH's HISTORICAL PANORAMA now OPEN every evening, at 8 o'clock, and Saturday morning at 3 o'clock, at St. James's-hall, with Descriptive Lecture and Music. This magnificent work of art pourtrays with life-like fidelity (from original sketches and photographs taken on the spot) the principal Battles, Sieges, and Naval Engagements, illustrating historically and impartially the civil war. Stalls, 3s. ; area, 2s. ; gallery, 1s. Tickets at Austin's ticket-office.

"Federals and Confederates," at the Polygraphic Hall, King William Street, Strand, and "Civil War in America — Church's Historical Panorama," at the St. James's Hall, Piccadilly, could both be seen in London in 1863. (*Times*, 11 March 1863 and 17 November 1863)

A detailed advertisement in the *Times* on the day it opened indicates a remarkably ambitious presentation, with thirty-seven scenes in three sections, which included the bombardment of Fort Sumter, the engagement between the *Monitor* and the *Merrimack* and the battle of Fredericksburg.[9] "In the battle-pieces, which are necessarily numerous," reported the *Times*, "a great deal of character and much skill in composition is displayed ... Far inferior to the battle-pieces are the landscapes, and again inferior to these are certain humorous pictures of life ... However ... as a work of art the 'Historical Panorama' ... will bear an interest of its own as a pictorial illustration of the sanguinary contest about which everybody talks and reads."[10] To sustain public interest, additional pictures, "with a new and highly interesting lecture," were announced in December. It appears to have closed in the middle of January 1864.

Photographers soon found that there was a ready market for Civil War portraits. In January 1862, McLean, Melhuish and Haes, in the Haymarket, were advertising "CIVIL WAR IN AMERICA — CARD PORTRAITS of all the CELEBRITIES, including President Lincoln, President Davis, Captain Wilkes [of the USS *San Jacinto*], Messrs. Mason, Slidell, &c."[11] The demand for these continued throughout the war, with Alfred W. Bennett of Bishopsgate offering "Cartes de Visite of American Celebrities, Federal and Confederate Statesmen and Generals" at one shilling each in August 1864.[12]

Some photographers seem to have specialized in Confederate celebrities, as the following announcement in December 1863 indicates:

> A series of very fine PHOTOGRAPHIC PORTRAITS, principally taken in camp within the last nine months, including Jefferson Davis, Generals Stonewall Jackson (photographed ten days previous to his death), R.E. Lee, Beauregard, Longstreet, Johnston, Bragg, A.P. Hill, Stuart, Ewell, Buckner, Price, Hood, Morgan, Kirby Smith, Fitzhugh Lee, etc are now published ... by MR WALKER, Photographer, 3 Pembridge Villas, Bayswater, of whom they may be obtained ... and from MESSRS MARION & SON, 23 Soho Square.[13]

A year later, photographer Henry Francis, in Great Russell Street, "opposite the British Museum," had for sale "A BEAUTIFUL PORTRAIT OF JEFF DAVIS, our FIRST PRESIDENT ... Also the twenty-three OFFICERS of the Confederate ship ALABAMA..."[14]

"Our First President" was also the subject of a large folio lithograph by Thomas Koppel, published in 1865 by Victor De La Rue, of Chandos Street, Covent Garden, presumably just before the final collapse of the Confederacy. Though described as being "From the Latest Photograph now in Possession of the Family," it was actually based on a pre-war portrait, and was probably intended for European rather than Confederate consumption, given the state of affairs in the South by then. Lithographs of Generals "Stonewall" Jackson and Joseph E. Johnston were issued by G. W. Bacon & Company, of Paternoster Row (who were also map publishers) and Day & Son, of Lincoln's Inn Fields, "lithographers to the Queen"; both were drawn from very out-of-date photographs. The war was already over when "A handsome steel engraving" of General Robert E. Lee, "from a portrait ... taken at Richmond, C.S.A., in October last," was announced as being "now ready" by Saunders, Otley of Brook Street, Mayfair in May 1865.[15]

Anyone wanting more than just a photograph or print could visit Thomas Revell's Fine Art Gallery in Leadenhall Street, where "STONEWALL JACKSON and other celebrated Confederate Generals. Authentic PORTRAITS, painted from life by B. F. Reinhardt [sic], Esq." were to be seen in June 1863.[16] Not just anyone could gain access: admission was by "address card" (visiting card) only. The generals represented included Robert E. Lee, Joseph E. Johnston, Pierre G. T. Beauregard, and for good measure, Jefferson Davis. Benjamin F. Reinhart was a Pennsylvania-born artist who exhibited at the Royal Academy, and as he spent the Civil War in London, his description "painted from life" should read, "painted from photographs."

Although more than seventy Confederate generals were killed in action or mortally wounded during the Civil War, none received more tributes than Thomas J. "Stonewall" Jackson, who was a victim of what we now call friendly fire. His accidental wounding by his own men at the battle of Chancellorsville in May 1863, and subsequent death a few days later from pneumonia, seemed to strike a particular chord with the British public. "Even on this side of the ocean," remarked the *Times*, "the gallant soldier's fate will everywhere be heard of with pity and sympathy," and it called him "one of the most consumate Generals that this century has produced." The paper went on to compare his death with that of Nelson at Trafalgar: "The national feeling of England recorded the victory of Trafalgar as dearly purchased by the death of Nelson. A similar feeling pervades the South for the loss of 'Stonewall' Jackson. The South will be exceptionally fortunate if it find another man with all the qualities and capacities General Jackson possessed."[17]

Americans living in London could not fail to notice the public mood. "Stonewall Jackson is dead of wounds. The British people are as sensibly affected by this last news as if the disaster were their own," an astonished Benjamin Moran recorded in his journal.[18] Henry Hotze expressed a similar view, in a letter to Secretary of State Judah Benjamin:

> The death of Jackson has elicited a feeling the depth and power, if not the very existence, of which had wholly escaped my observation before, a feeling altogether incommensurate to anything ever manifested on any previous event of the war. I am quite prepared to believe, what I am assured on all sides, that the death of no foreigner has ever so moved the popular heart ... The Press but inadequately expresses popular emotion which appears to be shared by all classes.[19]

On June 4, 1863, the *Index* announced: "It is proposed to raise a subscription in England for the erection in the Confederate States of A BRITISH MONUMENT to this gallant man." A committee of sixteen prominent Confederate sympathizers was formed to manage the "British Jackson Monumental Fund," with Alexander Beresford Hope as treasurer and William

Gregory, M.P., as secretary and an account for it was opened at Coutts Bank in the Strand. Its prospectus spoke admiringly of Jackson's fame, which had won the respect of his enemies as well as the admiration of the Old World, but it was careful to point out that subscriptions to the statue would not, of course, imply any bias in the great struggle taking place across the Atlantic. The eminent, Irish-born sculptor John H. Foley, R.A., whose most famous work is the figure of the Prince Consort on the Albert Memorial in Hyde Park, and who also designed the Great Seal of the Confederacy, was commissioned to make the statue, which would be based on a recent photograph.

The staff of the *Index* contributed ten guineas and the donations received each week were published in its columns; by the end of August 1863, more than £600 had already been subscribed. According to the records of the "Stonewall Jackson Memorial Account" at Coutts Bank, 114 named individuals, two firms and a few anonymous donors contributed to it, mostly during the second half of 1863. The most generous donations came from James Spence, Alexander Collie and J. Henry Schroder, who each gave £50.

In July 1865, in reply to an enquiry from a subscriber, Alexander Beresford Hope was able to report in the *Index* that sufficient money had now been raised, and that "Mr Foley is at work, with the confident expectation of a very successful result" at his studio in Osnaburgh Street, near Regent's Park. In spite of this optimistic statement, there were to be many more delays, caused by the sculptor's desire for perfection, other commissions competing for his time, and increasing ill health, and Jackson's statue was not completed until a few months before the sculptor's own death in 1874. It was exhibited at the Royal Academy in London the following year, before being shipped to Richmond, where it was erected in the grounds of the Capitol in October 1875, "in the hundredth year of the Commonwealth" (of Virginia). The bronze statue, signed by Foley, shows Jackson standing, uniformed and hatless, holding his sword; an inscription on the plinth records that it was "presented by English gentlemen as a tribute of admiration."

In view of the continuing public interest, a photographer announced in April 1864 the publication, by private subscription, of a photograph of the fallen general:

> LIEUTENANT-GENERAL STONEWALL JACKSON
> THE ONLY AUTHENTIC AND FAITHFUL LIKENESS YET PUBLISHED
> MESSRS. W. WALKER & SONS, 64 MARGARET ST, CAVENDISH SQ ... have lately been furnished by the Hon. J.M. Mason, of the Confederate States, with the only original likeness of the late lamented General Thomas Jefferson [sic] Jackson, photographed from life a week before the General received his fatal wound ... This portrait remains emphatically as The Likeness of the illustrious General. It has been seen and highly approved by many Southern Gentlemen who knew the General personally.[20]

Half of the net profits from the sale of the photographs, it was stated, were to go to the Southern Prisoners' Relief Fund, which had been set up to improve the lot of Confederate prisoners of war "in the Federal American States."

Another scheme to raise money for this was the reproduction of a bust of President Jefferson Davis, in a limited edition of 500 (quarter size), available in four versions — plaster; enameled plaster; *à l'ivoire* (wax and plaster); and marble — to order:

> The only Bust extant ... modelled by Volk, at Richmond ... has been kindly lent by the owner for reproduction for the benefit of the Southern Prisoners' Relief Fund ... The Bust may be seen at the studio of James Redfern, 29 Clipstone St., Fitzroy Sq. ... and at the *Index* office.[21]

Large numbers of songs were written and published in the South during the war and some of these were reprinted by London music publishers to satisfy popular demand. As Colonel Peyton later recalled: "Music dealers got out rapidly, Southern songs, set to music, and dedicated to Confederate exiles in Europe. Young ladies were taught to sing and play them, and everywhere was heard 'Dixie,' 'Bonnie Blue Flag,' 'Down among the Cotton,' 'My Maryland,' &c."[22]

Songs for the piano, as well as marches, quadrilles, polkas and quicksteps, all with Confederate themes, were published by firms like Boosey & Sons, Brewer & Company, Cramer, Beale & Wood and Joseph Williams, and advertised in weekly magazines like the *Illustrated London News*. Thomas Boosey & Sons, musical instrument makers, music sellers and publishers, who were established in 1816, and still exist as Boosey & Hawkes, brought out Victor Colline's "Maryland Quadrille" (1864) and George Forbe's "Maryland: A Confederate March for the Piano" (1864), as well as *Twelve Songs of the American War*, which contained six Confederate pieces, including "Old King Cotton" and "A Battle Hymn."

Cramer, Beale & Wood, music and musical instrument sellers and publishers, who had started in 1844 as Cramer, Beale & Chappell, and are now known as Cramer Music, published James Randall's "Maryland, My Maryland," which competed with Daniel Emmett's "Dixie" and Harry Macarthy's "Bonnie Blue Flag" as the Confederate national anthem. They also brought out "War Song of Dixie" (1862), written by Frederick Buckley, a member of the minstrel group known as Buckley's Serenaders, "with an illuminated frontispiece showing the Confederate flag and standard."

Joseph Williams, who had taken over his mother's music-printing business in 1844, published Henry Farmer's "Dixie's Land Polka" (1861) and Henri F. Hemy's "The Picket of the Potomac" (1864): "The beautiful and touching words of this song were found in the pocket of one of the Confederate volunteers who died in the camp on the Potomac from a rifle wound while on picket duty," claimed the publisher, who continued in business until at least 1954.[23] Another firm, Hopwood & Crew, advertised "Dixey's Land Gallop" (1861), by Charles Coote, Jr., and "The Boy of the Rappahannock" (1865), by Charles Blamphim, as well as those songs quoted by Colonel Peyton.

General Robert E. Lee rarely featured in songs, though his portrait appears on the cover of Carl Weiner's "Confederate War March," published by J. Jewell towards the end of 1864. "Stonewall" Jackson, on the other hand, was the inspiration for a number of pieces of music, not least after his death in 1863. Joseph Williams issued "The General Jackson Schottische" ("as played by the 600 performers at the Brass Band Contest, Crystal Palace") in 1862 and Foster & King brought out "The Stonewall Jackson Quadrille" in the same year. Charles Blamphim's "Death of Stonewall Jackson" was published by Samuel Brewer & Company in 1864; illustrated with the general's portrait, it is not surprising to learn that this was "sung by all the leading vocalists with rapturous applause."

As well as these reprinted pieces, at least two Confederate songs were published in London.[24] "A Confederate Raid" and "Our Queen Varine" were written by 'EM', an unidentified Southerner living in England, and brought out by Christopher Lonsdale, who had been in business on his own as a music seller and publisher since 1834, though the firm, previously known as Birchall, Lonsdale and Mills, dated back to c.1811.

"A Confederate Raid," dedicated to "General J. E. B. Stuart of the Confederate Cavalry," was the shorter of the two:

> Then hurrah for Stuart, hurrah!
> And his bold cavaliers of the West,
> 'Tis his twentieth raid, hurrah!
> No rest for brave Stuart, no rest!

"Our Queen Varine" was dedicated to "Varina, wife of the President of the Confederate States of America":

> Here's to the fair and brilliant one,
> Who by his side is seen
> Long may she be,
> Long may we see
> Varine our Queen!
> Our Queen, Varine!

Copies of the two songs were deposited in what is now the British Library in March and July 1864. "A Confederate Raid" was perhaps written about the beginning of 1864, fairly late in Stuart's career as a cavalry leader, and would have been published two months before his death, following his wounding at Yellow Tavern in May 1864. It is difficult, however, to imagine a song like "Our Queen Varine" being published as late as July 1864; the adulatory and overly optimistic sentiments suggest a much earlier date — perhaps the spring or summer of 1861, when Confederate nationalism was in full flow — long before disillusionment with Davis and his leadership had set in. The colored cover, showing the earliest version of the first Confederate national flag, the "Stars and Bars," with seven stars (adopted in March 1861), and reused for the second song, tends to reinforce this idea.

Although maps and atlases published by American firms like J.T. Lloyd were available in England — they included *Lloyd's Great Coloured Military Map of the Southern Confederacy* ("engraved on steel for the use of the War Department") and *Lloyd's American Railroad Map, showing the Whole Seat of War,* both issued in 1861— London map publishers also responded to public interest in events across the Atlantic.

Most of the Civil War maps published appeared in the first two years of the conflict. Some showed the boundary of the seceded states, or the area and extent of the "free and slave-holding states," others the seat of war in America. They were produced for a public which was initially unfamiliar with the geography of the war, though by 1864 the *Times* could remark: "The country between the Rappahannock and the Potomac [i.e., between Fredericksburg and Washington] has become as familiar [to] the English public as the space between St Paul's and South Kensington."[25]

G.W. Bacon & Company of Paternoster Row, who described themselves as "American Map Publishers and Importers" and were the London agents for the American mapmaking firm of J.H. Colton, issued a *New Army Map of the Seat of War in Virginia* (1862), which showed the battlefields and fortifications near the Potomac. James Wyld, whose Great Globe had been such a prominent feature of Leicester Square throughout the 1850s, published a number of military maps of the war, including several editions of one of the Southern states, showing forts, harbors and military positions. H.G. Clarke, a bookseller and publisher in the Strand, issued *Woolley's New Map of the Seat of War in the Confederate States of America,* possibly in 1861. There seem to have been very few maps of individual battles, probably because the ones which appeared in magazines like the *Illustrated London News* made them largely unnecessary, though G.W. Bacon did issue one of the battle of

Fredericksburg, as well as his *Map shewing the entire Field of Operations under Grant, Sherman and Thomas* (1865).[26]

Articles about the Civil War, many of them sympathetic to the South, began to appear in the weekly and monthly magazines published in London. They were usually unsigned, as was the practice of the time, and some of the accounts of the Confederacy were based on recent, first-hand experience, particularly ones written by serving army officers, who had gone there as unofficial observers or military tourists.

The *Illustrated London News*, which had begun publication in 1842, was the first and one of the most successful of the new illustrated weekly magazines, a pioneer in pictorial journalism. Its emphasis was on current affairs and in the spring of 1861, after the start of the Civil War, it sent a representative to America in the person of Frank Vizetelly, an experienced special correspondent who had already covered wars in Austria, Italy and Sicily. He began by reporting from the Northern side, but lack of cooperation from the Federal authorities caused him to go South in the summer of 1862.

He became a great admirer of the Army of Northern Virginia, with "its wonderful endurance ... its utter disregard for hardships," and made little attempt to hide his support for the Confederacy. Regardless of whether the *Illustrated London News* itself was hoping for a Southern victory, many of its readers probably were. With his taste for amateur theatricals and charades, this gregarious journalist was popular wherever he went. His sketches and reports sometimes failed to get through the blockade, and pirated ones occasionally appeared in Northern papers. Vizetelly returned to London three times during the war, on each occasion bringing with him collections of drawings made during the previous months. The only foreign artist–correspondent in the Confederacy, he accompanied President Davis and his party during part of their flight from Richmond, and his drawings of the "Last Days of the Confederate Government" (July 22, 1865) are a unique record of that event.

In December 1861 a favorable review of James Spence's book, *The American Union*, appeared in the widely-read weekly magazine, *All the Year Round*. Its founder and editor, Charles Dickens, was no admirer of the South, but his magazine did feature a couple of articles of Confederate interest: "The Diary of a Confederate Boy" (May 17, 1862) dealt with the early months of the war, about the time of First Manassas, and "A Waif from Dixie" (October 29, 1864) was based on the contents of Confederate newspapers from Mobile.

The humorous weekly *Punch*, which had been founded a year before the *Illustrated London News*, responded to the formation of the Confederate States of America by referring to them disparagingly as "confederates in the crime of upholding slavery" (March 9, 1861), but after the commencement of hostilities, it began to adopt a more ambivalent attitude, condemning both sides for what it saw as their stupidity:

> Yankee Doodles, oh, you noodles!
> Why prolong this idle strife? (September 28, 1861)

By the end of 1861, as a result of the blockade and the *Trent* affair, *Punch* was becoming increasingly anti–Northern and beginning to prophesy the defeat of the North. Nevertheless, it was still firmly opposed to slavery, which it regarded as doomed. When it was reported in 1862 that plantation bells were being donated to be melted down for cannon, it cautioned its readers:

> But pause on that last gift, can good come of cannon cast
> From the bells that waked the slaves to their heavy, hopeless toil? (April 26, 1862).

9—*Artistic Reflections, Literary Echoes*

VERY PROBABLE.

LORD PUNCH. "THAT WAS JEFF DAVIS, PAM! DON'T YOU RECOGNISE HIM?"
LORD PAM. "HM! WELL, NOT EXACTLY—MAY HAVE TO DO SO SOME OF THESE DAYS."

As late as August 1864 it was still thought that Confederate recognition was a possibility, as this *Punch* cartoon by John Tenniel seems to suggest.

In spite of its guarded, pro–Southern stance, it advised the people of Southampton not to welcome the Southern Commissioners Mason and Slidell openly when they arrived there, lest it be seen as "a declaration on the part of the people of England for the Confederate side" (January 18, 1862), advice which appears to have been heeded. It also published a poem called "The Tuscarora" (February 8, 1862), occasioned by the unwelcome presence at Southampton of both the CSS *Nashville* and the USS *Tuscarora*.

Latterly, it seemed to allow wishful thinking to cloud its judgment, with cartoons such as "Very Probable" (August 27, 1864), suggesting that recognition of the Confederacy was still a possibility, and "The American Juggernaut" (September 3, 1864), showing Union troops being crushed by a huge Southern gun-carriage, at a time when Grant had Lee bottled up in Petersburg, Sherman had taken Atlanta and Sheridan was starting to drive Early out of the Shenandoah Valley. There were also cartoons on the contentious subject of black troops in the Confederate Army, "The Black Conscription" (September 26, 1863) and "The Black Draft" (November 19, 1864).

The verses accompanying its cartoon of Lee's surrender admitted that it had often "misread the chances of the fight" (April 29, 1865), and *Punch's* editor conceded privately that "we have been a bit mistaken" when, after ridiculing Lincoln for four years, the magazine was obliged to do a lightning *volte-face*, after news of his assassination reached London.

The *Fortnightly Review* began publication the year the war ended, and was unusual for its time in that its articles were signed. "The Last Six Days of Secessia," an account of Lee's retreat to Appomattox, which appeared in the issue of August 15, 1865, was written by Francis Lawley, who had covered the war for the *Times*. Noted for his pro–Confederate reports, he was in Richmond when it fell, and apparently followed Lee's retreating army, the only journalist to do so.

A well-respected literary monthly which had been established as long ago as 1817, *Blackwood's Magazine* published a number of articles by British visitors to the Confederacy. "A Month with the Rebels," by the Hon. Robert Bourke, an Irish barrister who was the brother of the Earl of Mayo, appeared in December 1861. Its mockery of Northern newspapers, in particular the *New York Herald*, "a paper which all Americans read, most abuse, and none believe," left readers in no doubt where its author's sympathies lay. Bourke was favorably impressed by what he saw during his travels in the autumn of 1861, and thought that "The perfect unanimity throughout the whole South in the belief that their cause is just, strikes the stranger as one of the most formidable symptoms which the Union has to fear." Like many, he hoped that, once the Confederate States had been admitted into "the family of nations," European influences would bring about the emancipation of the slaves. Apparently at the request of propagandist Edwin De Leon, the same author also contributed a eulogistic piece about Jefferson Davis, "one of the few great men that this war has produced," to the September 1862 issue of the magazine.

Edward Seymour arrived in the Confederate capital at the end of June 1862, just as the Seven Days' Battles were about to start. He described them in "Ten Days in Richmond" (October 1862), and in particular the battle of Gaines' Mill, then went on to discuss the state of public opinion in the South. As far as he was concerned, "Separation is now not a question of right, or even of expediency, but a simple matter of fact. The people of the Confederate States are a separate nation." Seymour, who was Twelfth Duke of Somerset and First Lord of the Admiralty, was a privileged visitor and able to move around fairly freely.

Army officers like Lieutenant Colonel Garnet Wolseley, who had served in the Second

Burma War, the Crimean War, the Indian Mutiny and the China War, and was assistant quartermaster general in Canada, took a professional interest in events. In the North, Wolseley found that his English appearance and speech aroused suspicion and that "we are all considered as rebel sympathisers," a rather revealing comment. "A Month's Visit to the Confederate Headquarters" (January 1863) describes his visit in September and October 1862, during which time he saw the scenes of the recent Seven Days' Battles and was able to meet with both Lee and Jackson. He noted the confidence and loyalty they inspired in their men; some surprise was expressed that England had not already recognized the Confederacy, particularly "after M'Clellan's failure before Richmond."

Edward Hamley, who was professor of military history at the Royal Military College, Sandhurst, contributed an article called "Our Rancorous 'Cousins'" (November 1863). This denounced the attitude of the Federal government and press as one of "shameless impudence" while "glorying *ad nauseam* in the success of their own effort to throw off their allegiance to Great Britain [in the War of Independence] they have never ceased to denounce the secession of the Sovereign States of the South as 'a wicked and unnatural rebellion.'" Like many of his brother officers, Hamley was full of admiration for "the gallant deeds of the Southern armies and generals, the noble devotion of the Southern people."

A number of articles which were published in *Blackwood's* during or shortly after the war subsequently reappeared in book form. These included "The Battle of Gettysburg and the Campaign in Pennsylvania: extract from the Diary of an English Officer present with the Confederate Army" (September 1863), by Lieutenant Colonel Arthur Fremantle; "A Visit to the Cities and Camps of the Confederate States" (December 1864 – February 1865), by Captain Fitzgerald Ross; and "Memoirs of the Confederate War for Independence" (September 1865 – June 1866), by Lieutenant Colonel Heros Von Borcke.

The *Cornhill Magazine*, another literary monthly, was a runaway success when it began publication in 1860. For the first two years, its editor was the famous novelist William M. Thackeray, and it also published several articles on the Civil War, again chiefly from a Southern standpoint. "The Cruise of the Confederate Ship 'Sumter' (From the Private Journal of an Officer)," by a journalist called Frank Drake, appeared in the August 1862 issue. Comparison with Raphael Semmes' *Memoirs of Service Afloat* shows it to be remarkably accurate, even including details not contained in that work.

When "How We Broke the Blockade" was published in October 1862, its author, Edwin De Leon, was the Confederate propaganda agent in Paris. At the time of his blockade-running adventure, in February 1862, he was returning home after serving as U.S. consul general in Egypt. He and his wife sailed from Southampton to Havana, where they joined a "long, low, black, rakish-looking steamer" called the *Victoria*, for their uncomfortable, and at times alarming, journey back to the Confederacy.

"A Run through the Southern States" (April 1863), by Lieutenant Colonel Henry Fletcher, of the Scots Fusilier Guards, gave an account of his often difficult journeys, mostly by train, through Mississippi, Alabama, Georgia, the Carolinas and Virginia, in the last months of 1862. Fletcher, who later wrote a three-volume *History of the American War* (1865–1866) and himself rose to the rank of major general, met Generals Price, Van Dorn, Beauregard and Admiral Buchanan along the way, and visited Vicksburg, Mobile, where he saw the CSS *Florida*, and Charleston. He concluded "that no danger will ever frighten, or bribes of power induce, the States of the Confederacy to join again the Northern Union."

Frank Vizetelly of the *Illustrated London News* was in Charleston in 1863, and witnessed the attack on Fort Sumter by Federal ironclads in April, the assault on Battery Wagner (Morris Island) by land and sea three months later and the bombardment of the city itself in August. These events were described in some detail in his article "Charleston under Fire" (July 1864).

In November 1864 the *Monthly Packet*, a periodical for young women, founded and for many years edited by the novelist Charlotte M. Yonge, began to publish a series of articles called "Home Life in a Confederate State." They were allegedly based on the journal of an Englishwoman who had gone to America at the beginning of 1861 to be a teacher at a plantation on the Georgia coast, and later had moved inland with her employers. The series stopped in December 1865, then resumed in August 1866 under a new title, "Extracts from the Journal of a Refugee in Georgia during the American War," when its author insisted that the earlier parts of her journal had not been intended for publication, but that her "zealous correspondent in England ... thought that a simple statement of facts would enlist the sympathies of the English people in [sic] behalf of the Southern Confederacy."[27] It continued intermittently until May 1867, when, still incomplete, it ceased altogether; no explanation for this was given. The journal covers the period March 1861– December 1864, and demonstrates a remarkable knowledge of conditions and events in wartime Georgia on the part of its anonymous author.

The *Quarterly Review*, another established and influential journal, had been founded by the famous publisher John Murray and that too published a number of articles about the war. "The Confederate Struggle and Recognition" (October 1862) has been attributed to Lord Robert Cecil, a member of the Southern lobby in Parliament, who wrote extensively for the magazine. He observed: "The Southerners have shown every characteristic that can mark an independent nation. They have made the costliest sacrifices that men can make to assure their freedom from a foreign rule, and they have fought for it with a gallantry that has not been surpassed in all the wars of liberation the world has seen."

An evaluation of "The Prospects of the Confederates," which appeared in the April 1864 issue, was by Robert Lawley, who summarized the difficulties facing the Confederates as "1. Insufficient supply of men, horses and food. 2. Jealousy between the armies of the Potomac [Northern Virginia] and Tennessee, and general dissatisfaction with President Davis and the Confederate Government." None was thought to be insurmountable. Some of the optimism may derive from his journalist brother, Francis Lawley, who is thought to have contributed to the article.

"The question naturally arises, what caused the failure of this great effort of the South to possess a government of its own?" asked James Spence, a leading British champion of Confederate independence, in "The Close of the American War" (July 1865). As well as "the great superiority of the North in numbers and resources ... their command of naval force ... soon felt in a country intersected by great rivers," and "that special weapon, the blockade"; there was also what he described as "excess of confidence ... lives of Southern soldiers were expended ... as if the supply were inexhaustible." (That was particularly true of generals like John Bell Hood.) The failure to recruit blacks into the Confederate army until it was too late was also thought to be a serious mistake, and "would have turned the scale in favour of the South," an opinion some military historians might question. He reiterated his belief that Confederate independence would have meant the end of slavery: it was "doubtless the real cause why the independence of the South was not recognized by the European powers." (Most historians would probably describe it as a contributory cause.)

These magazines all had a predominantly middle- and upper-class readership and by and large reflected the views of their readers; they were also relatively expensive. The *Illustrated London News*, for instance, cost sixpence a copy, while the *Cornhill Magazine* was a shilling, nearly a third of a day's wages then for many workingmen. The abolition of the stamp duty on newspapers and magazines in 1855, followed by that on raw paper in 1861, resulted in a crop of weekly magazines, usually costing little more than a penny and often illustrated with cheap woodcuts, which aimed to provide both instruction and recreation for respectable working-class readers. They included the *London Journal, Cassell's Illustrated Family Paper,* the *London Reader, Once a Week* and the *Leisure Hour,* which all published articles on the Civil War, usually cobbled together from other sources by journalists who had probably never set foot in America, but presented convincingly, nonetheless. It has been pointed out that, on the whole, working-class journals were hostile to the North, certainly before the Emancipation Proclamation, and to some extent, after it as well.[28] Some evidence for this can certainly be seen in their tendency to devote more space to articles about Southern topics.

"The South American Confederation" [sic], which gave a biographical sketch of Jefferson Davis, and a summary of his address to the Confederate Congress, appeared in the *London Journal* as early as March 30, 1861, and the magazine continued to take an interest in events across the Atlantic. There were illustrated pieces about the *Merrimack* and her encounter with the *Monitor* (April 19, 1862), and several more chronicling the exploits of the *Sumter* (March 1, 1862), and the *Alabama* (December 13, 1862 and February 28, 1863). Subjects like the latter lent themselves easily to journalistic hyperbole, with descriptions of "the brave Captain Semmes, his gallant ship the Alabama, and his daring crew of—as the Americans style us— Britishers." The same magazine also published a detailed account of the New York draft riots (August 22, 1863) and a discussion of General Grant's plan to capture Richmond (May 21, 1864).

Cassell's Illustrated Family Paper published articles about the *Merrimack* (January 11, 1862), the *Arkansas* (October 18, 1862), and the *Alabama* (July 30, 1864), whose "fate, though terrible, was glorious ... a suitable termination to her daring and brilliant career." There were also pieces about Charleston (February 15, 1862 and April 16, 1864), and an excellent map of "The Seat of War in America" (December 20, 1862), which would have done credit to the *Illustrated London News*. These articles were not necessarily uncritical; the author of "Richmond, on the James River" (October 3, 1863), for instance, made his feelings about slavery very clear.

An article about the late-lamented "Stonewall" Jackson (June 13, 1863), in the *London Reader*, a similar publication to the *Journal*, caught the mood of the moment; there were also pieces about Charleston (June 6, 1863 and September 26, 1863), and Robert E. Lee (August 27, 1864), which described him, somewhat prematurely, as "The Confederate Commander-in-Chief," rather than commander of the Army of Northern Virginia. It was published at a stage in the war when it really did seem as if "the one will never submit, and the other, it is now evident, is wholly unable to conquer," and there were calls that the "bugbear of nonintervention should be flung aside, and words of friendly counsel strongly urged on both sides."

Once a Week published two articles on the subject of "The American Generals" (November 15 and 22, 1862), which gave brief details of the lives of the main Confederate and Federal commanders, while the *Leisure Hour* featured "The American Blockaded Ports" (April 16, 1864), written, it was claimed, by a British settler in Texas, and dealing chiefly with

Galveston, Wilmington and Charleston, and another piece on "American Generals" (June 25, 1864), which examined the careers of Jackson, Lee, McClellan and Grant.

Books by visitors to the South were also starting to appear. Samuel Phillips Day, the special correspondent of the *Morning Herald* from June through September 1861, was the author of *Down South: or, An Englishman's Experience at the Seat of the American War*, published by Hurst & Blackett in 1862. He spent most of his time in Richmond, and made no secret of his pro–Confederate sympathies, stating that "The Northern attempt to conquer the South is a labor equally as futile as that of Sisyphus [i.e., an endless, heart-breaking task] ... It is not only mere folly, but little short of sheer insanity, to think of over-running 750,000 square miles of territory, and subjugating the 9,500,000 people who now compose the eleven states of the Confederacy."[29]

Many of these books were published in 1863, when Confederate independence still seemed a possibility. The Rev. William Wyndham Malet's book, *An Errand to the South in the Summer of 1862*, was brought out by Richard Bentley & Son, a firm which had started in 1829 and was well-known for its multivolume novels, published for circulating libraries. Malet, a Hertfordshire clergyman, had traveled to South Carolina to visit his sister who was married to Captain Plowden C.J. Weston, a plantation owner serving with the Confederate Army. His readable account of a sometimes difficult trip, which lasted from May through November 1862, was based on a diary. While living in the South, he visited Richmond, where he met President and Mrs. Davis, and "Mr. Vizetelly, the accomplished sketcher for the *Illustrated London News*; he was lamenting over the loss of some sketches, from the bearer having to throw them with other papers into the Potomac, to avoid seizure by the enemy."[30] *An Errand to the South* is a rewarding account which would be worth reprinting.

Neither Samuel Day nor the Rev. William Malet found fault with slavery. That was not the case with William Howard Russell of the *Times*. As a representative of that opinion-forming newspaper, Russell was regarded as an important person on both sides of the Potomac, but succeeded in offending Northerners, with his outspoken account of the battle of Bull Run, and Southerners, with his denunciation of slavery. Unlike most English visitors to the Confederacy, Russell's name was already well-known there, since his reports on the Crimean War (1854–1856) had been reprinted in American newspapers. He spent three months in the South (April–June 1861) and was impressed by many of the civilian and military leaders he met. Ostensibly impartial, his sympathies, were really with the North, though like many he doubted that the Confederacy would ever be defeated. His experiences as special correspondent during the first year of the war were described in *My Diary North and South*, published by Bradbury & Evans.

Lieutenant Colonel Arthur James Lyon Fremantle's *Three Months in the Southern States: April — June 1863* was published by William Blackwood & Sons after extracts from it had appeared in *Blackwood's Magazine*. The firm had first been established at Edinburgh in 1804 and had opened a London branch in 1840. Colonel Fremantle, an officer in the Coldstream Guards, traveled from Texas, through Louisiana, Mississippi, Alabama, Georgia and the Carolinas, to Virginia, joined Lee's Army during its invasion of Pennsylvania, and was present as an observer, along with Fitzgerald Ross, at the battle of Gettysburg. As well as Generals Lee, Ewell and Longstreet, he met Johnston and Beauregard, and was impressed by them and their troops. It has been called "the best commentary on the wartime South by an English visitor," and Constance Harrison, the wife of Jefferson Davis's secretary, Burton Harrison, recalled how "its charming spirit and interesting presentment of the situation was greatly welcomed" when copies of the book were brought through the blockade.[31] Two copies, inscribed to President Davis and Secretary of State Benjamin, were taken to Richmond by Commander Maury, who traveled there in February 1864.

Two Months in the Confederate States, including a Visit to New Orleans under the Domination of General Butler was also published by Richard Bentley. It was written by "An English Merchant," who has now been identified as William Carson Corsan, a member of the Sheffield firm of Corsan, Denton & Burdekin, hardware merchants and manufacturers. From October through December 1862, Corsan traveled, mostly by train, from New Orleans to Richmond, stopping off at various towns along the way, to investigate the financial status of his firm's customers and perhaps find some new business. The *Sun* thought that it provided "a most opportune peep into the Confederate States."[32]

George Alfred Lawrence, already a successful novelist, decided to go to America in 1863 and join the Confederate Army. Before he could do so, however, he was captured in Maryland and spent eight weeks in the Old Capitol Prison in Washington, where one of his fellow prisoners was Belle Boyd. *Border and Bastille*, an account of his misadventures published by Tinsley Brothers after his release and return to England later that year, was not a novel, though it has been described as fiction *manqué*.

English residents in the South also wrote of their experiences. The Rev T.D. Ozanne, an Episcopalian minister who had lived in Mississippi since 1841, decided to return to England in 1862. *The South as it is; or, Twenty-one Years' Experience in the Southern States of America*, was published the following year by Saunders, Otley & Company. The firm had been established in 1826 by Simon Saunders and Edward John Otley, and had been a successful publisher of nonfiction, drama, poetry and novels, though by the time of the Civil War neither of its founders was still alive and it was no longer in the front rank of London publishers. Ozanne's book is mostly a discourse on slavery, which he presents in a favorable light, the resources, government and social life of the South, and secession; only the last three chapters constitute a personal narrative, though these do include his spell as a wartime hospital chaplain, and a description of life in occupied New Orleans, while he was waiting for a steamer for New York. He too was convinced that the South could never be subdued.

After several appointments teaching the "ornamental branches" (i.e., polite accomplishments) in Virginia, Catherine Cooper Hopley, who had been in America since the late 1850s, became governess to the children of Governor John Milton of Florida. *Life in the South: from the Commencement of the War*, apparently written in the space of ten weeks after her return to England in the autumn of 1862, was brought out the following year by Chapman & Hall, who were also Dickens' publishers. She tried to give an "impartial account of the 'domestic institution'" (i.e., slavery), observing: "The most calamitous and unmerciful affliction that could befall both master and servant, would be the *sudden* emancipation of the slaves of the Southern States."[33] In Richmond she saw President Jefferson Davis, and Secretary of the Navy Stephen Mallory, who did not impress her, and also met journalist Samuel Day. She ended her well-observed account by inviting her readers "to regard with more leniency and justice the people of the Southern Confederacy."[34] Throughout her narrative she refers to herself as Sarah L. Jones, a pseudonym she also used in later publications.

Edward Fitzgerald Turton Ross, a "captain of hussars in the Imperial Austrian Army," spent eleven months in the South, from May 1863 to spring 1864, witnessed the battle of Gettysburg with Arthur Fremantle, and traveled in South Carolina, Georgia, Tennessee and Alabama. All but the last four chapters of his *Visit to the Cities and Camps of the Confederate*

TWO MONTHS

IN

THE CONFEDERATE STATES,

INCLUDING

A VISIT TO NEW ORLEANS

UNDER

THE DOMINATION OF GENERAL BUTLER.

BY

AN ENGLISH MERCHANT.

LONDON:
RICHARD BENTLEY, NEW BURLINGTON STREET,
Publisher in Ordinary to Her Majesty.
1863.

Two Months in the Confederate States, an account of life in the Civil War South by an English businessman, was published in London in 1863.

States had previously appeared in *Blackwood's Magazine* and the book itself was published by William Blackwood in May 1865. The timing, however, was unfortunate: there had been a large readership for earlier accounts of Confederate life, but with the defeat of the South, the subject had lost its appeal. "The present moment is hardly favourable to the success of a book which was written while the Confederate cause still seemed prosperous; and which ... throws no light on the circumstances which disappointed the hopes so long and so confidently entertained, and brought the final catastrophe to pass so much more suddenly and decisively than ordinary observers could have expected ... When the fate of the Southern people is finally decided ... books of this class will have another and more melancholy interest. But at this conjuncture we do not need them," said the *Saturday Review* discouragingly.[35] When Lieutenant Colonel Johann August Heinrich Heros Von Borcke, an aristocratic Prussian officer, who was "lately Chief of Staff to General J.E.B. Stuart," arrived in London in February 1865 on a mission for the Confederate government (the nature of which has not been ascertained), Fitzgerald Ross suggested to publisher William Blackwood that Von Borcke's diary might be turned into a book. *Memoirs of the Confederate War for Independence* was translated, and in fact ghostwritten, by the journalist John Thompson, and first appeared in *Blackwood's Magazine* before being published, with "Map of the Seat of War in Virginia," in 1866.[36] Von Borcke participated in many battles, from Seven Pines to the beginning of the Gettysburg campaign, when he was wounded; there are descriptions of Confederate camp life and he met various English observers, and correspondents like Frank Vizetelly and Francis Lawley.

The death of Stonewall Jackson in 1863 had created considerable public interest, and Chapman & Hall commissioned a short biography of him from Catherine Hopley. It came out later that year, and though it went through three editions, *Stonewall Jackson, late General of the Confederate States Army: a Biographical Sketch and an Outline of his Virginian Campaigns,* was not well received, one reviewer calling it "steeped in sentimentalism and short on scholarship."

Another subject of great public interest was the CSS *Alabama*, which, in the words of her captain, "attracted the attention of the book-makers — those cormorants ever on the lookout for a speculation." They were soon at work. A pamphlet entitled *The Cruise of the Alabama*, based on the journal of her boarding officer, George Townley Fullam, was published at Liverpool in 1863. This formed the basis of a long article in *All the Year Round*, and another edition was brought out by a London printer, Adolphe Schulze, under the title of *Our Cruise on the Confederate States War Steamer Alabama*.[37]

The Alabama and the Kearsarge. An Account of the Naval Engagement in the British Channel, on Sunday, June 19, 1864 was compiled by Frederick Milnes Edge, who had interviewed both Union and Confederate survivors in Cherbourg, as well as French eyewitnesses, and published by W. Ridgway. *The Career of the Alabama, No. 290. From July 29, 1862 to June 19, 1864* was also cobbled together from reports in the *Times, Standard* and *Daily News*, and rushed out by Dorrell & Son, a firm of booksellers and stationers.

The illustrated weeklies published drawings of the sinking of the *Alabama* by the *Kearsarge* and a reconstruction of it, painted by a naval artist called Captain J. W. Anderson, was photographed and published by Oxford Street photographer Frederic Jones as a carte-de-visite, entitled "Action off Cherbourg, 19th June 1864."[38]

Before the battle, Captain Semmes had given his journals for safe keeping to a representative of the firm of Saunders, Otley, who had also published *Ordnance Instructions* for the Confederate States Navy. He was now persuaded to allow the publication of extracts from them, and *The Cruise of the Alabama and the Sumter. From the Private Journals and Other Papers of Commander R. Semmes, C.S.N., and Other Officers*, was out by the beginning of August. One of the first people to read it was Benjamin Moran: "Last night I bought and read the 'Cruise of the Alabama and Sumter, by Semmes' ... As a literary performance it is poor; but it contains certain facts that will be very useful some day against GB," he observed vindictively.[39]

Despite Moran's disparaging comments, it was a success, a second edition following within weeks, as well as a special "Confederate States edition" on thin paper, intended to be shipped through the blockade. It was reprinted in America (New York, 1864), and translated into French (Paris, 1864) and, somewhat surprisingly, into Dutch (Zwolle, 1865). An abridged edition called *The Log of the Alabama and the Sumter* was published in December 1864. In spite of all this, Semmes apparently made no money out of it, and later, in the preface to his *Memoirs of Service Afloat* (1869), made it clear he disapproved of it, calling it "a meagre and barren record." He claimed that its anonymous author, whoever he was, had neither the knowledge nor the experience to interpret his journals properly and do justice to the subject.

When Captain Semmes arrived in London in June 1864, Mrs. Rose Greenhow had been there for some months. Born in Maryland in 1817, Rose O'Neal Greenhow was a Washington political hostess with all the right connections. A widow with a reputation for intrigue, and known to some as "Rebel Rose," she was arrested and imprisoned for some months for operating a spy ring in the Federal capital. Deported to Richmond in 1862, in August of the following year Mrs. Greenhow was sent to Europe as an unofficial emissary for the Confederacy. With her youngest daughter and several other passengers from the Confederate States, she traveled, via Bermuda, in the steamer *Harriet Pinckney* and arrived at Falmouth, Cornwall, in September 1863.

She divided her time between London and Paris, writing and lecturing on behalf of the Southern cause, and also arranged for the publication of her book, *My Imprisonment and the First Year of Abolition Rule at Washington*. Published in November 1863 by Richard Bentley, who had already brought out two accounts of travel in the Confederate States, as well as the influential writings of James Spence, it was dedicated to "the brave soldiers who have fought and bled in this our glorious struggle for freedom." In spite of its rather uninspiring title, *My Imprisonment* enhanced its author's growing reputation, making her into a celebrity in both England and France, where she had a private audience with Emperor Napoleon III.

On her way to England, Rose Greenhow had encountered Georgiana Walker, the wife of Major Norman Walker, the Confederate agent in Bermuda. In December 1863 Mrs. Walker noted in her diary:

> I recd. a letter from Mrs. Greenhow. She has been wonderfully well received in England and her book is pronounced a "success." I do not wonder at that, for she is a very clever woman, and has the ability to show those Yankees up in their true character. She says a smart thing in her letter. She writes "I consider the cultivation of my good looks a duty which I owe to my country." She needs no cultivation of *beauty*, for Providence has blessed her with a high order of *that*. She is one of the most beautiful women I ever saw. She knows this and like a sensible woman, does not pretend to think the contrary.[40]

An imposing figure, theatrical in manner, and quick-witted, Rose Greenhow enjoyed the social and literary life of London, becoming a familiar figure at fashionable gatherings.

Both Mrs. Rose O. Greenhow and Mrs. Georgiana G. Walker lodged at this house in Sackville Street, Piccadilly, in 1864. (Author's photograph)

When she herself came to London, in July 1864, Mrs. Walker found herself living for a while in the same house in Sackville Street as Mrs. Greenhow, and observed:

> She has certainly had the *entrée* to the very highest society. The Lords & Ladies & Duchesses are her constant visitors, & her invitations to dinner parties & balls are innumerable. She is to dine with Lady Palmerston soon, & has gone thro the rounds of most of the others.[41]

One of her neighbors in Sackville Street was Commander Maury, and other Confederate associates included Henry Hotze and the Rev. Francis Tremlett. Lord Wharncliffe recalled a dinner conversation with her at Lady Chesterfield's house in Grosvenor Square, in a letter she was destined never to receive.[42]

In August 1864 Mrs. Greenhow joined the steamer *Condor* at Greenock, Scotland, to return to the Confederacy. One of Alexander Collie's blockade-runners, the *Condor,* was commanded by Captain William N.W. Hewett, an officer on leave from the Royal Navy, who used the alias Samuel P. Ridge. Off Fort Fisher, North Carolina, the vessel ran aground and Rose Greenhow was drowned while struggling to get ashore.

Although the event took place on October 1, it was not reported in the *Times* until November 5. One of those who knew of it before then was James Spence, who expressed his deep regrets in a letter to Lord Wharncliffe:

> I am sure you would feel as I did, deeply grieved at the tidings of Mrs Greenhow's death ... I believe she was drowned in getting on shore and the only one lost ... Poor thing — so bright and ... so cold now. None in this country ... will so much regret her sad fate. She had faults, and who has not, but she had great qualities far beyond the average ... I have known her to speak with an eloquence and power I have never heard the equal to in a woman.[43]

Alexander Collie's comment, written after the report of her death had appeared in the *Times*, was more matter-of-fact: "Mrs. Greenhow's fate is decided at last and we can lament her loss without laying blame on those who though near at hand were powerless to aid her."[44]

In the meantime, another well-known Confederate had appeared in London. Isabelle Boyd, better known as Belle Boyd, or, as French newspapers called her, "La Belle Rebelle," was a former spy and courier who had been imprisoned in the same Washington jail as Mrs. Greenhow. Sent to England in March 1864 with Confederate dispatches, the blockade-runner in which she was traveling was captured, and she was subsequently banished to Canada. When she finally reached London, she called on Henry Hotze to inform him that the dispatches she was carrying had been destroyed. Belle then surprised everyone by proceeding to marry a former Union naval officer, Samuel W. Hardinge, who had been involved in her capture.

The wedding took place on August 25, 1864 and the next day the *Morning Post* reported:

A Confederate Wedding

> St James's Church, Piccadily was yesterday the scene of a romantic episode in the fratricidal war now raging on the American continent; as, at the altar of that sacred edifice, Miss Belle Boyd ... pledged her troth to Mr Sam Wylde Hardinge, formerly an officer in the Federal naval service.

The wedding guests included Major Caleb Huse, Henry Hotze, John L. O'Sullivan and James Williams. There was also Captain John Fearn, who after yet another abortive mission,

St. James's Church, Piccadilly, where Belle Boyd was married in November 1864. (Author's photograph)

this time to Mexico, was now back in London as a Confederate agent. After the ceremony, everyone adjourned to the Brunswick Hotel in Jermyn Street for the wedding breakfast.

On November 7, to Benjamin Moran's astonishment, Sam Hardinge appeared at the U.S. legation in Upper Portland Place, in search of a loan. Two days later he was there again and Moran thought it extremely impudent of him, after "associating with rebels and marrying a spy," to be begging for money.[45] Hardinge returned to the United States later that month, but was arrested and imprisoned until the following February.

With her husband in a Federal prison, Belle now found herself increasingly short of money, and turned to George Augustus Sala, a prolific, freelance journalist, who in 1863–1864 had covered the Civil War for the *Daily Telegraph*. Visiting her in her Jermyn Street lodgings, he found her, "not quite friendless, in this great wilderness of London, but, what is worse, absolutely destitute of that indispensable and all-prevailing friend—*money*." Sala, who was pro–Southern, drew attention to her predicament in a letter to the *Morning Herald*, "that able and consistent defender of the Southern cause," headed "A Word to Confederate Sympathizers."[46] Some assistance was forthcoming from friends and admirers, but it was only a temporary respite, and Belle now embarked on a memoir describing her wartime adventures. Sala announced her forthcoming work in his "Echoes of the Week" column in the *Illustrated London News*:

> That famous Amazon of Secessia, Belle Boyd, now Mrs Hardinge — and whose marriage to the gallant but susceptible lieutenant whom she converted ... to Southern proclivities was one of the fashionable events of last season — is in London, and proposes, it is said, to publish her memoirs as a Secesh partisan and aide-de-camp to Stonewall Jackson. These memoirs cannot fail to be very interesting. Belle Boyd ... has suffered captivity, exile and poverty for the cause which she believes to be the true one.[47]

Belle Boyd in Camp and Prison. Written by Herself, with an introduction by "A Friend of the South" (Sala), was advertised in the *Index* on May 25, 1865 as "now ready" by Saunders, Otley.[48] In his introduction Sala claimed that the work was entirely her own, "with the exception of a few suggestions in the shape of footnotes."

Whatever the extent of Sala's contribution, the book was not well received. The *Athenaeum* thought Belle's story revealed her hardness and vanity, and disapproved of her exploits; it was, the reviewer concluded, "a very dull book."[49] The *Spectator* condemned the "unladylike qualities and saucy tone" of the narrative; "few books," wrote the reviewer, "are likely to disenchant Englishmen more thoroughly with the Confederate cause than the memoirs before us."[50] Even the *Index* remarked: "It is not according very high praise to say that it is among the best of its kind that the American war has thrown upon a glutted market," then tempered that by going on to describe it as "pleasantly, and upon the whole modestly, written, in a style ... free from any serious objection."[51]

One of the first novelists to write about the Civil War was William Stephens Hayward, who in 1862 wrote what was to be the first in a series of novels dealing with the exploits of Captain George, a pro–Confederate English adventurer. In *Hunted to Death, or Life in two Hemispheres*, the hero meets with various adventures in New York before marrying a Creole beauty in New Orleans. By the time of the second novel, *The Black Angel: a Tale of the American Civil War* (1863), he is serving with the Confederate Army in Virginia and South Carolina in the early weeks of the war, and in *The Star of the South* (1864) he is a cavalry commander at First Manassas. *The Fiery Cross; a Tale of the Great American War*, the next

George Augustus Sala, who reported the Civil War for the *Daily Telegraph* and assisted Belle Boyd with her memoirs. (Author's collection)

novel in the series, which deals with the battle of Shiloh and the capture of New Orleans, did not appear until 1866, while the final one, *The Rebel Privateer; or the Last Cruise of the Black Angel*, which includes Lincoln's assassination, was not published until 1874. The first two novels in the series were published by Ward & Lock, the last three by Charles H. Clarke.

The Elopement: A Tale of the Confederate States of America (1863) was brought out by William Freeman, the first publisher of the *Index*. It was by "Miss L. Fairfax," a pseudonym which hid the identity of Celia Logan, an American journalist, novelist and dramatist, who came to Europe in 1858, married an artist called M.K. Kellog, and worked as a reader and editor for a London publishing house. The subtitle is rather misleading: most of the novel is set in pre-war America, much of it in the North, and only the last two chapters are concerned with the war itself. It is the story of the unfortunate Amanda, "a white negress" from Georgia, whose lover is killed at the first battle of Manassas, and who later, at New Orleans, throws herself into the Mississippi to save her virtue. "General Felun," the military governor there, is a thinly veiled portrait of Benjamin Butler.

Nothing seems to be known about Florence J. O'Connor, the author of *The Heroine of the Confederacy; or Truth and Justice* (Harrison, 1864), a literary curiosity, part novel, part historical narrative which incorporates official notices and correspondence. It is dedicated to Colonel Robert H. Barrow, C.S.A., "The Hero of Belmont" (an early, inconclusive engagement in Missouri), and illustrated with photographs of the author, Colonel Barrow and Lieutenant Beverley Kennon, C.S.N. The "heroine" is Natalie de Villerie, an orphan "who shone as a star of the first magnitude in every assembly," and background events include First Manassas, the *Trent* incident and the fall of New Orleans.

A number of other novels about the Civil War South, by authors like Ouida (Marie Louise de la Ramée), Benjamin Disraeli, R. D. Blackmore and Percy Greg (who had written for the *Index*), appeared in the 1870s and early 1880s. One American critic has commented on "the duration of this pro–Confederate tradition in English fiction," remarking, "it is surprising that so much sentiment and romance could be concentrated on a way of American life which before the war had attracted almost no attention from English novelists." Though "the wartime novels had ... only fictionalized the view of the war spread by *The Times*, the *Saturday Review* and most of the other influential journals of England," they were really continuing an anti–Yankee tradition which had started as far back as the 1830s.[52]

In the end, the cultural impact of the Civil War turned out to be fairly short-lived. It found its most enduring expression in the published accounts of life in the Confederate South written by observers like Arthur Fremantle, Fitzgerald Ross and William Russell, and its most visible one in John Foley's statue of Stonewall Jackson, erected at Richmond, Virginia, in 1875, with money collected in London from British sympathizers.

10

Support for the South?

A word or two of sympathy, that costs us not a penny,
We give the gallant Southerners, the few against the many,
We say their noble fortitude of final triumph presages,
And praise in Blackwood's Magazine *JEFF DAVIS and his Messages.*
—Punch, *September 5, 1863*

The humorous magazine *Punch* clearly thought that English support for the South did not run very deep. The extent of that support is still a matter of debate among historians, some of whom now think it was not just limited to the middle and upper classes, as was once supposed, but was more widely spread throughout the population.

There was a natural tendency by some Confederates, both during and after the war, to exaggerate the amount of support they thought they enjoyed. Caleb Huse believed that English sympathy for the South was universal and James Mason was also certain that the Confederacy enjoyed the entire support of those sections of society which had an opinion. In his memoirs, James Bulloch wrote: "Northern men often complained of the sympathy exhibited ... in England for the Confederate cause. I have reason to believe that at least five out of every seven in the middle and upper classes in England were favourable to the South...," though how he arrived at that estimate is impossible to say.[1]

Other Confederates saw things rather differently. In a letter written in January 1863, Matthew Maury remarked: "Many of our friends here have mistaken British admiration of Southern pluck and newspaper spite at Yankee insolence as Southern sympathy. No such thing. There is no love for the South here. In its American policy the British government fairly represents the British people."[2] A few months later Douglas Forrest noted in his diary: "There is a great deal of sympathy felt for us in England & there it ends. As a distinguished gentleman said the other day to me, 'England will aid us when her aid can avail us nothing & not before.'"[3]

On his return from England in January 1864, J.E. Ward of Georgia told Robert Kean, head of the Confederate Bureau of War, that he had met no Englishman who did not wish the Confederates success, but at the same time, none who wanted Great Britain to intervene.[4] After the war, John Peyton offered an equally skeptical view of support for the South, concluding, "They [the English] patted her on the back as the weaker of the two combatants ... not because they loved her, but because they disliked the Yankees," though he admitted, "Confederate flags, manufactured by wholesale, were at many houses hoisted at dinner, over dishes of smoking roast beef, and hung gracefully from the walls of parlours and saloons."[5]

Like the Confederates, Northerners also sometimes exaggerated the extent of public sympathy for the South. In June 1862, Benjamin Moran observed despairingly, "British officials openly aid rebel sympathizers to violate the blockade, and the Queen's proclamation [of neutrality] ... It is clear ... that the entire British people ... have openly and shamefully aided the rebels while hypocritically professing neutrality."[6] The following month, the sight of well-dressed Britons celebrating recent "rebel successes" (probably the Seven Days' Battles) at Blanchard's restaurant in Soho enraged him.

"The late cessation of our progress has had the effect of encouraging the hopes of the people here who sympathize with the rebellion. I think there can now be little doubt that they constitute much the greater part of the active classes of this kingdom," remarked U.S. minister Charles Francis Adams to Secretary of State William H. Seward in July 1862. In December of that year, writing his son in the Union Army, he expressed the opinion that "the great body of the aristocracy and the wealthy commercial class are anxious to see the United States go to pieces." In another letter, written in September 1863, he elaborated on this theme, observing that while the aristocracy were very much against the United States, they did "little or nothing to sustain the rebellion," whereas "the commercial and moneyed people go a step further and furnish more or less of material aid."[7]

"All the mercantile & upper classes are entirely against the North," remarked U.S. agent John Forbes, in a sweeping generalization in March 1863, but added, "the emancipation movement is coming to our rescue, and the people are with us and ... the vicious London *Times* shakes to hear them."[8] Some ten years after the war the *New York Tribune* observed, "The public feeling in London [then] was almost universally in favour of the South."[9]

As the war continued, the level of support for the South fluctuated according to its military fortunes. In a dispatch to Washington in July 1862, Consul Freeman Morse wrote: "Our check, if it be not a reverse, before Richmond [the Seven Days' Battles] has caused increased activity among the rebel agents here, and given them and their numerous friends here great confidence in the early establishment of 'Southern Independence.'"[10]

"When Lee was known to be on his march," Morse observed in August 1863, "it excited very general interest here and a strong desire in influential circles for his success. This desire was openly proclaimed in chop houses, club rooms, railway carriages and in most places of resort for what is called here the better class of society."[11] The Confederate defeat at Gettysburg, together with the loss of Vicksburg, caused consternation. "The news of the check sustained by our forces at Gettysburg, coupled with the reported fall of Vicksburg, was so unexpected as to spread very general dismay not only among the active sympathizers of our cause, but even among those who take merely a selfish interest in the great struggle," reported Henry Hotze to Judah Benjamin, while Henry Adams, writing his brother, described, no doubt gleefully, how the salons of London were in tears when the surrender of Vicksburg became known.[12]

"Selfish interest" undoubtedly played an important part in the support which either side enjoyed. Even James Spence, whose efforts on behalf of the Confederacy resulted in the neglect of his own business, was not immune from this. In a letter to Judah Benjamin, Henry Hotze remarked that Spence "contends that while his espousal of our cause arises from sincere conviction ... he never pretended that he sought a financial connection with the Government without expectation of profit to himself as well as to us ... and he complained that he is not only disappointed in his just expectation but a loser to a ruinous extent by reason of that connection."[13] He was subsequently compensated by the Confederate government for his losses.

Secession had been regarded by many English people as inevitable and irreversible; it was something the North should accept, and the war was therefore futile and unjustified. When it came, however, there was no lack of admiration for the South's military skills and gallantry, its bid for nationhood seen as a struggle for freedom, on a par with that previously witnessed in several European and South American countries. "The Confederates are doing their own work alone, nobly and successfully, and they have deserved and obtained the admiration and sympathy of the world," wrote banker John S. Gilliat to a correspondent in Richmond.[14]

Support for the South was not necessarily seen as an endorsement of slavery; indeed, once the South was independent and subject to European influences, many believed the "peculiar institution" would disappear. "It will surely depart as a result of Southern independence and the world's action upon it, as a taper will die out in the sunlight," predicted James Spence in one of his letters to the *Times*.[15]

Furthermore, as an advocate of free trade, the Confederacy was perceived as Britain's natural ally, as opposed to the Northern States, whose democratic system and growing economic power were viewed with dislike and apprehension. Few doubted that the South would achieve her independence, either on the battlefield or as the result of a negotiated settlement with a North grown weary of the struggle to force her back into the Union. Indeed, for much of the war, the possibility that the South might be defeated was not one which was regarded as worthy of serious consideration.

The thinking within some sections of the British government is illustrated by correspondence between Edmund Hammond, Permanent Under-Secretary at the Foreign Office, and Sir Austen Layard, M.P., Under-Secretary of State for Foreign Affairs. In mid–July 1862, after General McClellan's failure to capture Richmond during the Seven Days' Battles, the pro–Southern Hammond was of the opinion that the Confederacy had almost completely established its claim to recognition, but that the British should not interfere until "the Northern cause is more thoroughly degraded." Ten days later he was discussing the matter of funds for a mission to the Confederacy, which before long, it appeared, "we must be prepared to accredit." Yet he failed to grasp the importance of Lee's failure at Antietam and the significance of the preliminary Emancipation Proclamation, and by the end of October had to admit that the idea of recognizing the South had been abandoned because of "its inexpediency."[16]

The British Cabinet itself, uncertain of the outcome of Lee's invasion of Maryland in September 1862, had indeed paused in its deliberations over mediation in the war and recognition of the Confederacy, and then postponed the matter indefinitely. In the circumstances, Chancellor of the Exchequer William E. Gladstone's speech at Newcastle-on-Tyne on October 7, which gave the impression he was speaking for the government, was particularly unfortunate:

> We may have our own opinions about slavery; we may be for or against the South; but there is no doubt that Jefferson Davis and other leaders of the South have made an army; they are making, it appears, a navy; and they have made what is more than either — they have made a nation (loud cheers) ... We may anticipate with certainty the success of the Southern States so far as regards their separation from the North ["Hear, hear"].[17]

Prime Minister Lord Palmerston who pursued a policy of British neutrality throughout the Civil War. (Author's collection)

10—Support for the South?

Although Lord Palmerston's Liberal government had adopted a policy of neutrality, there was considerable support for the Southern cause in Parliament. It was not a party political issue—individual members of Parliament in both Liberal and Conservative parties were sympathetic to the Confederacy. For instance, William Lindsay and John Roebuck, who were two of the principal spokesmen for the Southern lobby during the Civil War, were, respectively, a Liberal and a Conservative, while William Gregory was a Liberal-Conservative (i.e., a Conservative who usually voted with the Liberals).

Exaggerated claims were sometimes made about the extent of Confederate support in Parliament. Henry Hotze's statement that five-sixths of the House of Commons and all but two members of the House of Lords supported them was undoubtedly wishful thinking. Similarly, William Gregory, who should have known better, wrote in his autobiography: "The feelings of the upper-classes undoubtedly preponderated in favour of the South, so much so that when I said in a speech that the adherents of the North in the House of Commons might all be driven home in one omnibus, the remark was received with much cheering."[18]

Prominent pro–Southern members of the House of Commons included Lord Robert Cecil, William E. Duncombe, Sir James Fergusson, Thomas C. Haliburton, John L. Hopwood, Sir Edward Kerrison, John Laird, William S. Lindsay, George M.W. Peacocke, Frederick Peel, John A. Roebuck and James Whiteside. In the early part of the war, they were led by William H. Gregory, M.P. for County Galway, Ireland. Born in Dublin in 1816, William

Cambridge House, Piccadilly, Palmerston's London residence, was visited by a number of Confederates, including propagandist Edwin De Leon and Commissioner James Mason. (Author's photograph)

Henry Gregory had first been elected to Parliament in 1842 and, though he lost his seat in 1847, was reelected ten years later. His predilection for the Confederate cause seems to have been formed during a visit to America in 1859–1860.

In the House of Lords there was support for the South from men like the Marquess of Bath, Lord Campbell, Lord Eustace Cecil, the Earl of Donoughmore, the Marquess of Lothian and Lord Wharncliffe. Two of these were moved to express their feelings in print: Lord Campbell's speech to the House about Confederate recognition was published in 1863, while the Marquess of Lothian was the author of a pamphlet, *The Confederate Secession*, published the following year.

A number of members of Parliament visited the Confederacy during the war. Among them, in the autumn of 1861, was Crimean War veteran Sir James Fergusson, M.P. for Ayrshire, who was accompanied by the Hon. Robert Bourke (not yet an M.P.). While there, they watched a review of the Stonewall Brigade by Generals Joseph E. Johnston, Pierre G. T. Beauregard and Gustavus W. Smith. The future author Catherine Hopley, whom they encountered, was told that, contrary to what she might have heard, they were there in an unofficial capacity and that England would remain neutral. They were followed, in February 1863, by the Marquess of Hartington, M.P. for North Lancashire; in December 1864 by radical reformer George Thompson, the former M.P. for Tower Hamlets, whose particular parliamentary interests had included free trade and the extension of the ballot; and in January 1865 by Thomas L. Conolly, the Irish M.P. for Donegal, who arrived in the blockade-runner *Owl*, just in time to witness the collapse of the Confederacy, which he recorded in his diary.[19]

The main topics of parliamentary interest in the early months of the war were Confederate privateering and the treatment of British subjects living in the South. These were being "encouraged" to enlist as early as the summer of 1861 according to journalist William H. Russell, and the introduction of conscription in 1862 exacerbated the situation. Foreigners who did not have permanent residence in the Confederate States were exempt from military service, but this was a controversial ruling which was not always adhered to, and was further complicated by state laws often requiring militia service from all able-bodied white males in the appropriate age group. In July 1863 the House of Commons heard how Robert R. Belsham, an Englishman living in Alabama, had been dipped repeatedly in a tank of water because of his reluctance to join the Confederate Army.[20] British consuls in the Confederacy, who had remained in their posts after secession, attempted to safeguard the rights of British nationals, but this brought them into conflict with both state and Confederate authorities and probably contributed to the decision to expel them in October 1863.

Not until March 7, 1862 did the first major Civil War debate, on the effectiveness of the blockade, take place. It was introduced by William Gregory, who contended that it was a paper blockade, maintained by warships cruising up and down the coast, and not by ones lying off the main ports, and that many vessels had already successfully evaded it. Though the motion was supported by M.P.s like Sir James Fergusson, Lord Robert Cecil and William Lindsay, the government clearly had no intention of challenging the legality of the Federal blockade, which was tantamount to recognizing the South, and the motion was withdrawn without a division.

Henry Adams, son of the U.S. minister, who frequently attended the House of Commons, was present on this occasion, and heard Gregory make his speech: "It was listened to as you would listen to a funeral eulogy. His attacks on us ... and on our blockade were cheered with just enough energy to show the animus that existed in a large proportion of the members, but his motion ... was tossed aside without a division," he wrote his brother, who was serving with the Union Army.[21]

Lindsay, who had supported Gregory's motion, was to introduce one of his own some four months later and on July 18, 1862 the matter of mediation came before the House. If only to save the cotton industry, England should intervene to stop the war, Lindsay argued. There was much opposition to this, and again the motion was withdrawn without coming to a vote.

By the beginning of 1863, leadership of the Southern lobby in the House of Commons had passed to William S. Lindsay and John A. Roebuck, Gregory having concluded that he could do nothing further for the Confederate cause. William Schaw Lindsay, who had been a member of Parliament since 1854 and currently represented Sunderland, was a self-made man. Born at Ayr, Scotland, in 1816 and orphaned at an early age, he started life as a merchant seaman, then in 1840 went into business at Hartlepool. Moving to London in 1845, he rose to become the head of William S. Lindsay & Company, one of the largest shipowning firms in the world.

John Arthur Roebuck was M.P. for Sheffield. Born in Madras, India, in 1802 and educated in Canada, he returned to England in 1824 and trained as a barrister. He first entered Parliament in 1832 and became well-known for his outspoken, radical views, rather priding himself on the nickname of "Tear 'Em," given him by *Punch* on account of his bulldoglike ferocity in debates. By the 1860s he was described as "a small man, shabbily dressed, leaning on a stick, his face careworn, his voice feeble; but not a man to be lightly encountered — one who ... is still able to withstand his foes, and to lend good aid to his friends."[22]

In his autobiography, Henry Adams recalled them both: "Lindsay, about whom the whole web of rebel interests clung — rams, cruisers, munitions, and Confederate loan; social introductions and parliamentary tactics"; and Roebuck, "an eccentric of eccentrics ... notorious for poor judgment and worse temper ... rather a comical personage — a favorite subject for *Punch* to laugh at — with a bitter tongue and a mind enfeebled ... by ... egotism."[23]

On June 30, 1863, Roebuck introduced the debate on his motion: "That an humble address be presented to Her Majesty, praying that She will be graciously pleased to enter into negotiations with the Great Powers of Europe, for the purpose of obtaining their co-operation in the recognition of the independence of the Confederate States of America."[24] There was a long debate which was adjourned, and not concluded until July 13, but the motion never came to a vote.

As if to encourage the Great Powers, Roebuck and Lindsay took it upon themselves to request an audience with the Emperor Napoleon III. Afterwards, there was some confusion about what was actually said in the course of it, and this attempt at would-be diplomacy was not well received.

Sir John Trelawny, M.P. for Tavistock, Devon, noted in his diary:

> Roebuck ... moved his resolution proposing to take diplomatic steps towards recognition of the Confederate States in America. I read his speech which was deemed to be a clever one & amusing, but I do not think that he will have a great many followers ... Roebuck rather startled the House by his account of his interview with the Emperor of the French. Certainly, R. takes extraordinary steps. [John] Bright described him as being not an ambassador extraordinary, but *most* extraordinary — & insinuated inaccuracy in the version given of what passed.[25]

Though he was not now in favor of European intervention, Gladstone still believed that Southern independence would ultimately be achieved, and said so:

> We do not believe that the restoration of the American Union by force is attainable. I believe that the public opinion of this country is unanimous upon that subject — well, almost unanimous ... I do not think there is any real or serious grounds for doubt as to the issue of this contest.[26]

The result was described with malicious glee by Henry Adams, when writing to his brother:

> We too have had our excitements this week, as it was the time of the regular annual motion for recognition by the English copperheads. There was a hot debate in Parliament, but the Southern spokesman succeeded in tripping himself up ... So far as our affair is concerned, Mr. Roebuck has done us more good than all our friends.[27]

This was to be the last major debate on the Civil War in the House of Commons, although over the following months there were questions about the Laird rams, the Confederate cruisers, the CSS *Georgia*, and, as late as July 1864, yet another about mediation from William Lindsay.

At a more popular level, Gladstone's speech of June 30, 1863 was echoed a day or two later in an editorial in the *Illustrated Times*:

> The conviction that the Confederate States must sooner or later be recognized by the rest of the nations of the world is every day becoming stronger, and is but faintly disputed even by the most zealous friends of the North ... who have now generally abandoned the hope that the Federals will ever be able to restore the Union by force of arms.[28]

On the day Gladstone made his speech, Lee's forces were nearing the little Pennsylvania town of Gettysburg, while the *Illustrated Times* editorial appeared on the day that Vicksburg surrendered.

As late as January 1865, Alexander Collie, a hard-headed businessman and far from being an idealistic dreamer, wrote to Lord Wharncliffe, a prominent Confederate supporter:

> Bad news have [sic] reached us as regards military matters from the South ... but my faith in its ultimate triumph is as strong as it ever was. We ought to be prepared to hear of Wilmington and Charleston being captured, and of Richmond being evacuated, for events reach in that direction; but, in spite of all, the South will wear the North out and gain its independence.[29]

Many British visitors to the South had been convinced of this: Samuel Day, a journalist, Fitzgerald Ross, a professional soldier, and William Corsan, a businessman, were all certain the Confederacy would never be defeated and would achieve her independence in due course.

The Confederate States of America was already being seen by many as a de facto nation, and when a new reference work, *The Statesman's Yearbook*, began publication in 1864, its publishers, Macmillan & Company, devoted sixteen pages to it, giving details of its constitution and government, revenue and expenditure, population, trade and commerce — not because the firm was pro–Confederate, but simply for reasons of completeness. It featured in the next edition as well, but within months of publication, the Confederacy was already part of history.

Reuter's News Agency had been started in London in 1851 by the German journalist Paul Julius Reuter. It had grown rapidly, and by 1861 was worldwide in its coverage of financial and commercial news. Its headquarters were in Fleet Street, but at the start of the Civil War it opened a second office near Finsbury Square to deal with American news. Towards the end of July 1861, it was visited by Dudley Mann, who was told it could use all the news from the Confederacy he was able to supply. There were allegations, then and later, that Reuter's was pro–Southern, something it strongly denied since its agents gathered news from both sides.

Benjamin Moran, however, was in no doubt he knew where Reuter's sympathies lay, noting in his journal in August 1861 that its telegrams always seemed to favor the South: "The German, Reuter ... has evidently been bought up by the rebels," he concluded. His comments in November were even more sweeping: "Reuter's telegrams of yesterday are all one-sided again. The slaveocracy have bought him over to their side, together with nearly the whole press of England."[30]

John A. Roebuck, one of the Confederacy's most vehement and outspoken supporters in the House of Commons. (*Illustrated London News*)

And the press, it is true, was not impartial. At the time of secession, leading newspapers had been fairly sympathetic to the North, but when it became clear that Lincoln's principal war aim was preserving the Union rather than freeing the slaves, press opinion shifted. This pro–Southern bias was reinforced by the Federal rout at First Manassas, when it began to look as if the Confederacy might indeed secure its independence. Nor was it greatly affected by the preliminary Emancipation Proclamation, which *Punch* derisively called "Abe Lincoln's Last Card," a public admission that the North's military tactics had failed.

"The English press is more Southern than the South itself," observed the German philosopher Karl Marx, then the London correspondent of the *New York Herald*, in November 1862. A year later, Major Edward Hamley came to much the same conclusion, remarking that "with a few not particularly respectable exceptions, the press here is favourable to the South." And writing just after the war, John Peyton also agreed that "the leading daily papers kept up a constant fire for the South."[31]

With many newspapers catering to a middle- and upper-class readership, there was a tendency on the part of editors to play down Northern successes and minimize Southern defeats. "So completely has the public become convinced of the correctness of the representations continually made in the London press of the desperate condition of our affairs, and of the triumphal progress of General Lee, that the expectation was almost universal to hear of his taking possession of Washington," wrote U.S. minister Charles Francis Adams to Secretary of State William H. Seward in July 1863.[32] When news of the surrender of Vicksburg was received that month, many newspaper editors at first refused to believe it.

At that time, the morning papers were usually regarded as more important and authoritative than the evening ones, and their editors were men of influence. Of the eight then published in London — the *Daily News* (Thomas Walker), the *Daily Telegraph* (Edward Lawson), the *Morning Advertiser* (James Grant), the *Morning Herald* (Thomas Hamber), the *Morning Post* (Algernon Borthwick), the *Morning Star* (Samuel Lucas), the *Standard* (Thomas Hamber) and the *Times* (John Delane) — only the *Daily News* and the *Morning Star*, which *Punch* referred to disparagingly as the "London New York Herald," supported the North, and even their proprietors, alleged Benjamin Moran, were "rebel in their tendencies."[33] They were mostly located in Fleet Street and its environs, though the *Morning Post* was further west, in Wellington Street, on the edge of Covent Garden, and the *Times* was in its famous home in Printing House Square, near Blackfriars Bridge.

The evening papers were similarly divided in their allegiance, with the *Evening Herald*, the *Evening Standard*, the *Globe* and the *Sun* favoring the South, and the *Evening Star* and the *Express* (the evening edition of the *Daily News*) backing the North. At the time of the *Trent* incident, the *London American* summarized the sympathies of what it regarded as the leading English newspapers as follows: *Morning Star* (Union); *Morning Post* (Secession); the *Times* (Secession); *Daily News* (Union); *Daily Telegraph* (Rabid Secession); *Morning Advertiser* (Secession); *Standard* (Rabid Secession); and *Globe* (Secession).[34]

Some Church of England clergymen were sympathetic to the Confederacy. They saw slavery as having a benign influence, bringing Christianity to its servile recipients, and the Rev. William Malet, whose account of his visit to the wartime South was published in 1863, was probably not untypical. It is not without significance that, when it began publication that same year, the *Church Times* also adopted a pro–Southern viewpoint.

The best-known pro–Confederate parson in London was the Rev. Francis W. Tremlett, the vicar of St. Peter's, Belsize Park. Francis William Tremlett was born in Newfoundland in 1821 and ordained there before coming to England in 1849. In 1861 he became vicar of what was then a new parish, and was sufficiently wealthy to pay for the building of a substantial vicarage, as well as most of the church itself. During the war, he became a close friend of Commander Matthew Maury, who later described him as "the best Confederate in England," and with whom he carried on an extensive correspondence. He also corresponded with other Confederate naval officers, including Captain Semmes, Commanders North, Sinclair and Pegram (the former captain of the *Nashville*) and Lieutenant Murdaugh.

A number of Confederates who visited London are known to have stayed at a house in nearby Buckland Crescent, which served as the vicarage until 1862, and others lodged in the vicarage itself, which became known as "the home of the Confederates" or "the rebels' roost." Captain Semmes, who had been introduced to the Rev. Tremlett by Commander Bulloch and Commander North, stayed with him twice, and described "the Confederate parson" in his *Memoirs of Service Afloat* (1869):

> a somewhat portly gentleman, with an unmistakable English face, and dressed in clerical garb — not over clerical either, for, but for his white cravat, and the cut of the collar of his coat, you would not have taken him for a clergyman at all ... The name of the Rev. Francis W. Tremlett, of the Parsonage, in Belsize Park, near Hampstead, London, dwells in my memory, and in that of every other Confederate who ever came in contact with him — and they are not few — like a household word.[35]

John Peyton dedicated his book, *The American Crisis* (1867), to "the Rev. F.W. Tremlett ... in admiration of ... his unbounded kindness, and hospitality to all Confederate exiles ..." and later praised him for "the liberal hospitality extended to all friends of the South then in

St. Peter's Church, Belsize Park, whose vicar, the Rev. Francis W. Tremlett, was a staunch supporter of the Confederacy. His sermon on *Christian Brotherhood*, delivered here in November 1863, made special reference to the Civil War in America and sold many thousands of copies. (Author's photograph)

London," while another Confederate, Commander Pegram, writing to Tremlett's sister, Louisa, remarked that he could never repay all the acts of kindness and generosity he had received at the hands of her and her brother.[36]

Sympathy for the Southern cause, however, did not usually extend to Nonconformist ministers. In December 1861, at the time of the *Trent* incident, the Rev. Dr. John Waddington, the pastor of Union Street Congregational Chapel in Southwark, wrote to Sir Austen Layard at the Foreign Office deploring the idea of British support for the South and the possibility of war with the North. He wrote again in November 1862, expressing his hopes that the British government would not give any help to the slavery cause.[37]

There was also support for the Confederacy among some writers and intellectuals. Those favoring the South included historian and essayist Thomas Carlyle, poet and critic Matthew Arnold, historian Sir John Acton (who was also a Liberal M.P. and friend of Gladstone), novelist Edward Bulwer-Lytton and the poet laureate Alfred Tennyson. Confederate journalist and poet John R. Thompson became a friend of Carlyle, "the Sage of Chelsea," who though publicly neutral, nevertheless hoped for a Southern victory. He questioned Thompson about the Confederacy, its resources, its army, and its supplies of food and powder, and made many inquiries about General Lee, whom he greatly admired, during his visits to Carlyle's house in Cheyne Row, Chelsea.

The first pro–Southern organization in the metropolis was the London Confederate States Aid Association, established in August 1862. Its rules and aims were set out in a pamphlet, *An Address to the British Public and all Sympathizers in Europe*, a copy of which was obtained by the U.S. minister and sent to the secretary of state in Washington. "Formed for the purpose of giving countenance and support to the Confederate States of America in their struggle to establish and maintain their independence ... all moneys received by the association [were to be] appropriated for purchasing and forwarding to the Confederate States of America the materials ... the best calculated to enable them to carry on the war, and to bring their present protracted struggle to a successful issue."[38]

Memorial to the Rev. Tremlett by Kathleen Shaw in St. Peter's Church. (Author's photograph)

Reporting on this new association, Charles Francis Adams observed wryly, in a letter to Washington, that "an office has been opened in a house in the next street to that in which I am writing, at which place meetings for discussion are held every Wednesday evening." This was in Devonshire Street, just around the corner from the U.S. legation, which was now in Upper Portland Place. The association's meetings were not open to the public at large; a card, countersigned by the secretary, was necessary for admission. Nor was open

A house in Buckland Crescent, Belsize Park, belonging to the Rev. Francis W. Tremlett, where a number of Confederate naval officers stayed during the war. (Author's photograph)

discussion encouraged: "At one of the earlier [meetings] one person appeared who ventured to question some remark made by one of the speakers, for which act he was immediately expelled."[39] Nothing more was heard of it after 1862.

The Society for Promoting the Cessation of Hostilities in America was founded in October 1863 by the Rev. Francis Tremlett, Mrs. Rose Greenhow and Commander Matthew Maury. The committee included Lord Robert Cecil, the Marquis of Lothian, Lord Wharncliffe, the Marquess of Bath, Alexander Beresford Hope and William Lindsay, and it held its meetings in Regent Street. The Society claimed to have 5,000 members, and was to prove the most active of the pro–Confederate organizations in London.

Its aims were set out in an article which appeared in the *Index* on February 11, 1864. "By wide association, by petition, by the publication of papers, by enlisting in its cause the great mass of the clergy and ministers of the gospel," it would "put all the moral pressure possible on the people and government of England, the peoples and governments in America, as by some means or other to restore the blessings of peace to that distracted country."

In May 1864 it sent a pamphlet to all members of Parliament, appealing for immediate action to end the war by mediation. Later that summer it embarked on its most ambitious enterprise, an Address from the people of Great Britain and Ireland to the people of the United States, which called on the latter to make peace with the Confederate States. Appended to the Address were 300,000 signatures, from "men of all ranks, classes, religions and politics" collected "within the short space of three weeks from its first appearance." In September Benjamin Moran noted in his journal the campaign for it, with large posters inviting people to sign the petition and men going from house to house to collect signatures. He thought the address was insulting to the loyal American people, and those who put their names to it, mostly "children and fools ... shop girls and servants."[40]

The petition, seventy-six lines in length, was published in the *Times* on October 12, 1864, together with a letter from Sir Henry De Hoghton, allegedly one of the principal subscribers to the Cotton Loan. By then it was on its way to America in the care of Joseph Parker of Manchester, to be given to the governor of New York, who, it was hoped, "would place [it] before the people of the United States of America ... with a view to secure the object of our appeal."[41] The initiative proved a failure, Secretary of State Seward refusing to accept anything not approved by the British government.

In December 1863 yet another pro–Southern organization had come into being, when a group of thirty influential gentlemen met at Arklow House in Connaught Place, the home of Alexander Beresford Hope. They were there in response to a circular signed by Beresford Hope, William Lindsay and the Hon. Robert Bourke, who had contributed articles about the Southern states and Jefferson Davis to *Blackwood's Magazine*. The object of the meeting was to form the Southern Independence Association of London. Among those present were some of the best-known names in London Confederate circles, including Lord Campbell, Lord Robert Cecil, John Gilliat, Lord Wharncliffe, the Earl of Donoughmore and William Gregory. All but two of those present agreed to join the association, whose aim was "to keep before the minds of the British public the policy and justice of recognizing the independence of the Confederate States at the earliest possible moment." Membership was to be one guinea a year, and at least eight members contributed additional funds, among them Alexander Collie.[42]

In its *Address to the Public*, issued in January 1864, the Association stated:

Their wisdom in council, their endurance in the field, and the universal self-sacrifice ... have won general sympathy for the Confederates as a people worthy of, and who have earned, their independence. Our commercial classes are also beginning to perceive that our best interests will be promoted by creating a direct trade with a people so enterprising as the Confederates ... Therefore ... the Southern Independence Association of London has been formed ... as the rallying-point of all who believe that the dignity and interest of Great Britain will best be consulted by speedily and cheerfully recognizing a brave people...[43]

"The committee which is appended to the Address," noted pro–Northern academic Goldwin Smith in a pamphlet, "is highly aristocratic in its character. The list of the members of the Association, which has also been published, contains a large proportion of men of title and family, whose names head the list, and a good sprinkling of clergymen, curiously associated with the Member for Sheffield" [John Roebuck].[44]

In spite of its well-intentioned aims, the new association was not universally welcomed by the Confederates. The *Address* included the assumption that "recognition by Europe must necessarily lead to a revision of the system of servile labour ... in accordance with the spirit of the age, so as to combine the gradual extinction of slavery with the preservation of property..."[45] Dudley Mann wrote indignantly to Judah Benjamin about the offending paragraph, which had supposedly been inserted by James Spence, "the same gentleman who has the reputation of being, *par excellence*, the British champion of our cause."[46]

Henry Hotze's expectations of "much solid good" from the new associations were to be disappointed. "I am sorry that I can not give you a very glowing account of the two Southern Independence Associations which started out with such favorable auspices," he wrote to

Wharncliffe House, Curzon Street, Mayfair, the residence of Lord Wharncliffe, president of the Southern Independence Association of London. (Author's photograph)

Judah Benjamin in March 1864. "Both languished, partly for want of money and partly for want of moral courage."[47] The two associations did, however, join together in July 1864 to send a deputation to Lord Palmerston. It was headed by the Marquess of Clanricarde and the Bishop of Chichester, and urged the Prime Minister to mediate in the conflict. The response was predictable: a reaffirmation of British neutrality.

Lord Wharncliffe, president of the Southern Independence Association, was also chairman of a committee formed to administer the proceeds of the bazaar held at Liverpool in October 1864 to raise funds for Confederate prisoners-of-war. In November he wrote to Charles Francis Adams to obtain permission for "an accredited agent" to visit Federal prison camps and alleviate the sufferings of the inmates. His request, forwarded to Washington, brought a chilling response from Secretary of State Seward and a denial that any such sufferings existed. "The refusal of the Federal Government will not practically affect the distribution of the fund, for which, unhappily, we can find but too many recipients," Lord Wharncliffe assured the *Times*, in a long letter in December 1864, which it published along with the correspondence from Adams and Seward.[48]

Potential recipients of the fund were, indeed, not long in making themselves known. In January 1865 Lord Wharncliffe received a number of letters from men claiming to be former Confederate prisoners-of-war or wounded soldiers, some of whom may have been English. Joseph Taylor, late Co. F, 5th Louisiana, described the terrible conditions at Fort Delaware, where he had been held prisoner after being captured at Gettysburg; William S. Warwick, formerly a captain in General Morgan's cavalry, had been wounded three times; James D. Arco had also been wounded three times, though he omitted to give any details; and T. Hampson, "late Capt., 13th Louisiana Regt., and Provost Marshal, Adams' (Louisiana) Brigade," had escaped from Vicksburg in August 1864, before making his way to England. Most of the men were unemployed or in poor health and requested financial help. Some of the letters were referred to the Society for the Relief of Distress, suggesting Lord Wharncliffe had doubts about their authenticity.[49]

Goldwin Smith had observed that the Southern Independence Association was "not so strong in representatives of the interests of the labouring classes." Writing in 1862, just after Second Manassas, Henry Hotze observed: "The sympathies of the intelligent classes are now intensified into a feeling of sincere admiration ... If it cannot be said that this feeling is generally shared by the lower classes, it is at least certain that they also are swayed by that British instinct which hurrahs for the combatant who deals the hardest blows."[50]

The extent of support for the South among the "labouring classes" is still being debated by historians. Once thought to have been almost nonexistent, that view has now been revised somewhat. One modern historian has stated that the evidence suggests that many British workingmen — possibly a majority — were, like Gladstone, sympathetic to the idea of Confederate independence.[51] Another, however, has concluded that, though many working-class newspapers may have supported the South initially, their readers probably did not.[52]

The *Bee-Hive*, a weekly paper aimed at London workingmen, which began publication in October 1861, was an example of this. Intended as the official organ of the London Trades Council, which had been set up in 1860 as a result, the previous year, of a strike and continuing unrest in the London building trades, it adopted a pro–Confederate stance under its first editor, George Troup, arguing that secession would end slavery, and advocating the breaking of the Yankee blockade. Other prominent labor leaders, including George Potter, a carpenter, Thomas Vize and T.G. Facey of the Painters' union, T.J. Dunning of the Bookbinders', and J.B. Leno, a former shoemaker and prolific versifier, all supported Troup's pro–Southern views.

Things began to change, however, in January 1863, when Troup was replaced by Robert Hartwell, a former Chartist, who supported the North. This was in line with the shift in public opinion which seems to have occurred following Lincoln's Emancipation Proclamation, and was demonstrated in London by the mass meeting held at the end of that month in support of it at Exeter Hall, in the Strand. "That meeting," wrote the radical M.P. Richard Cobden, one of its organizers, perhaps a little prematurely, "has had a powerful effect on our newspapers and politicians. It has closed the mouths of those who have been advocating the side of the South."[53] By April 1863 the *Bee-Hive* was of the opinion that support for the Southern cause was now confined to "a very small section among the least thinking of the working millions."[54]

The huge trades union meeting which took place at St. James's Hall, Piccadilly, in March 1863 was "the most notable one in support of the North held throughout the whole course of the war."[55] It led to at least one union, the Bookbinders, disaffiliating itself from the London Trades Council the following year in protest at this pro–Northern agitation. "The trades of London," announced its secretary, T.J. Dunning, who was known as "the Father of London Trades Unionism," "have no confidence in Mr. Lincoln, either an an opponent to slavery or as a friend to the Negro. His Emancipation Proclamation ... they consider less intended to benefit the negro, than to destroy, if possible, the Confederates. Of course we say nothing as to their correctness, but such are the opinions of nine out of every ten workmen we have heard speak on the matter."[56]

Sympathy for the South certainly existed in considerable measure, both inside and outside Parliament. Whatever the actual extent of it, the British government was unlikely to grant the Confederacy diplomatic recognition until her independence was assured by military success. And that recognition would have meant, at the very least, the long-term enmity of the United States, not something that would have been seen as being in Britain's best interests.

Epilogue

Everybody was delighted or feigned delight with the news of Lee's surrender.
— Benjamin Moran, April 24, 1865

With the Civil War coming to an end, former Confederates began to arrive at the U.S. legation in Upper Portland Place, hoping to take the oath of allegiance and obtain passports, with a view to returning home. In May 1865, Benjamin Moran recorded the appearance there of M. Hildreth Bloodgood, "a rebel auditor of accounts," who two years previously had been sent to assist Colin McRae in his investigation of Major Huse's business transactions, and Commander William A. Webb, who had captained three Confederate warships, including "the rebel ram *Atlanta*," and was in England waiting to take command of another when the war ended.[1] Both were fortunate and were given passports; the amnesty issued by the U.S. government at the end of that month did not apply to Confederates who had worked abroad, and fearing persecution or even imprisonment, many who were in London when the war ended chose to remain there for the time being.

Later that year they were joined by others who had fled, either because they feared indictment for treason, or no longer wished to live in a defeated and devastated South. They included two former members of the Confederate government — Secretary of War Major General John C. Breckinridge and Secretary of State Judah P. Benjamin, who arrived in London separately in August 1865 — and an assortment of ex-senators, state governors and former generals.

For many, it was a stay of months rather than years and they moved on; Paris, with its large Confederate community, was a favorite destination. Writing to James Mason in May 1867, Judah Benjamin estimated that few former Confederates now remained in London, and most of those on the Continent seem to have departed by the middle of the following year.[2] Many had already gone back to America by the time of the universal amnesty of Christmas 1868, but some did not return until the 1870s.

A number of Confederates, of course, had gone back to the South while the war was still in progress. After serving as both a Confederate and state purchasing agent, Major Edward Anderson returned to Georgia in late 1861 and ended the war as a colonel. He was Savannah's first postwar mayor, became a director of both the Atlantic & Gulf and Central Railroads, and died in 1883; he was buried in Laurel Grove Cemetery, Savannah. Thomas King, who had been sent to Europe early in 1861 as a state commissioner for Georgia, returned the following year without having achieved very much; he did not outlive the war, but died in 1864 at Waresboro, Georgia. William Yancey, one of the first Confederate commissioners to be sent to Europe, went home in 1862, a deeply disillusioned man, and was only 49 when he died at his plantation near Montgomery, Alabama, the following year; he was buried there in Old Oakwood Cemetery. Lucius Lamar, one of the Confederacy's lesser-known diplomats, returned in 1863 and served as a judge-advocate in the Army of Northern Virginia in 1864–1865. After the war he became a member of the House of Representatives and a Senator, was Secretary of the Interior in Grover Cleveland's administration, 1885–1888, and was an Associate Justice of the Supreme Court when he died at Macon, Georgia, in 1893. John Fearn, who in turn had been secretary to Commissioners Yancey, Rost and Lamar, also had an impressive postwar career. He established an international law firm with offices in London and New York, held several diplomatic appointments, and was involved in planning the great Chicago Exposition of 1893; he died at Hot Springs, Virginia, in 1899.

Ordered back to the Confederacy in 1864 after the *Georgia* was decommissioned, Midshipman James Morgan tried his hand at many things after the war, including helping to train the Egyptian Army. His celebrated book, *Recollections of a Rebel Reefer*, appeared in 1917 and he lived to the age of 83, dying in Washington in 1928. Mrs. Rose Greenhow had also attempted to return to the Confederacy in 1864, but with tragic consequences; the blockade-runner *Condor* in which she was traveling ran aground off the North Carolina coast near Wilmington, and she was drowned while struggling to get ashore. Her grave is in Oakdale Cemetery, Wilmington.

After a period of recovery following the loss of the *Alabama*, Raphael Semmes and John Kell returned to the South. Semmes ended the war with the dual ranks of Rear Admiral, C.S.N., and Brigadier General, C.S.A. After being arrested on charges of treason and piracy in late 1865 and detained for three months, he was released and eventually able to return to Mobile to practice law; his *Memoirs of Service Afloat* was published in 1869. He died at Mobile in 1877 and was buried there in the Catholic graveyard. Kell, who had been promoted to commander, was on sick leave when the war ended. He became a farmer in his native state of Georgia and died there at Sunnyside in 1900, the year his *Recollections of a Naval Life* appeared.

A number of other Confederate naval officers were on their way back to the South when they learned that the war was over. Flag Officer Samuel Barron, the most senior of them, settled down to the life of a farmer in Essex County, Virginia, and died in 1888. Assistant Paymaster Douglas Forrest, who became an Episcopalian minister and served as rector of a number of churches in different parts of the United States, died while on a visit to Virginia in 1902. Commander James North chose to return to England and rejoin his family, but eventually went back to the United States and also became a farmer in Virginia, dying there in 1893.

Commander Matthew Maury went to Mexico after learning of the Confederate collapse, but after nine months in the impressive-sounding but largely meaningless role of Imperial Commissioner of Immigration, he returned to London in 1866 to be reunited with his family. There, he was guest of honor at a testimonial dinner attended by English naval officers, "scientific men of the highest distinction," and ex–Confederates like General Pierre G. T. Beauregard, and was presented with a purse of 3,000 guineas in appreciation of his services to the maritime world. He was commissioned to write a series of geography textbooks for a New York publisher, and in 1868 was awarded an honorary doctorate by Cambridge University. Later that year he returned to the United States, where he was appointed Professor of

Meteorology at the Virginia Military Institute, Lexington. He died there in 1873 and was buried in Hollywood Cemetery, Richmond.

Albert Bledsoe, one of Henry Hotze's associates, returned to the South in 1865 and went to live in Baltimore, becoming a fierce promoter of the Lost Cause. In 1867 he founded the *Southern Review*, dedicated to "the despised, disfranchised, and down-trodden people of the South," and remained its editor until his death ten years later. After the *Index* ceased publication, John Thompson found work in London with the *Standard* newspaper, but returned to the United States in 1866, becoming literary editor of the *New York Evening Post*. He died in New York in 1873 at the early age of 49 and, like Matthew Maury, was buried in Hollywood Cemetery, Richmond.

Hiram Fuller, who had also worked on the *Index*, did not go back to America until 1874, but his attempt to reestablish himself there by means of a book called *Grand Transformation Scenes in the United States, or Glimpses of Home after Thirteen Years Abroad* (1875) was not successful and he returned to Europe. His last few years were spent in Paris, working as a journalist, and he died there in obscurity in 1880. After the Civil War, John O'Sullivan, another of Hotze's journalist colleagues, remained in Europe for some years, dividing his time between London, Paris and Lisbon, before returning to America in 1879. He spent the remainder of his life in New York, dying there in 1895 at the age of 82. After living abroad for a number of years, Confederate propagandist Edwin De Leon also went back to the United States in 1879 and died in New York in 1891. His *Secret History of Confederate Diplomacy Abroad*, originally written in 1867 as a series of articles for the *New York Citizen*, was finally published in book form in 2005.

James Mason remained in London until 1866, when he went to Canada to be reunited with his wife and family in Montreal. Two years later he was able to return to his native Virginia, dying near Alexandria in 1871. Sent to London in the closing weeks of the war, in a last desperate attempt by the Confederate government to secure diplomatic recognition in return for the abolition of slavery, Duncan Kenner returned to his ruined Louisiana sugar plantation to rebuild his life. He was so successful that when he died in New Orleans in 1887 his estate was more valuable than it had been before the war. Pierre Rost, who after his unsuccessful postings to Paris and Madrid, seems to have spent the rest of the war in self-imposed exile in provincial France, also returned to Louisiana and died in New Orleans in 1868.

The flamboyant Belle Boyd, who had taken to the English stage to support herself, returned to America in 1866.[3] For a while she continued with her work in the theater, but retired from it three years later. Then, in 1886, she embarked on a new career, giving recitations of her wartime experiences entitled "The Perils of a Spy," dressed in a Confederate uniform of her own design. She continued with these until her death in 1900, at Kilbourne, Wisconsin, while on tour.

Colonel John Peyton, who had served as a state agent for North Carolina, moved to Guernsey in 1866; his book, *The American Crisis,* appeared the following year. Apart from his travels on the Continent, he remained there until his return to America in 1876. He settled near Staunton, Virginia, devoting his remaining years to farming and literary pursuits until his death in 1896. Lieutenant Thomas Crossan, who had also been a purchasing agent for the Tar Heel state, died in 1865; his colleague, John White, resided in Liverpool for some time after the war, working in the cotton business, but later returned to his native North Carolina, dying there in 1894.

Left almost penniless at the end of the war, with a large family to support, Major Caleb

Huse lived at Auteuil, near Paris, before returning to the United States in 1868, where he started a military school, preparing pupils for entry to West Point. His pamphlet, *The Supplies for the Confederate Army*, was published in 1904, and he died the following year at Highland Falls, New York. Captain William Crenshaw also remained in Europe until 1868. An astute businessman, he became wealthy in the 1880s mining pyrites for the manufacture of sulphuric acid, and built the first furnace for that purpose in the United States at Richmond; he died there in 1897. James H. Burton, another purchasing agent for the Ordnance Bureau, lived in England for some time after the war before returning to Loudoun County, Virginia, where he farmed for some years; he died in Winchester in 1894.

Among the arrivals in 1865 from the former Confederacy, the most remarkable success story was that of Judah P. Benjamin. In January 1866, at the age of 55, he embarked on a new career, enrolling as a law student at Lincoln's Inn, then going on to become a highly successful lawyer and Queen's Counsel. His *Treatise on the Law of Sale of Personal Property* ("Benjamin on Sales"), first published in 1868, became a standard legal textbook which went through many editions and helped make his reputation. When he retired in 1883, a farewell dinner was given in his honor at the Inner Temple, a rare occurrence. He died in Paris the following year and was buried in Pere Lachaise Cemetery.

Judah Benjamin's postwar recovery was exceptional; for most ex–Confederates abroad, it was a matter of trying to rebuild their lives in a foreign land, with varying degrees of success. Major Norman Walker, the former agent in Bermuda, arrived in England in May 1865 with his wife, Georgiana, and their children and went to live at Leamington Spa, Warwickshire, where a number of other Southern families were residing.[4] The following year he established a cotton-importing business at Liverpool with his father-in-law, though it is not clear how successful this was. In any event, the Walkers returned to America in 1878, eventually settling in New York, where Georgiana died in 1904 and her husband in 1913; they were both buried on Staten Island.

At the other end of the scale was Louis T. Wigfall of Texas, a former Confederate brigadier and senator, and one of Jefferson Davis's bitterest opponents. He arrived in England about March 1866 and was joined by his family in October, to begin a miserable, poverty-stricken exile in London. One of those who never accepted defeat, he seems to have spent much of his time in a state of intoxication and it was no doubt a relief to all concerned when, in 1872, he was persuaded to return to America. He settled first in Baltimore, then moved to Galveston, Texas, where he died in 1874; he was buried there in the Episcopal Cemetery.

And there were those Confederates who never went back to America at all. After the *Index* ceased publication in 1865, Henry Hotze moved to Paris, where he continued working as a journalist, and three years later married Ruby Senac, the daughter of a former paymaster in the Confederate Navy. He returned to London for a while at the time of the Franco-Prussian War in 1870, and is known to have visited Constantinople (Istanbul) in 1872 for a newspaper assignment, but eventually he went back to his native Switzerland, dying at Zug in 1887 at the early age of 53. James Williams, one of his associates, who had also written for the *Times* and the *Standard* and remained in Europe after the war, died at Graz, Austria, in 1869.

Dudley Mann, one of the first Confederate commissioners, also settled in Paris after the war, and made a living as a journalist; he died there in 1889 at the age of 88. John Slidell, another of the commissioners, chose to remain in Paris, with occasional visits to England, until the fall of the Emperor Napoleon III in 1870; he died the following year on the Isle of

Wight. Buried originally in Brighton Cemetery, he was subsequently reinterred at Villejuif (Seine), France.

Commander James Bulloch stayed on in Liverpool, where he had many friends and associates, and became a cotton broker. His book, *The Secret Service of the Confederate States in Europe*, was published in 1883 and he died at Liverpool in 1901, the year in which his nephew, Theodore Roosevelt, became the twenty-sixth president of the United States. His grave in Toxteth Park Cemetery is marked by a modern headstone erected by the United Daughters of the Confederacy in 1968.

When the Civil War ended, Confederate finances in Europe were exhausted, other than for a certain amount credited to the Navy Department. U.S. Consul Freeman Morse proposed that Fraser, Trenholm & Company, the Confederacy's bankers, should submit their books and accounts to official inspection, and also provide details of any remaining Confederate property still in their possession, such as cotton and steamers, which could then be sold. This arrangement, however, was vetoed by Secretary of State William H. Seward, and instead legal proceedings against Charles Prioleau, one of the principals of Fraser, Trenholm, were set in motion in July 1865, ending two years later with a failed attempt at an out-of-court settlement and bankruptcy.[5]

Colin McRae was sued unsuccessfully in the English courts by the Federal government for Confederate assets believed to be in his possession at the end of the war, and in June 1866 the government also began proceedings against him as the agent of the Confederate Cotton Loan. The case dragged on for three years, but McRae was able to prove that he had accounted to his own government for "the entire proceeds of the loan in payment of supplies and munitions of war to various commissary and quartermaster officers in this country" and it was finally dismissed in May 1869.[6] In both cases, one of the defending lawyers was Judah Benjamin; the irony of that situation cannot have been lost on those involved. McRae never returned to the United States, but emigrated to British Honduras (Belize) in 1867, and died there ten years later.

In an attempt to settle outstanding Confederate government debts, John Breckinridge and Judah Benjamin tried to recover funds thought to be in the possession of Jacob Thompson, the former commissioner in Canada. He had been in London for a while—William E. Gladstone had met him there in early April 1865—but moved to Paris in July. Exactly how much money he had was a matter of conjecture, but former associates in Canada claimed it was as much as $300,000. Both Breckinridge and Benjamin went to Paris and interviewed Thompson separately, but with only limited success. To avoid a public scandal, they were forced to compromise: Thompson agreed to pay them £12,000, but insisted on retaining another £23,000, which he admitted having, as compensation for the destruction of his plantation in Mississippi.[7]

More information about missing Confederate funds also came to light in November 1865, when Consul Morse learned that "one or two persons here, who appear to have full knowledge of some of the financial operations of the late rebels, say that from £50,000 to £60,000 of Confederate government gold is now held in this city, by some person, house or bank, and that the holders refuse to deliver it to any ex–Confederate agent whatever ... [saying] that it belongs to the United States, if they can find it."[8] He requested authorization to negotiate with the persons in question, though whether the gold, if it ever existed, was eventually retrieved is not known.

Of the men who championed the Confederate cause in Parliament, William Lindsay was forced to give up both political life and the shipping business in 1864 when he lost the use of his legs. He retired to his home at Shepperton Manor, Middlesex, where he devoted his remaining years to writing his four-volume *History of Merchant Shipping and Ancient Commerce* (1874–1876); he died in 1877. John Roebuck continued to serve as an M.P. until 1868, and again from 1874 through 1879. Later a supporter of Benjamin Disraeli, he was made a privy councillor a year before his death in London in 1878; he was buried at Bushey, Hertfordshire. William Gregory remained in Parliament until 1871, then was appointed Governor of Ceylon (Sri Lanka). He held this post for five years and was knighted during the visit there of the Prince of Wales in 1875. His remaining years were spent chiefly in Ireland, though he died at his London home in 1892. *Sir William Gregory: an Autobiography*, edited by Lady Gregory, was published two years later.

Alexander Beresford Hope, treasurer of the British Jackson Monumental Fund, returned to Parliament in 1865 and remained an M.P., combining his parliamentary duties with his literary and artistic interests, until his death at Bedgebury Park, Kent, in 1887; he was buried nearby at Kilndown. Lord Wharncliffe, another prominent Confederate supporter, died at his London residence in 1899.

John Gilliat, head of J. K. Gilliat & Company, whom James Mason called "my bankers," had been appointed a director of the Bank of England in 1862 and was Governor in 1883–1884; between 1886 and 1900 he also served as an M.P. He died in London in 1912, at what the *Times* described as "the ripe age of 82," and was buried at Chorley Wood, Hertfordshire. Archibald Hamilton, the head of Sinclair, Hamilton & Company, and also a director of the London Armory Company, died at Southborough, Kent, in 1880. Edgar Stringer remained a partner in the firm of Stringer, Pembroke & Company until 1879, then continued in business on his own. After his retirement in 1882, he lived in a succession of large houses in west London, but died at Brighton in 1894. He left his widow well-provided for: Mrs. Julia Stringer was worth nearly £27,000 at her own death in 1906.

Thomas Hamber, the "Swiss Captain," continued to edit the *Morning Herald* until 1869, and the *Standard* until 1870, and went on to be the editor of three more newspapers over the next twenty years. He died at Mortlake, Surrey, in 1902. John Hopkins, who had been business manager, assistant editor, and eventually publisher of the *Index*, was a prolific journalist and after the war worked for the *Standard* for three years, as well as contributing to other newspapers and periodicals; he was also the author of several novels and plays. He died in London in 1888. John Witt, who was also an assistant editor on the *Index*, became a lawyer and a Queen's Counsel, dying in 1906. Percy Greg, another of the *Index's* contributors, wrote for many other periodicals, as well as publishing essays, novels and poems. His *History of the United States to the Reconstruction of the Union* (1887) left its readers in no doubt about his earlier pro–Southern views. He was only 53 when he died in London in 1889.

James Spence continued in business as an iron merchant and cotton broker at Liverpool, but in 1872 moved to London, "so as to be within reach of the literary circle of the metropolis." Later he seems to have returned to Liverpool, but by 1890 was living in South Wales, where he had a tinplate works. He finally retired to London, where he died in 1893.

The Rev. Francis Tremlett, who provided support and hospitality for many Confederates and former Confederates in London, during and after the war, died in 1913 at the remarkable age of 91, after serving for 52 years as vicar of St. Peter's, Belsize Park, and was buried in Hampstead Cemetery. There is a monument to his memory in St. Peter's Church.

John and William Dudgeon, who were among the principal London builders of blockade-runners, continued to operate their business until 1875, when their yards at Millwall and Cubitt Town were closed on the death of William and the mental illness of his brother John; the latter was admitted to an asylum in Edinburgh, where he died in 1881.

Zachariah Pearson was completely ruined by his blockade-running ventures and his disastrous involvement with the CSS *Rapphannock*. He never recovered his position as a leading shipowner and in later years found work as a ship's surveyor, though in 1882 he was described as "United States commercial agent, ship broker and coal exporter." He died in obscurity in Hull in 1891, though his name lives on in Pearson Park, which he had presented to the people of Hull in 1860; it contains an obelisk to his memory, bearing a relief portrait of him, and a statue of Queen Victoria which he commissioned. Thomas Begbie, though not actually bankrupted by the war, also lost a number of his blockade-runners, and does not seem to have prospered much afterwards as a merchant; he died in London in 1899 in relative poverty.

Though Samuel and Saul Isaac, of Isaac, Campbell & Company, were largely ruined by the war and their firm was forced into liquidation in 1871, both men had married wealthy second wives, so were able to start again and they made a remarkable recovery. Samuel acquired the rights to the unfinished Mersey Tunnel, between Liverpool and Birkenhead, and lived to see it opened in 1885; when he died in London the following year, he left more than £200,000. His younger brother, Saul, was M.P. for Nottingham, 1874–1880, and also had coal-mining interests in that area; he died in London in 1903. Both men were buried in Willesden Cemetery.

Alexander Collie survived his financial difficulties at the end of the war, only to go bankrupt in 1875. It was reported that his mansion in Kensington Palace Gardens, including the furniture and effects, was worth £28,755, while his pictures, watercolor drawings and paintings were valued at a further £14,500.[9] Charged with obtaining £200,000 from a bank by false pretenses, Alexander Collie broke bail and disappeared, leaving his partner, William Collie, to face the bankruptcy proceedings. They dragged on for nearly three years, by which time Alexander Collie had still not been traced.

The Rev. William Malet, the Hertfordshire clergyman whose visit to the Confederacy was described in *An Errand to the South in the Summer of 1862*, died in 1885, aged 81. The merchant William Corsan, who also visited the Confederacy that same year and wrote of his experiences in *Two Months in the Confederate States*, died at Sheffield in 1876 at the early age of 51. Lieutenant Colonel Arthur Fremantle, of the Coldstream Guards, author of *Three Months in the Southern States,* went on to have a distinguished military career, retiring with the rank of general. Subsequently knighted, he served as Governor of Malta from 1894 through 1899, and died on the Isle of Wight in 1901. All three of these books appeared in 1863, but Fitzgerald Ross, with whom Arthur Fremantle had watched the Battle of Gettysburg, did not publish his *Visit to the Cities and Camps of the Confederate States* until 1865. After its publication he vanished into genteel obscurity, dying at Kensington in 1895; he was buried at Little Bookham in Surrey.

* * *

The men sent to London by the Confederate government varied greatly in their abilities. Some were outstanding, others mediocre, almost verging on the incompetent. Representing a government not yet recognized, and one, furthermore, which endorsed slavery, they worked under difficult conditions, hampered by poor communications, financial problems and increasingly efficient Federal surveillance. In spite of their achievements — and in some cases they were considerable — international political considerations and military developments worked against them, and meant that they were unable to influence the outcome of what their English contemporaries called "the sanguinary contest about which everybody talks and reads."

Appendix A

London Firms with Confederate Links

Numbered postal districts were not introduced in London until 1917, but they are used in the appendices and Gazetteer for ease of reference.

Robert Adams, 76 King William Street (EC4): gun, rifle and pistol manufacturer.

Sir William G. Armstrong & Co., 59 Fenchurch Street (EC3); and Newcastle-upon-Tyne: engineers and armaments manufacturers.

James Ash & Co., Cubitt Town (E14): iron ship builders.

J.H. Ashbridge & Co., Adelaide Chambers, 52 Gracechurch Street (EC3); later 148 Leadenhall Street (EC3); and Liverpool: dealers in bonds and securities.

Baiss Bros. & Co., 102 Leadenhall Street (EC3): wholesale and export druggists.

Barker Bros. & Co., 4 Abchurch Lane (EC4): merchants.

John E. Barnett & Sons, 134 Minories (EC3); Brewhouse Street, Shadwell (E1): wholesale gunmakers.

William J. Barron & Co., 66–67 Aldermanbury (EC2): elastic web makers and wholesale shoe dealers.

Benjamin Beasley, 4 St. James's Street (SW1): gun, rifle and sword maker; also manufacturer of Whitworth rifles ("By appointment to HM War Department").

Thomas S. Begbie, 4 Mansion House Place (EC4); later 36 Walbrook (EC4): shipowner and merchant.

Bennett & Wake, 77 Cornhill (EC3): ship and insurance brokers.

Thomas Bensusan, 75 Old Broad Street (EC2): dealer in stocks and shares.

Thomas Bissell, 75 Tooley Street (SE1): gun, rifle and pistol manufacturer.

Blakely Ordnance Co., 35 Parliament Street (SW1); 28 Gravel Lane and 1 Bear Lane, Southwark (SE1)(works): cannon manufacturers.

Joseph Buckley, 156 Cheapside (EC2): dealer in securities.

R. Gordon Coleman & Co., 28 Clements Lane (EC4): shipowners.

Alexander Collie & Co., 22A Austin Friars (EC2); later 17 Leadenhall Street (EC3); and Liverpool: cotton merchants & commission merchants.

Coutts Bank, 57–59 Strand (WC2).

Crowder, Maynard, Son & Lawford, 57 Coleman Street (EC2): lawyers.

Curtis & Harvey, 74 Lombard Street (EC3); Hounslow Heath (works); and Tonbridge, Kent: gunpowder manufacturers and merchants.

Thomas De La Rue & Co., 109–113 Bunhill Row (EC1): printers & wholesale stationers.

Dent & Co., 61 Strand (WC2); 34–35 Royal Exchange (EC3): chronometer, watch and clock makers.

John T. Dobson, 34 Great St. Helens (EC3): merchant.

John & William Dudgeon, 10 London Street (EC3); Sun Iron Works, Millwall (E14); Cubitt Town (E14): engineers, boilermakers and iron shipbuilders.

Firmin & Sons, 153–155 Strand (WC2); 13 Conduit Street (W1); 12 White Horse Yard, Drury Lane (WC2) (factory): army and navy button manufacturers.

Foster, Porter & Co., 47 Wood Street (EC2); 25 Addle Street (EC2); 21 Aldermanbury (EC2): wholesale hosiers & glovers.

Freshfields & Newman, 5 New Bank Buildings, Princes Street (EC2): lawyers.

John K. Gilliat & Co., 4 Crosby Square (EC3): merchants and bankers.

Goody & Jones, 40 Pall Mall (SW1): military and naval outfitters.

Charles W. & Wentworth Gray, 31 Great St Helens (EC3): merchants.

Greenwood & Batley, 20 Cannon Street (EC4); and Leeds: machinists.

John Hall & Son, 23 Lombard Street (EC3): gunpowder manufacturers.

Sydney Hodgkinson & Co., 4 Laurence Pountney (EC4): general merchants.

Thomas & Charles Hood, Iron Wharf, Earl Street, Blackfriars (EC4): iron merchants and contractors for iron ordnance and munitions of war.

Lambert Hotchkiss, 16 Bishopsgate Street Within (EC2): shipbroker.

Hughes & Kimber, 5 Red Lion Passage, Fleet Street (EC4): importers of lithographic stones, manufacturers of lithographic and copperplate presses, and engravers' and lithographers' materials.

Isaac, Campbell & Co., 71 Jermyn Street (SW1): commission merchants and army contractors; promoters of the Atlantic Trading Company.

Jones, Loyd & Co., 43 Lothbury (EC2): bankers.

M. Kramer, 10 Old Jewry Chambers (EC2): dealer in securities.

William Ladd, 11-12 Beak Street (W1): electrical engineer.

Charles W. Lancaster, 151 New Bond Street (W1); 2 Little Bruton St. (W1) (factory): gunmaker; patentee of the British Lancaster short rifle.

John Lane, Hankey & Co., 25 Old Broad Street (EC2): merchants.

Laurence, Son & Pearce, Auction Mart, Bartholomew Lane (EC2): stockbrokers.

William S. Lindsay & Co., 8 Austin Friars (EC2); 54 Old Broad Street (EC2): shipowners and insurance brokers.

London Armory Co., Henry Street, Bermondsey (SE1); later 36 King William Street (EC4); Victoria Park Mills, Old Ford Road (E2): armaments manufacturers.

Charles Lungley & Co., 4 Brabant Court, Philpot Lane (EC3); Deptford Green Dockyard (SE8); Commercial Dry Dock, Rotherhithe (SE16): shipbuilders.

Henry F. Mackintosh, 11 Crane Court, Fleet Street (EC4): printer.

Morgan Brothers, 21 Bow Lane (EC4): merchants; dealers in bonds.

Frederick Napton, Glass House Yard (EC4): gun carriage maker.

Negretti & Zambra, 1 Hatton Garden (EC1); 59 Cornhill (EC3); 122 Regent Street (W1); 153 Fleet Street (EC4): meteorological, mathematical, surveying, electrical, nautical, chemical and photographic instrument makers.

Overend, Gurney & Co., 65 Lombard Street (EC3): bankers and money dealers.

Z. C. Pearson & Co., 34 Great St. Helens (EC3); later 32 Nicholas Lane (EC4); and Hull: shipowners and brokers.

Peek Brothers & Co., 20-21 Eastcheap (EC3); 31 Love Lane (EC2); 4 St. Mary-at-Hill (EC3): wholesale tea, coffee and spice dealers.

Pile, Spence & Co., 2 Cowper's Court, Cornhill (EC3); and West Hartlepool: shipowners, shipbuilders and ship repairers.

Quilter, Ball, Jay & Co., 3 Moorgate Street (EC2): accountants.

Rayden & Reid, 12 King William Street (EC4): shipbrokers.

Reuter's News Agency, 1 Royal Exchange Buildings (EC3); 2 King Street, Finsbury Square (EC2) (American office).

Richardson Bros. & Co., 17 St. Helens Place (EC3) (counting house); 11 East Road (N1): merchants; saltpeter refiners.

Robinson & Cottam (late Bramahs), 7 Parliament Street (SW1): Lower Belgrave Place (SW1): engineers, iron founders and railway plant contractors.

Robinson & Fleming, 21 Austin Friars (EC2): merchants.

Alexander Ross & Co., Grange Mills, Grange Road, Bermondsey (SE1): army contractors, tanners and leather merchants, accoutrement makers, artillery harness, cavalry equipment.

John Scott Russell & Co., 20 Great George Street (SW1); Blackwall (E14): civil engineers and shipbuilders.

Martin Samuelson & Co., 8 Adam Street (WC2); later 28 Cornhill (EC3); and Hull: engineers and iron shipbuilders.

J. Henry Schroder & Co., 145 Leadenhall Street (EC3): merchants and bankers; members of the European Trading Company.

Stephen W. Silver & Co., 3-6 Bishopsgate (EC2); 66-67 Cornhill (EC3); Silvertown (E16): patentees and manufacturers of telegraphic wire insulators; army and navy contractors; clothing and accoutrement makers.

Sinclair, Hamilton & Co., 11 St. Helen's Place (EC3); later 17 St. Helen's Place: commission merchants.

George A. Spottiswoode, 5 New Street Square (EC4): printer.

Samuel Straker & Sons, 80 Bishopsgate Street Within (EC2); 26 Leadenhall Street (EC3):

printers, lithographers, engravers, wholesale and export stationers.

Stringer, Pembroke & Co., 8 Austin Friars (EC2); 54 Old Broad Street (EC2): ship and insurance brokers; directors of the Mercantile Trading Company.

Charles Tennant, Sons & Co., 9 Mincing Lane (EC3): chemical manufacturers and agents; West India merchants.

Turner Bros., Hyde & Co., Falcon Factory, Whitecross Street (EC1/EC2); and Northampton: boot and shoe manufacturers.

James White, 12 Narrow Street, Limehouse (E14): sailmaker.

Joseph Whitworth & Co., 28 Pall Mall (SW1); and Manchester: engineers, machine tool, cannon and rifle manufacturers.

Wilkinson & Son, 27 Pall Mall (SW1): gun and sword manufacturers and army contractors.

William Wilson & Sons, 3 Aldermary Churchyard, Bow Lane (EC4): wholesale boot and shoemakers.

Joseph S. Wyon, 287 Regent Street (W1); 3 Langham Chambers, Langham Place (W1): medalist and engraver of seals.

Elizabeth Yeomans & Son, 7 St. Mildred's Court, Poultry (EC2); Tenter Street West, Goodmans Fields (E1): gunmakers to Her Majesty's Honorable Board of Ordnance; wholesale gun, pistol and rifle makers and sword cutlers; ships' armaments fitted up and supplied.

Appendix B
Pro-Confederate Publications and Their Publishers

Richard Bentley & Son, 8 New Burlington Street (W1): James Spence. *The American Union* (1861). (Also translated into French & German.); James Spence. *On the Recognition of the Southern Confederation* (1862); John L. O'Sullivan. *Union, Disunion and Reunion* (1862); An English Merchant [William C. Corsan]. *Two Months in the Confederate States, including a Visit to New Orleans under the Domination of General Butler* (1863). Reissued by Louisiana State University Press, 1996; Rose O. Greenhow. *My Imprisonment and the First Year of Abolition Rule at Washington* (1863); William W. Malet. *An Errand to the South in the Summer of 1862* (1863); James Spence. *Southern Independence* (1863); James Williams. *The Rise and Fall of the Model Republic* (1863); *The Southern Bazaar, Liverpool, October 1864* (1864).

William Blackwood & Sons, 37 Paternoster Row (EC4): Arthur J. L. Fremantle. *Three Months in the Southern States* (1863). Reissued by University of Nebraska Press, 1991; Marquis of Lothian. *The Confederate Secession* (1864). (Also translated into French.); Fitzgerald E.T. Ross. *A Visit to the Cities and Camps of the Confederate States* (1865). Reissued by University of Illinois Press, 1958; Heros Von Borcke. *Memoirs of the Confederate War for Independence* (1866).

Chapman & Hall, 193 Piccadilly (W1): A Blockaded British Subject [Catherine C. Hopley]. *Life in the South: From the Commencement of the War* (1863). Reissued by A.M. Kelly, 1971; [Catherine C. Hopley]. *Stonewall Jackson, Late General of the Confederate States Army: A Biographical Sketch and an Outline of the Virginia Campaign* (1863); Hiram Fuller. *North and South* (1863); Frederick A. Maxse. *Pro Patria* (1863).

William Freeman, 102 Fleet Street (EC4): *The Index* (1862).

Robert Hardwicke, 192 Piccadilly (W1): John W. Cowell. *Southern Secession* (1862); Hugo Reid. *The American Question in a Nutshell* (1862).

Hurst & Blackett, 13 Great Marlborough Street (W1): Samuel P. Day. *Down South: Or, An Englishman's Experiences at the Seat of the American War* (1862). Reissued by B. Franklin, 1971.

Longman, Green, Longman, Roberts & Green, 14 Ludgate Hill (EC4): James Williams. *The South Vindicated* (1862). (Also translated into German.)

Henry F. Mackintosh, Crane Court (EC4): *The Index* (1862–1864). A Northern Man [Hiram Fuller]. *Curiosity Visits to Southern Plantations* (1863). Charles Mitchell & Co., 12 & 13 Red Lion Court (EC4): P.C. Centz (Plain Common Sense) [Bernard J. Sage]. *Davis and Lee: A Vindication of the Southern States, Citizens and Rights* (1865).

James Ridgway, 169 Piccadilly (W1): Thomas C. Grattan. *England, and the Disrupted States of America* (1861); Alexander J.B. Beresford-Hope. *The American Disruption* (1862); Hiram Fuller. *The Causes and Consequences of the Civil War in America* (1862); Hiram Fuller. *The Flag of Truce: Dedicated to the Emperor of the French* (1862); Lord Campbell. *Speech in the House of Lords, March 1863* (1863).

Saunders, Otley & Co., 66 Brook Street (W1): Lord Robert Montagu. *A Mirror in America* (1861); T.D. Ozanne. *The South as It Is, or Twenty-One Years' Experience in the Southern States of America* (1863); *The Cruise of the Alabama and the Sumter, from the Private Journals and Other Papers of Commander R. Semmes, C.S.N., and Other Officers* (1864); *The Log of the Alabama and the Sumter* (1864); *Ordnance Instructions for the Confederate States Navy Relating to the Preparation of Vessels of War for Battle, to the Duties of Officers and Others When at Quarters, to Ordnance and Ordnance Stores, and to Gunnery*, 3rd ed. (1864); Belle Boyd. *Belle Boyd in Camp and Prison* (1865). Reissued by Thomas Yoseloff, 1968; Louisiana State University Press, 1998; John L. Peyton. *The American Crisis; or, Pages from the Note-book of a State Agent During the Civil War* (1867).

Tinsley Brothers, 18 Catherine Street (WC2): George A. Lawrence. *Border and Bastille* (1863).

Appendix C

Confederate Music Published in London

Boosey & Sons, 28 Holles Street (W1) [now Boosey & Hawkes]: "A Battle Hymn" (*ILN*, Dec. 1864); "Bonnie Blue Flag" (Harry Macarthy) (*ILN*, Dec. 1864); "Dixey's Land" (arr. Frederick Buckley) (*ILN*, Jan. 1865); "Maryland" (George Forbes) (*ILN*, Dec. 1864); "Maryland Quadrille" (Victor Colline) (*ILN*, Dec. 1864); "Old King Cotton" (*ILN*, Jan. 1865)

Brewer & Co., 23 Bishopsgate Street (EC2): "The Death of Stonewall Jackson" (Charles Blamphin) (*ILN*, Aug. 1864)

Cramer, Beale & Wood, 201 Regent Street (W1) [now Cramer Music]; "War Song of Dixie" (Frederick Buckley); "The Confederates' National Air, Maryland" (James R. Randall)

Foster & King, 16 Hanover Street (W1): "Stonewall Jackson Quadrille" (Henri Talbot) (*ILN*, Nov. 1862)

Hopwood & Crew, 42 New Bond Street (W1): "The Bonnie Blue Flag" (Harry Macarthy) (*ILN*, Oct. 1864); "The Boy of the Rappahannock" (Charles Blamphin) (*ILN*, Jan. 1865); "Dixie" (Daniel D. Emmett) (*ILN*, Nov. 1864); "Dixey's Land Gallop" (Charles Coote, Jr.) (*ILN*, Nov. 1861); "Down Among the Cotton" (*ILN*, Nov. 1864); "It is My Country's Call" (*ILN*, Oct. 1864); "My Maryland" (*ILN*, Oct. 1864); "My Southern Home" (*ILN*, Jan. 1865)

J. Jewell, 104 Great Russell Street (WC1): "The Confederate War March" (Carl Weiner) (*ILN*, Oct. 1864)

Christopher Lonsdale, 26 Old Bond Street (W1): "A Confederate Raid" (E.M.); "Our Queen Varine" (E.M.)

Joseph Williams, 123 Cheapside (EC2): "Dixie's Land Polka" (Henry Farmer) (*ILN*, Nov. 1861); "General Jackson's Schottische" (Tidwell, arr. Henry Farmer) (*ILN*, Sept. 1862); "The Picket of the Potomac" (Henri F. Hemy) (*ILN*, Jan. 1864)

ILN = *Illustrated London News*

For details of songs, see *Catalogue of Printed Music in the British Library to 1980*. 62 vols. (London: K.G. Sauer, 1981–1987). Brief histories of some music publishing firms can be found in Charles Humphries & William C. Smith, *Music Publishing in the British Isles from the Earliest Times to the Middle of the Nineteenth Century*. (London: Cassell, 1954).

Appendix D
The Southern Lobby in Parliament

House of Commons: Lord Robert Cecil, Conservative M.P. for Stamford (Lincolnshire), 1853–1868; William E. Duncombe, Conservative M.P. for the North Riding of Yorkshire, 1859–1867; Sir James Fergusson, Bt., Conservative M.P. for Ayrshire (Scotland), 1859–1868; William H. Gregory, Liberal-Conservative M.P. for County Galway (Ireland), 1857–1872; Thomas C. Haliburton, Conservative M.P. for Launceston (Cornwall), 1859–1865; John T. Hopwood, Conservative M.P. for Clitheroe (Lancashire), 1857–1865; Sir Edward C. Kerrison, Bt., Conservative M.P. for Eye (Suffolk), 1852–1866; John Laird, Liberal-Conservative M.P. for Birkenhead, 1861–1874; founder of J. Laird, Sons & Co., shipbuilders; William S. Lindsay, Liberal M.P. for Sunderland, 1859–1865; shipowner; George M.W. Peacocke, Conservative M.P. for Maldon (Essex), 1859–1868; Frederick Peel, Liberal M.P. for Bury (Lancashire), 1859–1865; financial secretary to the Treasury; John A. Roebuck, Independent M.P. for Sheffield, 1849–1868; James Whiteside, Q.C., Conservative M.P. for Dublin University, 1859–1866

House of Lords: John A. Thynne, 4th Marquis of Bath; William F. Campbell, 2nd Baron Campbell, 2nd Baron Stratheden; Lord Eustace Cecil; Richard J. Hely-Hutchinson, 4th Earl of Donoughmore; William S. Kerr, 8th Marquis of Lothian; author of *The Confederate Secession* (1864); Edward M. Stuart-Wortley-Mackenzie, 3rd Baron Wharncliffe

Appendix E

The Southern Independence Association of London

Committee[1]: Edward Akroyd; Marquis of Bath; A.J.B. Beresford-Hope; Hon. Robert Bourke; Lord Campbell; Lord Eustace Cecil; Lord Robert Cecil, M.P.; Hon. C.W.W. Fitzwilliam, M.P.; W.H. Gregory, M.P.; Col. F.S. Greville, M.P.; T.C. Haliburton, M.P.; W.S. Lindsay, M.P.; Marquis of Lothian; G.M.W. Peacocke, M.P.; William Scholefield, M.P.; James Spence; William Vansittart, M.P.; Lord Wharncliffe.

Chairman: A.J.B. Beresford-Hope
Secretary: A. Kintrea
Treasurer: Lord Eustace Cecil
Temporary office: 24 St. James's St. (SW1)

Appendix F

The British Jackson Monumental Fund

Committee[1]: Lord Campbell; Lord Eustace Cecil; Earl of Donoughmore; Hon. W.E. Duncombe, M.P.; Sir James Fergusson, Bt., M.P.; Hon. C.W.W. Fitzwilliam, M.P.; J.S. Gilliat; Col. F.S. Greville, M.P.; Sir E.C. Kerrison, Bt., M.P.; Sir Coutts Lindsay, Bt.; W. S. Lindsay, M.P.; G.M.W. Peacocke, M.P.; G.E. Seymour; James Spence.
Hon. Treasurer: A.J.B. Beresford-Hope
Hon. Secretary: W. H. Gregory, M.P.

There is a slight discrepancy between the weekly lists published in the *Index* and the records of the Stonewall Jackson Memorial Account at Coutts Bank. The former show a total of £1,040 donated between June 1863 and August 1864; the latter lists £965 subscribed between June 1863 and May 1864, with a further £55 in July and August 1865, making a total of £1,020. Coutts' account also shows various expenses, amounting to some £44, probably for printing and advertising. The account appears to have become dormant in 1877.

Some subscribers to General Jackson's Statue

Edward Akroyd	£5	A. J. B. Beresford-Hope*	£20
D. Forbes Campbell	£5.5s	Lord Campbell*	£10
Lord Eustace Cecil*	£5	Alexander Collie	£50
Sir Henry De Houghton, Bt.	£22.10.6	W.H. De La Rue	£1.1s
Earl of Donoughmore*	£5	Sir Eardley Eardley, Bt.	£10.10s
Sir James Fergusson, Bt., M.P.*	£5	W.H. Gregory, M.P.*	£5
Col. F.S. Greville, M.P.*	£5	Sir E.C. Kerrison, Bt., M.P.*	£10
Marquis of Lothian	£5	H.F. Mackintosh	£1.1s
W.J. Rideout	£1.1s	J.H. Schroder	£50
G.E. Seymour*	£25	James Spence*	£50

*Member of the British Jackson Monumental Fund committee; not all members of it contributed to the fund.

Appendix G

A Note on British Currency

In the early 1860s, the basic unit of currency, as now, was the pound sterling. It then took the form of the gold sovereign, which was divided into 20 shillings or 240 pence. The actual coins in circulation were as follows:

Gold: Sovereign (20 shillings); Half-sovereign (10 shillings)

Silver: Florin (2 shillings); Shilling (12 pence); Sixpence; Threepenny piece

Bronze: Penny; Half-penny; Farthing (quarter-penny)

Bank of England notes for £5, £10, £20, £50, £100, £200, £300, £500 and £1,000 were also issued.

Guineas (21 shillings) and half-guineas (10 shillings and 6 pence), which were gold coins, had been withdrawn from circulation in the early nineteenth century, but the practice of charging in guineas was still common in the 1860s, and lingered on well into the twentieth century.

The exchange rate with the U.S. dollar throughout the Civil War was $4.85. Though there was no official exchange rate with the Confederate dollar, there was an attempt at an unofficial one, which at the time of the Erlanger Loan in 1863 was quoted as $13.33.

Chronology

1861

April	Dudley Mann, one of the three Confederate commissioners appointed for Europe, arrives in London and two weeks later is joined by William Yancey and Pierre Rost, who subsequently proceeds to Paris.
May	The commissioners have two unofficial meetings with Foreign Secretary Lord John Russell.
	Captain Caleb Huse arrives in London to buy weapons for the Confederate Army.
	Queen Victoria issues a Proclamation of Neutrality, granting both sides belligerent status. In Parliament, Lord John Russell points out that recognizing the Confederate States as belligerents does not imply diplomatic recognition.
	Charles Francis Adams, new U.S. minister to Great Britain, arrives to take up his post, as does consul Freeman Morse.
June	James Bulloch, purchasing agent for the Confederate Navy, arrives at Liverpool and subsequently calls on the commissioners in London.
	Lieutenant James North and Major Edward Anderson reach London, North to buy ships for the Confederate Navy, and Anderson to oversee Army purchasing operations.
	Private detective Ignatius Pollaky is hired to keep watch on the Confederates.
July	Major Benjamin Ficklin is sent to London to engage craftsmen and buy equipment for printing treasury notes.
August	Pierre Rost rejoins William Yancey and Dudley Mann in London, for another meeting with Lord John Russell, but their request to see him is refused.
September	After new commissioners James Mason and John Slidell are appointed for Europe, William Yancey resigns, but is asked to remain in London until his replacement arrives.
October	Henry Hotze visits London to check on arms shipments.
	James Spence's *The American Union* is published.
	The *Bee-Hive*, a workman's paper with a pro–Confederate bias, begins publication.
	Major Anderson leaves London for Liverpool, to return to the Confederacy.
November	William Yancey and Dudley Mann are guests of honor at a banquet given at Fishmongers' Hall.
	The CSS *Nashville* arrives at Southampton, carrying spare officers for Confederate ships being built in England and Colonel John Peyton, state agent for North Carolina, who proceeds to London.
	Reports of the seizure of Mason and Slidell from the British mail steamer *Trent* cause a public outcry, with newspaper placards proclaiming "outrage on the British Flag."
	Pierre Rost again returns to London in the hope of further dialogue with Lord Russell.

December	A royal proclamation, prohibiting the export of arms and munitions, is published. Lord John Russell declines to enter into any further communication with the Confederate commissioners.

1862

January	New Confederate commissioner James Mason finally reaches London. Henry Hotze, Confederate States commercial agent, also arrives. Effigies of Mason and Slidell go on display at Madame Tussaud's waxworks. The Federals dispense with Ignatius Pollaky's services.
February	The *Nashville* finally leaves Southampton. The order prohibiting the export of arms, ammunition and military equipment is revoked. Pierre Rost moves to Madrid; William Yancey returns to the Confederate States. James Mason has a meeting with Lord Russell. Henry Hotze's first editorial is published in the *Morning Post*. The first letter by "S" (James Spence) appears in the *Times*.
March	A debate takes place in Parliament about the effectiveness of the blockade. Samuel Day's *Down South* is published. The *Oreto* (CSS *Florida*) sails for Nassau.
April	Commander Raphael Semmes, of the CSS *Sumter*, arrives in London for a stay of a few weeks. John Swisher is sent to London by the Texas State Military Board.
May	Henry Hotze begins publication of the *Index* in Fleet Street. Colonel Peyton has an unofficial interview with Prime Minister Lord Palmerston. A bark, the *Agrippina* (a "Scotch collier"), is chartered by Commander Bulloch as a tender for the *Alabama* and loaded in the London Docks.
June	Edwin De Leon arrives in London as head of Confederate propaganda in Europe.
July	He has a meeting with Lord Palmerston before proceeding to Paris. British mediation in the Civil War is debated in Parliament. The *Enrica* (CSS *Alabama*) leaves Liverpool, supposedly for a trial run.
August	The London Confederate States Aid Association is formed. At a banquet, Lord Palmerston reiterates that Britain will maintain its policy of "a strict and rigid neutrality."
October	James Spence is appointed European financial agent for the Confederacy. The *Index* moves to Bouverie Street.
November	*A Southerner Just Arrived* is produced at the Olympic Theater. Commander Matthew Maury comes to England to buy ships and materials for the Confederate Navy. Major Norman Walker is sent to London by the Ordnance Bureau.
December	The Quartermaster Bureau sends Major James Ferguson to London.

1863

January	North Carolina state agents John White and Thomas Crossan arrive in London. The *Bee-Hive* gets a new editor and no longer supports the Confederacy.
February	James Mason makes a speech at the lord mayor's banquet at the Mansion House. Lieutenant William Maury arrives in London with $1.5 million in cotton certificates to purchase and equip a commerce raider, and stays with his cousin, Commander Matthew Maury.

March	The Seven Per Cent Cotton Loan is floated in London, Liverpool, Paris, Amsterdam and Frankfurt; "a great carnival" is held at Morley's Hotel to celebrate the event. The *London American* ceases publication.
	Colonel Lucius Lamar, Confederate commissioner to Russia, arrives in London, and remains until mid-April, when he leaves for Paris.
	Federals and Confederates opens at the Polygraphic Hall and runs until May. Texas state agent Nelson Clements arrives in London.
April	The *Alexandra*, being built for the Confederates at Liverpool, is seized.
	Catherine Hopley's *Life in the South* is published.
	Confederate naval officers assemble in London prior to joining the CSS *Georgia*.
	The South as It Is, by the Rev. T.D. Ozanne, is published.
June	Colin McRae comes to London to manage the Confederate loan and investigate alleged irregularities in the purchasing operations.
	Henry Hotze organizes a Confederate flag poster campaign as a prelude to the forthcoming parliamentary debate about diplomatic recognition.
	Parliament debates the recognition of the Confederate States.
	The trial takes place at the Court of Exchequer concerning the case of the *Alexandra*.
	An exhibition of Confederate portraits by Benjamin F. Reinhart is held at Revell's Fine Art Gallery.
	Colonel Lamar returns to London after his mission is aborted and works with Henry Hotze.
July	The British Jackson Monumental Fund is launched.
	Assistant Paymaster Douglas Forrest arrives in London, prior to being assigned to the CSS *Rappahannock*.
	The Rev. William Malet's *Errand to the South* is published.
September	Charles Francis Adams sends a note to Lord John Russell, pointing out that to allow the Laird rams to sail might mean war with the United States; meanwhile the seizure of the vessels is already under way.
	Mrs. Rose Greenhow arrives in England as an unofficial Confederate emissary.
	The London Confederate States Commercial League is formed.
	James Mason informs Lord John Russell of his instructions to withdraw from London; he leaves for Paris, but returns from time to time.
	Albert Bledsoe comes to London and writes for the *Index*.
October	Captain Samuel Barron arrives in London, en route for Paris, where he is to be Flag Officer Commanding Confederate States Naval Forces in Europe.
	The Society for Promoting the Cessation of Hostilities in America is founded.
	The Confederate States Exchange Rooms are proposed.
November	Church's Historical Panorama at the St. James's Hall features *The Civil War in America*.
	Colonel Lamar returns to the Confederacy.
	Mrs. Greenhow's *My Imprisonment* is published.
	Charles Francis Adams makes representations to Lord John Russell about the CSS *Rappahannock*.
December	Colin McRae replaces James Spence as chief financial agent in Europe.
	The Southern Independence Association of London is formed.
	Colonel Arthur Fremantle's *Three Months in the Southern States* is published.

1864

January	Colonel Josiah Gorgas, head of the Ordnance Bureau, visits London.
March	*The Alabama: A Nautical Extravaganza* is performed at the Theater Royal, Drury Lane.
May	The Society for Promoting the Cessation of Hostilities addresses an appeal to M.P.s for immediate action.

June	Captain Semmes arrives in London, following the loss of the CSS *Alabama* in a battle off Cherbourg; he and Commander Maury are guests of the Rev. Francis W. Tremlett in Belsize Park. The steamer *Hawk*, intended as a privateer in the Virginia Volunteer Navy, leaves London for Bermuda. A Confederate bank in London is proposed by J. Henry Schroder and Emile Erlanger.
July	The Society for Promoting the Cessation of Hostilities and the Southern Independence Association of London make a joint appeal to Lord Palmerston for mediation in the war. James Mason meets Lord Palmerston. John Seymour is acquitted of violating the Foreign Enlistment Act in the *Rappahannock* affair. John Thompson comes to London to work on the *Index*. *The Cruise of the Alabama and Sumter* is published.
August	A Confederate wedding takes place at St. James's church, Piccadilly. Major Walker comes to London again on Confederate business. Mrs. Greenhow leaves London to return to the Confederate States.
September	John Witt is appointed assistant editor of the *Index*.
October	The *Index* moves to the Strand. Captain Semmes returns to the Confederacy. The *Sea King*, soon to become the CSS *Shenandoah*, sails from London.
November	Mrs. Greenhow is reported drowned. Lord Wharncliffe asks permission for an "accredited agent" to be allowed to visit Confederate prisoners-of-war in Federal prison camps, but is unsuccessful.

1865

January	The *Hawk*, now returned to London, is sold at auction to pay its debts.
February	Lieutenant Colonel Heros Von Borcke arrives in London on a special mission for the Confederate government. William Rumble, an Admiralty official, is found not guilty of a breach of the Foreign Enlistment Act in connection with the CSS *Rappahannock*.
March	Duncan Kenner comes to London on a secret mission from President Davis. Officers take over from the CSS *Florida* arrive in London, on their way to join the ironclad CSS *Stonewall*. Reports of the fall of Charleston create consternation among Confederate supporters. James Mason and Duncan Kenner meet Lord Palmerston to discuss diplomatic recognition. The last payment of interest on the Confederate loan is made.
April	Flag Officer Barron, Commanders North, Sinclair and Pegram, Assistant Paymaster Forrest and other naval officers leave for Havana. A dinner is held in honor of Commander Maury prior to his return to the Confederacy. News of Lee's surrender reaches London. The reports of Lincoln's assassination cause intense excitement in the West End, leading John Thompson to remark that he "never witnessed such a sensation in London."
May	*Belle Boyd in Camp and Prison* is published. Captain Ross's *Visit to the Cities and Camps of the Confederate States* also appears.
June	The *Times* publishes an official circular, declaring the Civil War to be at an end.
August	*The Confederate's Daughter* opens at the Britannia Theater, Hoxton. The *Index* ceases publication.
November	The CSS *Shenandoah* surrenders at Liverpool.

Gazetteer

The following principal Confederate sites in London, mentioned in the text and described below, can still be seen: Arklow House, W2; 3 Belsize Square, NW3; 35 Buckland Crescent, NW3; 38 Clarendon Road, W11; 15 Half Moon Street, W1; 162 New Bond Street, W1; 40 Pall Mall, SW1; St. James's Church, W1; St. Peter's Church, NW3; 34 Sackville Street, W1; 17 Savile Row, W1; Wharncliffe House, W1.

Adelphi Theater see **Strand**

Albemarle Street (W1)

At the time of Commander Maury's stay in December 1862, the Albemarle Hotel, on the corner of Piccadilly, was owned by Louis Schill. The hotel, which was rebuilt in 1889, closed about 1905 and is now a suite of offices called Albemarle House.

The first Confederate commissioner to arrive in London, Dudley Mann had found lodgings at 40 Albemarle Street by May 1861; the premises then belonged to William Markwell, a wine and spirit merchant. Although subsequently commissioner to Belgium and the Vatican, Mann nevertheless appears to have been in London for much of the war, living at this address.

Arklow House see **Connaught Place**

Austin Friars (EC2)

The offices of W. S. Lindsay & Co., leading shipowners and insurance brokers, were at 8 Austin Friars; Commissioner Yancey went there in May 1861 and had "a long & interesting interview" with Mr. Lindsay. Edgar Stringer and Edward Pembroke, employees of Lindsay, set up the firm of Stringer, Pembroke & Co. c1864, and took over these premises, as well as others in Old Broad Street, when Lindsay retired.

Alexander Collie & Co., cotton merchants and major operators of blockade-runners, had a London office at 22A Austin Friars until 1864, when they moved to 17 Leadenhall Street. Agents like Major Huse and Captain Crenshaw seem to have used the premises as an accommodation address for correspondence.

Baker Street (W1)

Since 1835 Madame Tussaud's Waxworks on Baker Street had been a leading tourist attraction and was visited by a number of Confederates, including Lieutenant North in July 1861 and Assistant Paymaster Forrest in August 1863; Forrest was much impressed, finding them housed in "a magnificent building and admirably appointed." The collection moved to its Marylebone Road site in 1884.

Belsize Square (NW3)

Designed by J.R. St. Aubyn Mumford for the new suburb of Belsize Park and consecrated in 1859, St. Peter's Church, Belsize Square, was built largely at the expense of its first incumbent, the Rev. Francis Tremlett, who paid for the nave, aisles and transepts. A staunch Confederate, his sermon, *Christian Brotherhood: Its Claims and Duties, with a Special Reference to the Fratricidal War in America*, delivered here in November 1863, was printed and sent to churches throughout the country; it sold many thousands of copies. There is a memorial to him by Kathleen Shaw, on the wall by the vestry door, erected in 1915; his sister, Louisa, who corresponded with Captain Semmes and Commander Pegram, died in 1912 and is commemorated by a brass tablet in the side chapel.

Usually referred to in the nineteenth century as the Parsonage, St. Peter's Vicarage was built in 1862, also by the Rev. Tremlett; even by mid–Victorian standards it was massive. Confederates and their supporters were frequent guests here during the Civil War, and it became known as "the home of the Confederates" and "the Rebels' roost."

Ex-Confederates who came here after the war included Jefferson and Varina Davis, and ex-generals Pierre Beauregard, William Pendleton and Walter Stevens. The Rev. Tremlett remained here until his death in 1913 and it was demolished the same year to make way for a new vicarage.

In March 1866 Matthew Maury returned from Mexico and was reunited with his family at 30 Harley Street, where they rented rooms. From there they moved to 41 Clarendon Terrace, Belsize Road, in July, then to more comfortable accommodation at 3 Belsize Square in November. It cost $40 a week for food and lodgings "for all hands" (the Maurys and their four children) and was conveniently close to St. Peter's Vicarage, where the Rev. Francis Tremlett lived. The Maurys were to remain here until their return to the United States in July 1868. The house still exists.

Berners Street (W1)

Assistant Paymaster Forrest stayed at the Berners Hotel when he arrived in London at the end of July 1863, and probably again after his return from Liverpool the following month; it was then owned by Mrs. Louisa Ashton, the widow of its founder, Thomas Ashton. The hotel, which was rebuilt c1909, is still in existence.

Bouverie Street (EC4)

The *Index* left Fleet Street in October 1862 and moved to 13 Bouverie Street, next-door-but-two to the pro–Northern *Daily News*; it was published there until October 1864, when it transferred to the Strand. The paper occupied two small rooms in a building it shared with other publishers, engravers and a kitchen-range manufacturer.

Britannia Theater see **Hoxton Street**

Brunswick Hotel see **Jermyn Street**

Buckingham Palace Road (SW1)

When Assistant Paymaster Forrest stayed at the Grosvenor Hotel in November 1863, it had only been open two years. The Grosvenor was reconstructed in 1892–1899 and extended in 1907, but externally is not greatly changed. It is still a major London hotel.

Buckland Crescent (NW3)

Built in the late 1850s, 11 (now 35) Buckland Crescent, Belsize Park, served as a temporary vicarage for St. Peter's Church until the one in Belsize Square was completed in 1862. It remained the property of the incumbent, the Rev. Francis Tremlett, a staunch supporter of the South, and a number of Confederates are known to have stayed there in the early weeks of 1863, among them Commander Sinclair and Lieutenants Chapman and Evans.

Bunhill Row (EC1)

The premises of Thomas De La Rue & Co., stationers and printers, at 109–113 Bunhill Row, were visited by various Confederate agents, including Commander Bulloch, Commander Sinclair and Major Ficklin, who may also have lodged there and used them as an accommodation address for correspondence. They were destroyed in the London Blitz in 1940.

Burlington Hotel see **Cork Street**

Bury Street (SW1)

Mrs. E. Preston, of 31 Bury Street, St. James's, advertised "Furnished apartments and bedrooms to let" in the *Index* from September 1862 to January 1863, and Henry Hotze himself stayed there when he arrived in London. At least two other Confederates, Lieutenants Chapman and Carter, are also known to have lodged with Mrs. Preston.

Cambridge House see **Piccadilly**

Chesham Place (SW1)

There is a plaque on 37 Chesham Place to mark the residence here, from 1841 until 1870, of Lord John Russell, foreign secretary during the Civil War, and twice prime minister. Here he had interviews with commissioners William Yancey, Pierre Rost and Dudley Mann in May 1861, and with their successor, James Mason, in February 1862.

Cheyne Row (SW3)

Confederate journalist and poet John Thompson visited 5 (now 24) Cheyne Row, Chelsea, the home of Thomas Carlyle, on a number of occasions during his stay in London between 1864 and 1866. The house, which was Carlyle's home from 1834 until 1881, is marked with a plaque; it has been the property of the National Trust since 1936 and is open to the public.

Clarendon Road (W11)

Major Huse had moved from Jermyn Street to 38 Clarendon Road, Notting Hill, by July 1862; this may have been because of the arrival of his wife and children, though evidence for this is lacking. He was still at this address in 1863, but by February 1864 was living in the suburbs of Paris, in a house provided rent-free by the banker Emile Erlanger; 38 Clarendon Road seems little changed externally.

Clifford Street (W1)

Captain Ross, who wrote *A Visit to the Cities*

and Camps of the Confederate States, was living at 3 Clifford Street when it was published in 1865; Lieutenant Colonel Von Borcke, author of *Memoirs of the Confederate War for Independence*, published the following year, also lodged there. The house was rebuilt in the late nineteenth century.

Connaught Place (W2)

Alexander Beresford Hope, a leading supporter of the South, lived at Arklow House, 1–2 Connaught Place. A number of Confederates came here during the war, including William Yancey, James Mason, Commander Bulloch, James Spence, Henry Hotze and Edwin De Leon. A plaque indicates that in 1883–1892 it was also the home of Lord Randolph Churchill, father of Sir Winston Churchill.

Cork Street (W1)

Flag Officer Barron, Commander Maury, Colin McRae, Hildreth Bloodgood and James Spence all stayed at the Burlington Hotel. The hotel was demolished in 1935, and a block of flats, later converted into offices, built on the site.

Covent Garden (WC2)

Assistant Paymaster Forrest was unimpressed with the Tavistock Hotel when he spent a night there in February 1864. It was rebuilt in 1868 and pulled down in 1928.

Crosby Square (EC3)

In September 1863, on the termination of his London mission, James Mason deposited "all the books and other things belonging to the commission" with J. K. Gilliat & Co., merchants and bankers, of 4 Crosby Square. At this time the head of the firm, which had various dealings with the Confederacy, was John Gilliat.

Curzon Street (W1)

The residence of Lord Wharncliffe, president of the Southern Independence Association of London, Wharncliffe House was the scene in February 1865 of a luncheon at which Confederate journalist John Thompson was present, and he commented in his diary on the sumptuous nature of the meal. The white-stuccoed mansion, which still exists, dates from about 1730, and was known for many years as Crewe House. In the twentieth century it was briefly home to two American ambassadors, including Frank Billings Kellog, of the Kellog-Briand Pact (1928), which attempted to outlaw war.

Devonshire Street (W1)

The home of Rev. Arthur Godson, curate of All Souls', Langham Place, 3 Devonshire Street, was where the London Confederate States Aid Association had an office and held its Wednesday evening meetings in the latter part of 1862.

A block of 1930s flats called Goodwood Court stands on the site of 54 Devonshire Street, where James Mason had taken rooms by the middle of May 1862; the house was then occupied by Frederick Hermann, a marquetery manufacturer. Mason was still there at the beginning of October, but a month later had moved to his next and final London address in Upper Seymour Street.

Drury Lane (WC2)

The Theater Royal, where John Morton's nautical extravaganza, *The Alabama*, was performed in March 1864, dates from 1812, though there have been many alterations since then. It is the oldest theater in London.

Euston Square (NW1)

On their first visit to London in May 1862, Commander Semmes and Lieutenant Kell took rooms in Euston Square. It was then still mostly in private occupation, though there was a boarding house on the north side and a private hotel on the east side. This latter building still exists, as does part of the south side of the original square, renamed Endsleigh Gardens in 1879.

Euston Street (NW1)

Lieutenant North stayed at the Euston Hotel in October 1861, on his way to and from Liverpool. The hotel was demolished in 1963 when Euston Station was rebuilt.

Evans' Music and Supper Rooms see **King Street**

Fenton's Hotel see **St. James's Street**

Fishmongers' Hall see **King William Street**

Fleet Street (EC4)

The *Index* was first published by William Freeman at 102 Fleet Street in May 1862, and continued to be published from this address until October 1862, when it moved to Bouverie Street.

Garrick Club see **King Street**

Grosvenor Hotel see **Buckingham Palace Road**

Half Moon Street (W1)

In May 1861 William Yancey came to lodge at 15 Half Moon Street, the home of Arthur Dare, a hosier and glover, who had a shop in nearby Piccadilly. The following month he was called on by James Bulloch, then by Major Anderson, Lieutenant North and Captain Huse. In August 1861 it was the scene of an altercation between Yancey and

Anderson, concerning the former's recommendation of unknown Englishmen for appointments as officers in the Confederate Army and the latter's apparent failure to purchase 20,000 French muskets as a result of slowness. Yancey seems to have remained here until he returned to the Confederacy the following February. The house is now used as offices.

Hampstead Cemetery (NW6)

The Rev. Francis Tremlett, the vicar of St. Peter's, Belsize Park, who died in June 1913, aged 91, is buried here. His grave, which also houses his mother and sister, is marked by a simple cross bearing the patronym "Tremlett."

Hanover Square (W1)

In August 1863, Assistant Paymaster Forrest attended morning service at St. George's Church and was thrilled to discover that one of his eighteenth century ancestors had been married there. St. George's was designed by John James and built in 1721–1724.

Hatchett's Hotel see **Piccadilly**

Haxell's Hotel see **Strand**

Haymarket (SW1)

Major Anderson visited the Theater Royal twice, in August and September 1861. Externally, the building is largely unchanged since then, though there have been two major reconstructions of the interior, in 1879 and 1904.

High Holborn (WC1)

In September 1861 Major Anderson visited the Holborn Casino, a place for dancing rather than gambling. It was rebuilt in 1874, when it became the Holborn Restaurant, a celebrated establishment which survived until 1955. The site is now occupied by offices and a supermarket.

Lieutenant Whittle stayed at Wood's Hotel in October 1864 and here he met his contact, prior to embarking in the *Sea King*, the future CSS *Shenandoah*. The hotel later featured in Charles Dickens' last, unfinished novel, *Edwin Drood* (1870), and was demolished in 1895. A plaque on what was formerly the Prudential Assurance building, which stands on the site, records its approximate location.

Hoxton Street (N1)

John Thompson saw Colin Hazlewood's play, *The Confederate's Daughter*, at the Britannia Theater in August 1865. For many years the Britannia was famous for its melodramas; from 1923 until its destruction by bombing in 1940 it was used as a cinema.

Jermyn Street (SW1)

The Piccadilly Arcade, built in 1910, stands on the site of the Brunswick Hotel, where Belle Boyd stayed from August 1864 until at least January 1865; the owner then was Charles Hughes.

Captain Huse found rooms at 58 Jermyn Street, a lodging house kept by William Wyborn, and in July 1861 he was joined by Major Anderson, who noted in his diary the following month that he was sharing the accommodation with Huse, James Bulloch, and John Fearn (Commissioner Yancey's secretary). Anderson left at the beginning of October, when he returned to the Confederacy, but Huse was still there in March 1862.

Isaac, Campbell & Co., commission merchants and army contractors, established about 1852, were at 71 Jermyn Street, on the corner of Bury Street, by 1861. It was used later by Captain Huse as an accommodation address for correspondence. The firm remained there until after the war, when they moved to East India Avenue, Leadenhall Street. 71 Jermyn Street was rebuilt in 1902.

Belle Boyd was staying at 102 Jermyn Street, a private hotel kept by Mrs. Eliza Wood, in February 1865.

In July 1861 Major Anderson found "cheap lodgings" for Lieutenant North and his family at 108 Jermyn Street, an establishment kept by Henry Porter.

Colonel Peyton, state agent for North Carolina, took furnished rooms in Jermyn Street in November 1861.

Kensington Palace Gardens (W8)

Built in 1845–1846, 12 Kensington Palace Gardens was bought in 1864 by Alexander Collie. He had previously lived in Sussex Gardens, Bayswater, but in January 1865, in a letter to Lord Wharncliffe, he announced that he had now moved to his palatial new abode. Collie lived there until 1875, when he disappeared following his bankruptcy and prosecution for a banking fraud. The house still exists.

King Street (WC2)

James Mason made several visits to the Garrick Club; he dined there in February 1862 as a guest of William Gregory, M.P., and again in April with Alexander Baring, M.P. The club was then at 35 King Street, Covent Garden, and did not move to its present building in Garrick Street until 1864.

Evans' Music-and-Supper Rooms, which Assistant Paymaster Forrest visited in August 1863, were at 43 King Street, Covent Garden, and operated until c1882. They occupied an early eighteenth-century house which has survived, though much restored.

King William Street (EC4)

William Yancey and Dudley Mann were guests of honor at a dinner given by the Fishmongers' Company at Fishmongers' Hall, by London Bridge, in November 1861, at which Yancey made a speech. Fishmongers' Hall, designed by Henry Roberts and completed in 1834, was badly damaged in the London Blitz in 1940.

Knightsbridge (SW7)

Henry Hotze met William E. Gladstone, Chancellor of the Exchequer, at a dinner party at Stratheden House, the residence of Lord Campbell, in July 1862. James Mason had dined there the previous April, and met General Sir James Scarlett, a Crimean War hero, and the novelist Mrs. Caroline Norton. Rutland Court, a block of mansion flats built in 1901, stands on the site.

London Pavilion see **Tichborne Street**

Mansion House (EC4)

The official residence of the lord mayor of London, the Mansion House was built in 1739–1753 to the designs of George Dance, the Elder. Its splendid Egyptian Hall was the scene of a banquet in February 1863, when Confederate commissioner James Mason was a guest and made an impromptu speech.

Morley's Hotel see **Trafalgar Square**

New Bond Street (W1)

The Time and Life Building stands on the site of 157 New Bond Street, where in early August 1863, Assistant Paymaster Forrest and three other Confederate naval officers were lodging. The building was then occupied at street level by Henry Browne, a tailor, but the upper part was let as rooms. Later, at the beginning of March 1865, a dozen officers from the *Florida* arrived there, on their way to join the CSS *Stonewall*.

William Houghton, a stationer, occupied 162 New Bond Street when Commander Maury stayed there in May 1863. The five-story building, used as shop and office premises, still exists.

Olympic Theater see **Wych Street**

Osnaburgh Street (NW1)

For many years 10 Osnaburgh Street was the home and studio of sculptor John Foley, and the statue of General "Stonewall" Jackson was made there for the British Jackson Monumental Fund. Work on the statue was in progress by July 1865, though it was not completed until shortly before the sculptor's death in 1874. No. 10 subsequently became No. 30 and there is now a block of flats on the site.

Oxford Street (W1)

Assistant Paymaster Forrest paid a visit to the Princess's Theater in July 1863, but was unimpressed, both with the theater itself and the play (*Romeo and Juliet*). The Princess's Theater was destroyed by fire in 1880; though rebuilt, it closed in 1902 and was converted into shops. A modern shopping complex called Oxford Walk stands on the site.

Pall Mall (SW1)

Goody & Jones, military tailors, of 40 Pall Mall, advertised the availability of "Confederate Grey Cloth" in the *Index*. Their narrow-fronted, five-story building, with a stuccoed facade, still exists.

Piccadilly (W1)

The Piccadilly Hotel stands on the site of the St. James's Hall where Hiram Fuller gave a lecture about secession in December 1861. It was then a new building, opened only three years previously. Built as a concert hall, it became famous for its minstrel shows, as well as being used for lectures and readings. It was demolished in 1905.

The only West End church to be designed by Christopher Wren, St. James's church was the scene of Belle Boyd's wedding in August 1864; it was rebuilt following bomb damage in World War II.

Major Anderson and Lieutenant North stayed at Hatchett's Hotel when they first arrived in London in June 1861, and Anderson stayed there twice more the following month. It was rebuilt in 1886 but proved unsuccessful and was forced to close, though Hatchett's Restaurant perpetuated the name for many years.

94 Piccadilly, then called Cambridge House, was the home of Lord Palmerston from 1857 until his death in 1865. Confederates who came to see Palmerston included Colonel Peyton in May 1862, Edwin De Leon in July 1862, and James Mason, who had two meetings with him, in July 1864 and March 1865. The house, which still exists, was occupied by the Naval and Military Club from 1866 until 2000. Palmerston's residence here is commemorated by a plaque.

By mid–February 1862 James Mason had moved to 109 Piccadilly, a rooming house kept by Robert Francis. There until at least the beginning of May, Mason subsequently moved to an address in Devonshire Street.

Polygraphic Hall see **William IV Street**

Portland Place (W1)

The Royal Institute of British Architects' building occupies the site of 24 (now 66) Portland Place, which housed the U.S. legation at the outbreak of the Civil War. Confederate commissioner Dudley Mann called there in April 1861, on his arrival in London, to see outgoing minister George Dallas.

The U.S. legation was at 5 Upper Portland Place (now 98 Portland Place) from 1862 until 1866. When the Civil War ended, several Confederates living in London went there to obtain passports to return to America, including Hildreth Bloodgood, Colin McRae's assistant, and Commander Webb, formerly of the CSS *Atlanta*. A plaque records its diplomatic role as well as the fact that it was the home of Henry Adams, who became a distinguished historian.

Princess's Theater see **Oxford Street**

Regent Street (W1)

The Society for Promoting the Cessation of Hostilities in America had its headquarters at 215 Regent Street. Other occupants of these premises included Bosworth & Harrison, who published the Rev. Francis Tremlett's topical sermon, *Christian Brotherhood*, in 1863.

Russell Square (WC1)

After their return from Paris in November 1861, Lieutenant North and his family lodged at 37 Russell Square, on the corner of Montague Place, a private residence occupied by the Misses Ellis. They were certainly there by January 1862, and remained until at least June, after which they moved to Scotland. Stewart House, neo–Georgian offices built for the University of London in the 1980s, now stands on the site.

Sackville Street (W1)

When Commander Maury came to London in 1862, he found rooms at 10 Sackville Street, a house whose main occupant was William Frohlich, a military tailor. He was still there in September 1863, but by the following month had moved across the road to 43 Sackville Street, where his landlady was a Mrs. Hopkinson. 10 Sackville Street was rebuilt in 1961–1962, and a modern block called Pegasus House occupies the site of No. 43.

In July 1864, on her arrival in England, Georgiana Walker lodged for a few days at 34 Sackville Street, where she found that one of the other residents was Rose Greenhow, whom she had met in Bermuda. Mrs. Greenhow left in August, but Mrs. Walker again stayed there in September with her husband, Major Walker. The premises then were partly occupied by John Johnstone, an army clothier, and today are still in commercial use.

St. George's Church see **Hanover Square**

St. Helen's Place (EC3)

Sinclair, Hamilton & Co., commission merchants, had been at 11 St. Helen's Place since the 1850s. A storeroom, where Captain Huse proposed depositing future purchases of arms, and which Major Anderson refers to as "our warehouse," may have been there. The firm later moved to 17 St. Helen's Place, where it remained for many years after the Civil War.

St. James's Church see **Piccadilly**

St. James's Hall see **Piccadilly**

St. James's Street (SW1)

Because of the *Trent* incident, James Mason found himself a celebrity, "called on by a great number of gentlemen within the first few days" of his arrival at Fenton's Hotel at the end of January 1862. How long he was there is uncertain, but by mid–February he had moved to an address in Piccadilly. Fenton's Hotel closed and was demolished in 1886.

St. Mildred's Court (EC2)

The short-lived London Confederate States Commercial League was located at 7 St. Mildred's Court, Poultry, in 1863. The honorary secretary was James Yeomans, of the firm of Elizabeth Yeomans & Son, wholesale gun, pistol and rifle makers, and sword cutlers, whose address it was.

St. Peter's Church & Vicarage see **Belsize Square**

Savile Row (W1)

A four-story, stucco-fronted house, 17 Savile Row contained the offices of the Confederate States Commercial Agency between 1862 and 1865. Henry Hotze also resided there and was visited by men like Lord Campbell, a leading member of the Southern lobby in the House of Lords; John Thompson, who came to London to work on the *Index*, lodged there in August 1864 and possibly until he returned to America in 1866. At that time, Savile Row was mainly occupied by physicians and surgeons, and had not yet become world-famous as the home of London's finest tailors. No. 17 was the home of Dr. Richard King, and after he left in 1867 the house served as the offices of London University, and then as the Burlington Fine Arts Club, but is now used for business purposes. 17 Savile Row was a center of Confederate activity in London and is one of the most important sites to survive. A plaque records that it was also the home of architect George Basevi, 1829–1845.

Seymour Street (W1)

By the beginning of November 1862 James Mason had moved to 24 Upper Seymour Street (later 46 Seymour Street), a rooming house kept by the Misses Frances and Elizabeth Davies, and this became his chief base in London. He left for Paris at the end of September 1863, after receiving instructions to terminate his mission to London, but returned briefly about the middle of October to clear up some outstanding matters. In a letter to Judah Benjamin written about this time, he speaks of "having given up my house"; whether this means he rented all the available accommodation, or is simply a figure of speech, is not clear. Nonetheless, he made so many return visits to London, always staying at this address, that he must have made special arrangements to have rooms kept ready for him. In 1864 he was there from mid–February through the beginning of April, from early June through early August, in late September, probably in mid–October and in December. He was there again in January 1865, but had returned to Paris when Duncan Kenner arrived in late February, and came back to London with him at the beginning of March. When the war ended he was still there, and remained until the end of April 1866, when he left for Liverpool, en route for Montreal, where he was reunited with his family.

Stable Yard (SW1)

James Mason twice visited Stafford House, "perhaps the largest and most sumptuous in London," as a guest of the Duke and Duchess of Sutherland in May 1862. The first occasion was a glittering affair, when "a great crowd of the nobility" and members of the royal family, *"it was said*, were present"; the second was a dinner party which included such guests as Baron Rothschild. Perhaps Mason might have been less enraptured had he known that it had also been the scene of a luncheon given in honor of Harriet Beecher Stowe in 1853, when she was presented with a gold bracelet made in the form of a slave's shackle. Stafford House was built between 1825 and 1841 and renamed Lancaster House after it was presented to the nation in 1913; it is now used for government conferences and receptions.

Strand (WC2)

An account was opened at Coutts Bank, at 59 Strand, for the British Jackson Monumental Fund in June 1863. Founded in 1692, the bank came into the possession of the Coutts family in 1755, and under the direction of Thomas Coutts (d. 1822), it became a leading financial institution, numbering many distinguished people, including members of the royal family, among its clients. Now at 440 Strand, it was rebuilt in 1904 and again in 1978.

In October 1864 the *Index* moved from Bouverie Street to a large rented house at 291 Strand, and from then until it ceased publication in August 1865 was published from there.

A large establishment ("upwards of one hundred rooms"), Haxell's Hotel advertised in both the *Index* and the *London American*. Confederate journalist John Thompson stayed there when he first arrived in London in July 1864. The hotel, which was in two parts, separated by Exeter Hall, closed in the late 1920s; the Strand Palace Hotel, still popular with American visitors, stands on the site.

Major Anderson visited the Adelphi Theater in September 1861, shortly before his return to the Confederacy. The present Adelphi Theater dates from 1930.

Stratheden House see **Knightsbridge**

Tavistock Hotel see **Covent Garden**

Tichborne Street (W1)

Assistant Paymaster Forrest visited the London Pavilion Music Hall in August 1863. It was demolished in 1885 when Piccadilly Circus and Shaftesbury Avenue were constructed. A new London Pavilion, whose facade still exists, was built, but on a different site.

Trafalgar Square (WC2)

Captain Huse stayed at Morley's Hotel in May 1861, when he first arrived in London; a Mr. Davis, president of a New Orleans bank, met Major Anderson there in September 1861 to talk about financial matters; "a great carnival" was held there in March 1863 to celebrate the initial success of the Confederate Cotton Loan; and Assistant Paymaster Forrest stayed there twice, in February and April 1864. In 1921 Morley's Hotel became the first South Africa House; it was replaced by the present building in 1935.

Tussaud's Waxworks see **Baker Street**

Victoria Street (SW1)

William Yancey and Pierre Rost stayed at the Westminster Palace Hotel in May 1861, and Yancey returned there in August, when there was a dinner for Dudley Mann, John Fearn, Major Anderson and Richard Meade (a former U.S. minister to Brazil), "a very handsome affair, given in honour of the Confederates." Later, in March 1863, Midshipman Morgan spent several weeks there, prior to joining his ship, the CSS *Georgia*. Converted into offices after World War I and renamed Abbey House, it was demolished in the 1970s.

Wharncliffe House see **Curzon Street**

William IV Street (WC2)

Henri Drayton's show *Federals and Confederates* was staged at the Polygraphic Hall, in what was then King William Street, from March until May 1863. The Polygraphic Hall, which had opened in 1854, was converted into a theater in 1869; it was demolished in 1896 for an extension to Charing Cross Hospital.

Wood's Hotel see **High Holborn**

Wych Street (WC2)

Major Anderson visited the Olympic Theater in August 1861. It was rebuilt in 1890 but demolished in 1905 when the area was cleared for the building of the Aldwych.

Chapter Notes

Introduction

1. First reports of the Battle of Gettysburg (July 1–3, 1863) did not appear in the *London Times* till July 17, and the fall of Vicksburg (July 4, 1863) till the 20th. The occupation of Richmond (April 3, 1865) was first reported in the *Times* on April 15, with official dispatches in full two days later. Lee's surrender (April 9, 1865) was first known about in London on April 23, with reports appearing in the *Standard* on April 24 and the *Times* the following day.

2. There was at least one proposal for an Atlantic cable during the war. In 1862 a man called Henry Cook put forward a scheme for a cable linking the Confederate States with Europe and the details were forwarded to Richmond; Cook was told that the idea would be considered when peace was secured. *Official Records of the Union and Confederate Navies* (ORN), ser. II, vol. 3, 545, 666.

3. Graham Storey, *Reuter's Century, 1851–1951* (London: Max Parrish, 1951), 33–34; Donald Read, *The Power of News: The History of Reuters, 1849–1989* (Oxford: Oxford University Press, 1992), 35.

4. In *The Secret Service of the Confederate States in Europe* (New York: Thomas Yoseloff, 1959), first published in 1883, naval agent James Bulloch mentions the delays in communicating by letter and the danger of writing at length about important topics because of the danger of correspondence being captured.

1— London in the 1860s

1. John Timbs, *Curiosities of London* (London: Longmans, Green, 1868), 27.

2. *Census of England & Wales, 1861, Vol. 3. General Report* (1863), Table 133.

3. See Gavin Stamp, *The Changing Metropolis: Earliest Photographs of London, 1839–1879* (Harmondsworth, Middlesex, UK: Viking, 1984), for illustrations of what 1860s London really looked like, including the chaos caused by the construction of the Metropolitan Railway, views of Battersea, Southwark and Waterloo Bridges, Morley's Hotel, Her Majesty's Theater and the International Exhibition in South Kensington.

4. Details of maps are in Ralph Hyde, *Printed Maps of Victorian London, 1851–1900* (Folkstone, UK: Dawson, 1975).

5. *Collins' Illustrated Atlas of London*, with introduction by H. J. Dyos, was reissued by Leicester University Press in 1973.

6. Quoted in William Kent, *London for Americans* (London: Staples Press, 1950), 141.

7. *Murray's Modern London 1860* (reprinted by Old House Books, 2003), xii.

8. Ibid.

9. Ibid., xiii.

10. Ibid., xiv–xv.

11. George F. Pardon, *The Popular Guide to London and Its Suburbs* (London: Routledge, Warne & Routledge, 1862), 25.

12. *Index*, January 5, 1865.

13. Timbs, 442.

14. Pardon, 47.

15. *Murray's*, xxxvii.

16. Pardon, 47.

17. Daniel Joseph Kirwan, *Palace and Hovel; or, Phases of London Life* (London: Abelard-Schuman, 1963), 15. First published 1870.

18. Pardon, 48.

19. Ibid., 37.

20. Francis Wey, *A Frenchman Sees the English in the 'Fifties* (1935), quoted in Alison Adburgham, *Shopping in Style* (London: Thames & Hudson, 1979), 112.

21. Pardon, 44.

22. Quoted in Ben Weinreb & Christopher Hibbert (eds.), *The London Encyclopaedia* (London: Macmillan, 1983), 513.

23. Douglas F. Forrest, *Odyssey in Gray: A Diary of Confederate Service, 1863–1865*, ed. William N. Still, Jr. (Richmond: Virginia State Library, 1979), 51.

24. George Augustus Sala, *Twice Round the Clock, or the Hours of the Day and Night in London* (Leicester: Leicester University Press, 1971), 157. First published 1859. A *bezesteen* is a bazaar or marketplace in the East.

25. Henry Mayhew, *The Shops and Companies of London* (London: Strand Printing & Publishing Co., 1865), 101.

26. *Lady's Newspaper*, December 21, 1850.

27. *Murray's*, xxi–xxii.

28. Quoted in M. Willson Disher, *Winkles and Champagne: Comedies and Tragedies of the Music Hall* (London: Batsford, 1938), 15.

29. Forrest, 46. "Welsh rarebit," or "rabbit," is toasted cheese.

30. Edward C. Anderson, *Confederate Foreign*

Agent, ed. W.S. Hoole (University, AL: Confederate Publishing, 1976), 67–68.
   31. *Murray's*, xlviii.
   32. Henry Mayhew, *London's Underworld*. Selections from *Those That Will Not Work*, vol. 4 of *London Labour and the London Poor*, ed. Peter Quennell (London: Spring Books, 1950), 38–39. First published 1862.
   33. *Murray's*, 26.
   34. Mayhew, op. cit. See also Kellow Chesney, *The Victorian Underworld* (Harmondsworth, Middlesex, UK: Pelican Books, 1972) for a detailed description of the criminal scene in the 1860s.

2 — A Diplomatic Presence

   1. *Charleston Mercury*, June 4, 1861, quoted in Thomas A. Bailey, *A Diplomatic History of the American People*, 9th ed. (Englewood Cliffs, NJ: Prentice-Hall, 1974), 333. A surplus of cotton in Britain when the Civil War began postponed the expected cotton famine until 1862. It has been suggested that the failure of the British wheat crop early in the war, resulting in greatly increased imports from North America, may also have helped undermine the power of King Cotton; though European wheat could have been imported, it would have been more expensive than that from America. Clement Eaton, *A History of the Southern Confederacy* (New York: Free Press, 1965), 68–69.
   2. Benjamin Moran, *The Journal of Benjamin Moran, 1857–1865*, eds. Sarah A. Wallace & Frances E. Gillespie, vol. 1 (Chicago: University of Chicago Press, 1948), 799.
   3. Frank L. Owsley, *King Cotton Diplomacy*, 2nd ed. (Chicago: University of Chicago Press, 1959), 52.
   4. Quoted in David P. Crook, *The North, the South and the Powers, 1861–1865* (New York: Wiley, 1974), 27–28.
   5. Brian N. Morton, *Americans in London* (London: Queen Anne Press, 1988), 208. "William L. Yancey's European Diary, March–June 1861," ed. W. Stanley Hoole, *Alabama Review*, 25 (April 1972):138. A report of both visits appeared in the *New York Tribune* and was reprinted in the *National Anti-Slavery Standard*, June 1, 1861. None of the histories of Barings makes any reference to the commissioners' visit.
   6. *London American*, May 8, 1861. This was one of the very few references to their activities by the Federal newspaper.
   7. "William L. Yancey's European Diary," 139. Each commissioner received a monthly allowance of $1,000, a generous amount, considering that the *annual* salary of commercial agent Henry Hotze when he first came to London in 1862 was only $1,500. The Confederate secret service fund accounts (*American Historical Review*, 35 [1930]:814–821) suggest that government officials in London were paid in U.S. currency because there was no British exchange rate with the Confederacy. How they actually received their money is uncertain, but it was probably via Fraser, Trenholm & Company, the Liverpool firm which acted as bankers to the Confederacy.
   8. Yancey to Hunter, August 7, 1861, in James D. Richardson, *Messages and Papers of the Confederacy*, vol. 2 (Nashville, TN: U.S. Publishing, 1905), 57.
   9. Russell had promised Adams in June that he would not see the "pseudo-commissioners" anymore. Richardson, vol. 2, 136.
   10. *Times*, November 12, 1861.
   11. Yancey, Rost and Mann to Hunter, December 2, 1861, in Richardson, vol. 2, 121.
   12. Richardson, vol. 2, 132.
   13. *Punch*, January 18, 1862. *Stone-jug* was slang for "prison"; "a free and an accepted mason" is a Masonic phrase.
   14. *Illustrated Times*, February 8, 1862. Charles P. Cullop, *Confederate Propaganda in Europe, 1861–1865* (Coral Gables, FL: University of Miami Press, 1969), 32.
   15. Yancey to Reid, July 3, 1861, quoted in the *Dictionary of American Biography* article on Yancey. John Bigelow, "The Confederate Diplomatists," *Century Magazine*, 42 (1891):117. "Mr Yancey ... left yesterday," reported the U.S. consul in London on February 5, 1862.
   16. Mary B. Chesnut, *Mary Chesnut's Civil War*, ed. C. Vann Woodward (New Haven, CT: Yale University Press, 1981), 170–171, 520.
   17. H. Adams to C. F. Adams, Jr., June 6, 1862, in Worthington C. Ford (ed.), *A Cycle of Adams Letters, 1861–1865*, vol. 1 (London: Constable, 1920), 154.
   18. Henry Adams, *The Education of Henry Adams* (Boston: Mariner Books, 2000), 184–185.
   19. Moran, vol. 2, 1212.
   20. Mason to Hunter, January 30, 1862, *ORN*, ser. II, vol. 3, 323.
   21. Virginia Mason, *Public Life and Diplomatic Correspondence of James Murray Mason* (Roanoke, VA: Stone Printing & Manufacturing Co., 1903), 340–342.
   22. *Times*, February 12, 1863.
   23. Mason, 185.
   24. H. Adams, 185.
   25. *Times*, June 18, June 23, 1863. William L. Garrison, *The Letters of William Lloyd Garrison*, ed. Walter M. Merrill, vol. 5, 1861–1867 (Cambridge, MA: Belknap Press of Harvard University Press, 1979), 88, 132–133, 161–162.
   26. C. F. Adams to C. F. Adams, Jr., September 25, 1863, in Ford, vol. 2, 85.
   27. Adams to Adams, Jr., February 17, 1865, ibid., 256–257.
   28. Adams to Seward, March 9, 1865, in *Papers Relating to the Foreign Relations of the United States, 1865*, vol. 1, 199.
   29. *Times*, January 16, 1865; Gladstone to Reynard, April 18, 1865, in C. Collyer, "Gladstone and the American Civil War," *Proceedings of the Leeds Philosophical & Literary Soc*iety, 6 (1948–1952):593.
   30. *Index*, January 19, 1865.
   31. Kenner's mission also included attempting to negotiate a second foreign loan of £15 million, following the proposed establishment of a Confederate bank in Europe.
   32. Moran, vol. 2, 1410.
   33. *Times*, April 17, 1865.
   34. Adams to Seward, April 20, 1865, in *Foreign Relations 1865*, vol. 1, 323.
   35. Moran, vol. 2, 1414.
   36. Mason to Benjamin, May 1, 1865, *ORN*, ser. II, vol. 3, 1277.
   37. Bulloch, vol. 2, 155.

3 — The Propaganda War

1. Mason to Benjamin, May 2, 1862, *ORN,* ser. II, vol. 3, 401. There was a similar flood of pro-Northern books and pamphlets; they are listed in Donaldson Jordan & Edwin J. Pratt, *Europe and the American Civil War* (Boston: Houghton Mifflin, 1931).
2. The German translation, and possibly also the French one, was paid for by the Confederate secret service fund; Hotze himself also contributed towards the cost of the German edition. J. F. Jameson, "The London Expenditures of the Confederate Secret Service," *American Historical Review, 35* (1930):814–815. *ORN,* ser. II, vol. 3, 536.
3. Mason, 340; John W. Cowell, *Southern Secession,* quoted in James T. deKay, *The Rebel Raiders* (New York: Ballantine Books, 2002), 122. Cowell's pamphlet was also paid for by the Confederate secret service fund (Jameson, 815–816).
4. Richardson, vol. 2, 115.
5. Hotze to Hunter, February 23, 1862, *ORN,* ser. II, vol. 3, 346–347.
6. Ibid. The "clubs" were the gentlemen's clubs of Pall Mall and St James's.
7. Ibid.
8. Sir Henry Brackenbury, *Some Memories of My Spare Time* (1909), 108, quoted in Basil L. Crapster, "Thomas Hamber, Tory Journalist," *Victorian Periodicals Newsletter, 8* (1975): 116.
9. Crapster, 117.
10. Hotze to Benjamin, September 26, 1862, *ORN,* ser. II, vol. 3, 535.
11. Hotze to Benjamin, April 25, 1862, ibid., 400–401. Both Brewer and Wetter were involved in the shipping business and later in blockade-running.
12. *Index,* May 1, 1862.
13. Hotze to Benjamin, May 15, 1862, *ORN,* ser. II, vol. 3, 423.
14. H. Adams to C. F. Adams, Jr., June 6, 1862, in Ford, vol. 1, 154.
15. Ephraim D. Adams, *Great Britain and the American Civil War,* vol. 2 (London: Longmans, 1925), 231.
16. *Index,* February 18, 1864.
17. Hotze to Benjamin, September 26, 1862, *ORN,* ser. II, vol. 3, 537.
18. Ibid., 535.
19. He died at Ealing, then a village in Middlesex, and was buried in the crypt of Kensington parish church. *Gentleman's Magazine,* August 1862. *Who Was Who in America, Historical Volume 1607–1896* (Chicago: Marquis, 1963).
20. *American Magazine Journalists, 1850–1900* (*Dictionary of Literary Biography,* vol. 79) (Detroit: Gale Research Inc., 1989), 61. Bledsoe traveled to England with Flag Officer Barron and Lieutenant Whittle in the steamship *Florida.*
21. The articles by "A White Republican" in *Fraser's Magazine* were as follows: "Universal Suffrage in the United States, and Its Consequences" (July 1862); "North and South: The Controversy in a Colloquy" (September 1862); "North and South: The Two Constitutions" (October 1862); "North and South; or, Who Is the Traitor?" (November 1862); "Negroes and Slavery in the United States" (February 1863).
22. S. H. Harris, "John L. O'Sullivan Serves the Confederacy," *Civil War History, 10* (1964):275–290.
23. Hotze to Benjamin, October 24, 1862, *ORN,* ser. II, vol. 3, 567; October 31, 1863, ibid., 944. John Slidell and Dudley Mann both complained about Spence, Slidell in connection with the Erlanger Loan and Mann regarding the Southern Independence Association of London's prospectus.
24. Some people apparently thought that "S" was John Slidell. There were at least forty-two letters, published on the following dates: 1862: February 5; March 18, 22; April 7, 28; May 5, 19, 29; June 4, 11, 16, 17; July 7, 17; August 1, 12, 29; October 3, 9, 11, 23; November 4, 27; December 30. 1863: January 16; June 19; July 2; August 13, 29; September 11, 26; October 9, 29; December 11. 1864: January 4; April 1; June 8; July 13; September 15; November 15; December 12. 1865: January 6.
There is no discernible pattern in their frequency and there may be others which have not yet been found.
25. Hotze to Benjamin, September 26, 1862, *ORN,* ser. II, vol. 3, 537.
26. Jameson, 812.
27. Ibid.
28. Ibid., 814, 816. The exchange rate was then US$4.85 to £1 sterling.
29. Moran, vol. 2, 1114. The *London American* survived for 2 years and 10 months, the *Index* for 3 years and 3 months.
30. Hotze to Benjamin, August 4, 1862, *ORN,* ser. II, vol. 3, 507. Why did Hotze travel all the way to Germany to consult an oculist when an eminent ophthalmic surgeon like William Bowman was just round the corner in Clifford Street?
31. William E. Gladstone, *The Gladstone Diaries,* vol. 6, 1861–1868, ed. H. C. G. Matthews (Oxford: Oxford University Press, 1978), 138; Richard Shannon, *Gladstone,* vol. 1, 1809–1865 (London: Hamish Hamilton, 1982), 463.
32. Hotze to Benjamin, August 4, 1862, *ORN,* ser. II, vol. 3, 506.
33. Jameson, 813.
34. Ibid., 816–817. The posters cost US$522, or approximately £108.
35. *Autobiography of Moncure D. Conway* (1904), vol. 1, 365, quoted in David A. Wilson, *Carlyle to Threescore-and-ten, 1853–1865* (London: Kegan Paul, 1929), 556.
36. *Antebellum Writers in New York and the South,* in *Dictionary of Literary Biography* (*DLB*), vol. 3 (Detroit: Gale Research Inc., 1979), 330–332. See also *American Magazine Journalists, 1741–1850* (*DLB,* vol. 73, 1988), 327–330, and *Antebellum Writers in the South, Second Series* (*DLB,* vol. 248, 2001), 364–369.
37. "From the Diary of John R. Thompson," *Confederate Veteran* (March 1929), 99.
38. *Index,* August 12, 1865. There is a complete file of the *Index* in the British Library Newspaper Library at Colindale, London NW9. The copies presumably came from the *Index* office as they bear the signatures of the publishers, Henry F. Mackintosh and John B. Hopkins.

4 — Supplies for the Confederate Army

1. Caleb Huse, *Supplies for the Confederate Army* (1904), quoted in Philip Van Doren Stern, *Secret Missions of the Civil War* (New York: Bonanza Books, 1990), 76.
2. Ibid., 77. In June 1863 Huse informed McRae he had been offered the opportunity to buy the London Armory Company; nothing came of this, though the following January it was recommended to Col. Gorgas that an unidentified armaments factory in England should be acquired (Thomas Boaz, *Guns for Cotton* [Shippensburg, PA: Burd Street Press, 1996], 72).
3. *Official Records of the Union and Confederate Armies* (ORA), ser. IV, vol. 1, 344.
4. Dunbar Rowland, *Jefferson Davis, Constitutionalist* (Jackson, MS: Mississippi Department of Archives & History, 1923), vol. viii, 311.
5. Victor A. Hatley, "Monsters in Campbell Square," *Northamptonshire Past and Present*, vol. 4 (1966), 54. Isaac, Campbell & Co. had a boot and shoe factory in Northampton from 1857 until 1861, which was then taken over by Turner Bros., Hyde & Co., a London firm which advertised in the *Index*. Part of the cargo of the *Justitia*, a blockade-runner owned by Thomas Begbie, which left London in November 1862, was supplied by them.
6. Anderson, 31.
7. Peggy Robbins, "Caleb Huse, Confederate Agent," *Civil War Times Illustrated* (August 1978):35.
8. Anderson, 31.
9. Ibid., 43. James Bulloch was a naval purchasing agent, John Fearn was Commissioner Yancey's secretary and George Jones was a visitor from Savannah.
10. Ibid., 61. At the end of the war, Helm returned to London with General Breckinridge, whom he had encountered in Havana (A. J. Hanna, *Flight into Oblivion* [Baton Rouge: Louisiana State University Press, 1999], 232).
11. Pardon, 177–178.
12. Ibid.
13. Anderson, 58. Archibald Hamilton's country residence was a house called Southbarrow, at Southborough, then a hamlet two miles from the village of Bromley, Kent.
14. Ibid., 62, 58.
15. Ibid., 67.
16. Ibid., 71. Henry Hotze was born in Zurich, in the German-speaking part of Switzerland.
17. Moran, vol. 2, 893.
18. Invoice dated January 1862, Pickett Papers, Library of Congress; *The American Civil War: A Centennial Exhibition* (Washington: Library of Congress, 1961), 26.
19. John W. Dubose, *Life and Times of William Lowndes Yancey* (Birmingham, AL: Roberts & Son, 1892), 661–664; *Foreign Relations, 1862*, 108.
20. William Diamond, "Imports of the Confederate Government from Europe," *Journal of Southern History*, 6 (1940):470–503.
21. *ORA*, ser. IV, vol. 3, 674.
22. Emma H. Ferguson, "Running the Blockade: A Confederate Reminiscence," *Lippincott's Monthly Magazine* (October 1893):493–502. Major Ficklin had previously been to England as a Treasury agent.
23. It was apparently the "magnificent new uniform" that Lee wore at Appomattox and which was also used by the French sculptor M. J. A. Mercie when modeling the equestrian statue of Lee which stands in Monument Avenue, Richmond, Virginia. Emma H. Ferguson, "Sketch of Major Ferguson," *Confederate Veteran* (March 1899):99–100.
24. John B. Jones, *A Rebel War Clerk's Diary*, ed. Earl S. Miers (Baton Rouge: Louisiana State University Press, 1993), 258.
25. He is sometimes referred to as General McRae: this was a pre-war rank in the Mississippi state militia and has nothing to do with the Civil War.
26. McRae to Seddon, February 19, 1864, *ORA*, ser. IV, vol. 3, 155. Before Bloodgood arrived, McRae was assisted in the initial examination by H. O. Brewer, a business associate from Mobile who was involved in blockade-running.
27. For the various ways in which the Confederates financed their overseas purchases, see Richard C. Todd, *Confederate Finance* (Athens: University of Georgia Press, 1954), particularly chapter 6, "Financial Operations Abroad."
28. Quoted in Todd, 187.
29. Georgiana G. Walker, *The Private Journal of Georgiana Gholson Walker*, ed. Dwight F. Henderson (Tuscaloosa, AL: Confederate Publishing, 1963), 104. The vessel's arrival was reported to the U.S. consul, Freeman Morse.
30. Ibid., 109.
31. Angus J. Johnston, *Virginia Railroads in the Civil War* (Chapel Hill: University of North Carolina Press, 1961), 178–180; *ORA*, ser. IV, vol. 2, 409–410, 841–842.
32. Anderson, 4.
33. Ibid., 66.
34. John L. Peyton, *The American Crisis*, vol. 1 (London: Saunders, Otley, 1867), 334.
35. *Times*, November 26, 1861.
36. Peyton to Vance, January 15, 1863, in *The Papers of Zebulon Baird Vance*, ed. Joe A. Mobley, vol. 2, 1863 (Raleigh, NC: State Dept. of Archives & History, 1995). John Wilson was a bookseller and minor publisher.
37. *The Papers of Zebulon Baird Vance*, ed. Frontis W. Johnston, vol. 1, 843–862 (Raleigh, NC: State Dept. of Archives & History, 1963), lii–liii, 288, 360; Stephen R. Wise, *Lifeline of the Confederacy* (Columbia: University of South Carolina Press, 1991), 105–106.
38. *ORA*, ser. IV, vol. 1, 545.
39. Louise B. Hill, *Joseph E. Brown and the Confederacy* (Chapel Hill: University of North Carolina Press, 1939), 119.
40. The invoice, dated May 15, 1863, is in *ORN*, ser. II, vol. 3, 940.

5 — Vessels Suitable for Our Purposes

1. Raimondo Luraghi, *A History of the Confederate Navy* (London: Chatham Publishing, 1996), 20–21. It may also have been difficult at this time to fund the purchase of the cotton or transport it to England (Lester, 91).

2. Because he had commanded a mail steamer, he was often referred to as Captain Bulloch, which has led to confusion over his rank: he left the U.S. Navy as a lieutenant and was later commissioned as a commander in the C.S. Navy, but he never held the naval rank of captain. There is also a query concerning the spelling of his middle name. In the introduction to the 1959 edition of his memoirs, the *Dictionary of American Biography* and the *Historical Times Illustrated Encyclopedia of the Civil War*, it is spelt Dunwody; elsewhere, including on his tombstone in Toxteth Park Cemetery, Liverpool, it is Dunwoody.

3. Bulloch to Mallory, August 13, 1861, *ORN*, ser. II, vol. 2, 86.

4. Bulloch, vol. 1, 100.

5. It has been suggested that Bulloch's informant was a Foreign Office clerk called Victor Buckley (Luraghi, 225, 422).

6. Lester, 110–112.

7. *Times*, January 26, 1865. There were also plans for the Dudgeon Bros. to build six torpedo boats for the Confederate Navy, but they were still under construction when the war ended (Milton F. Perry, *Infernal Machines* [Baton Rouge: Louisiana State University Press, 1965], 178).

8. *Times*, March 16, 1865.

9. Bulloch to Whittle, October 6, 1864, *ORN*, ser. II, vol. 2, 731–732.

10. A number of Confederates who came to England during the Civil War brought, or were joined by, their wives and children. In addition to Mrs. North, there was Mrs. Bledsoe, Mrs. Bulloch, Mrs. Clements, Mrs. Ferguson, Mrs. Hobson, probably Mrs. Huse, Mrs. Peyton and Mrs. Walker; Dudley Mann's son, Grayson, also came to London to act as his secretary, and Cdr. Maury was accompanied by 13-year-old Matthew, Jr.

11. James H. North Diary, July 29, 1861, #862, Southern Historical Collection, Wilson Library, University of North Carolina at Chapel Hill.

12. Anderson, 66.

13. North Diary, October 7–10, 1861. Bulloch came to England as a civilian; it was not until January 1862 that he became a commander in the Confederate Navy.

14. North to Mallory, March 29, 1862, *ORN*, ser. II, vol. 2, 176–177.

15. Quoted in Lester, 122.

16. *Times*, April 7, 1863, quoted in Douglas H. Maynard, "The Forbes-Aspinwall Mission," *Mississippi Valley Historical Review*, 45 (1958):74. Confederate commissioner James Mason had also been informed of their mission by a contact in New York.

17. Edgar Stringer seems to have specialized in introductions: apart from the two naval contracts with J. & G. Thomson, he also introduced Nelson Clements, a Texas state purchasing agent, to Sinclair, Hamilton & Co.

18. Sinclair to North, February 2, 1863, *ORN*, ser. II, vol. 2, 350.

19. Douglas H. Maynard, "The Confederacy's Super-Alabama," *Civil War History*, 5 (1959): 80–95. Some of the guns intended for it were later installed in the *Shenandoah*.

20. Raphael Semmes, *Memoirs of Service Afloat*, ed. John M. Taylor (Baton Rouge: Louisiana State University Press, 1996), 347–348. It is interesting to compare Semmes' rose-tinted view of Mason with that of Benjamin Moran and Henry Adams. Apart from newspaper reports, an article about the *Sumter* had appeared in the *London Journal* in March 1862, and there were several more pieces mentioning Semmes by name later that year.

21. Ibid., 785.

22. Part of this took the form of letters to the newspapers, e.g., *Times*, "A Voice from Secessia," December 23, 1862; "Prospects of the Confederates," August 20, 1863; and "The War in America," September 19, 1863, all of which were signed.

23. Bulloch, vol. 2, 261. After the war, Maury handed over the rights to his electric torpedoes to Nathaniel J. Holmes, "electrical engineer and contractor," who patented them in December 1865 (Perry, 191).

24. James M. Morgan, *Midshipman in Gray: Selections from Recollections of a Rebel Reefer*, ed. R. Thomas Campbell (Shippensburg, PA: Burd Street Press, 1997), 85. Maury remained a lieutenant in the U.S. Navy for many years and was not promoted to commander till 1858. In the Virginia State Navy and the C.S. Navy, he also held the rank of commander; sometime after his return to America in 1868, he was apparently given the honorary rank of commodore. His letter to the *Times*, December 23, 1862, was written from the Albemarle Hotel, where presumably he was staying for a few days.

25. Maury, Jr., to Mrs. Ann Herndon Maury, March 14, 1863, in Frances L. Williams, *Matthew Fontaine Maury* (New Brunswick, NJ: Rutgers University Press, 1963), 405.

26. Morgan, 85.

27. Ibid., 88.

28. Ibid., 89. Lt. William L. Maury was promoted to commander about this time.

29. Maury to Carter, July 24, 1863, *ORN*, ser. II, vol. 2, 471.

30. Forrest, 39.

31. Ibid., 45. Paymaster Felix Senac subsequently served in Paris under Flag Officer Barron; his daughter, Ruby, married Henry Hotze after the war. Lt. Charles Graves served with Forrest on the *Rappahannock*, and Lt. Charles M. Morris was on his way to take command of the *Florida*.

32. According to Douglas Forrest's diary, Hobson appears to have died in the early part of 1865, though no record of his death in England has been found.

33. The Confederates were not the only ones trying to recruit in London: in November 1864 the *Times* carried reports of attempts to engage men, in both London and Lancashire, supposedly for a glassworks in New York, but in reality for the Union Army. Several hundred men were already on board an emigrant ship at Liverpool when this violation of the Foreign Enlistment Act was discovered; they were subsequently sent home. The Federals were also attempting to recruit in Ireland at this time.

34. *Foreign Relations*, 1864, pt. 1, 18–19.

35. *Times*, February 7, 1865.

36. Adams to Seward, April 28, 1864, in *Foreign Relations, 1864*, 1, 642.

37. *ORN*, ser. II, vol. 2, 671.

38. Morse to Adams, June 15, 1864, in *Foreign Relations, 1864*, 185–187.

39. Bulloch, vol. 2, 253.

40. Ibid., 253–254, 256–258.

41. A consular dispatch at the beginning of March

1865 reported rather belatedly that ten or more officers from the CSS *Florida* had arrived in London and were lodging in New Bond Street prior to joining the CSS *Stonewall* (London consular dispatches, March 4, 1865).

42. Wharncliffe Muniments, WhM 461. The honorary secretary of the testimonial fund was probably the Rev. Francis Tremlett. The circular was sent from 28 Charles Street, the offices of Du Pasquier & Tremlett, a firm of lawyers, one of whom, George Tremlett, was the Rev. Tremlett's cousin; it does not indicate where the dinner was to be held.

43. There are useful descriptions of the *Florida*, the *Alabama*, the *Georgia*, the *Rappahannock* and the *Shenandoah* in Lester, 212–221.

6 — *The Spying Game*

1. Harriet C. Owsley, "Henry Shelton Sanford and Federal Surveillance Abroad, 1861–1865," *Mississippi Valley Historical Review, 48* (1961–1962):212–213.
2. Ibid., 213.
3. *Times*, January 23, 1862. Pollaky, who was later assisted by his son and namesake, subsequently moved his office to Paddington Green, where it functioned until the 1880s. He appears in Gilbert & Sullivan's light opera *Patience* (1881) as "Paddington Pollaky."
4. "On Duty with Inspector Field," *Household Words*, June 14, 1851. He was also the original of Inspector Bucket in Dickens' *Bleak House* (1853).
5. Owsley, 217.
6. It had been in operation since at least August; Major Anderson noted in his diary on September 26 that he, as well as Bulloch and Huse, had been followed for the past month by detectives employed by the U.S. minister.
7. Moran, vol. 2, 946.
8. At the time of the Civil War, the United States had nine consulates in England. In addition to London and Liverpool, they were located at Falmouth, Plymouth, Southampton, Bristol, Leeds, Manchester and Newcastle. There were also three in Scotland, one in Wales and five in Ireland.
9. London consular dispatches, November 1, 1861.
10. Ibid., November 2, 1861.
11. Ibid., January 24, 1862.
12. Ibid., March 14, 1862.
13. Ibid., June 5, 1863.
14. Ibid., November 7, 1862.
15. Ibid., July 16, 1864. Bunting is mentioned several times in Douglas Forrest's diary. According to him, "that dog Bunting" was a former doctor who had been expelled from Canada for performing an abortion.
16. Ibid., July 6, 1864.
17. Forrest records a visit to them on April 12, 1864, when he met "Thomas Gordon," a name sometimes used by Thomas Bold, Cdr. Maury's cousin.
18. Morse to Adams, June 15, 1864, in *Foreign Relations, 1864*, pt. 2, 185.
19. Ibid., 186.
20. Ibid., 202.
21. Ibid., 187. The ship had, in fact, been intended for the Virginia Volunteer Navy, but the money to pay for it was not forthcoming.
22. London consular dispatches, July 18, 1862, July 25, 1862.
23. Ibid., September 23, 1864.
24. Ibid., July 19, 1861. Chester G. Hearn, *Gray Raiders of the Sea* (Baton Rouge: Louisiana State University Press, 1992), 154.
25. Owsley, 214.
26. Bulloch, vol. 1, 102.
27. Ibid., vol. 2, 38.
28. Ibid., vol. 1, 425.
29. Luraghi, 225, 422; Adams, vol. 2, 120. Buckley's name also appears in the list of supposed Confederate bondholders published in the *New York Herald*, December 9, 1865, with the comment: "This man is a clerk in that department of the Foreign Office through which passed all correspondence with or about the United States." Major Anderson also claimed to have a contact in the Foreign Office, a relative of a Mr. Bond, a member of the firm of Sinclair, Hamilton & Co.
30. Anderson, 63–64.
31. Ibid., 64.
32. Ibid., 64.
33. Ibid., 65.
34. Ibid., 68–69.
35. K. Bourne (ed.), *British Documents on Foreign Affairs: Reports and Papers from the Foreign Office Confidential Print*. Pt. 1, ser. C, vol. 6, *The Civil War Years 1862–65*, doc. 58, Huse to Major (?), April 1, 1862.
36. London consular dispatches, March 5, 1864. Edward (or Edwin) Archer's name does not appear in the list of commissioned and warrant officers in J. Thomas Scharf's *History of the Confederate States Navy* (1887), 819–820; like Daniel Talley, he was probably an officer in the Virginia Volunteer Navy.

7 — *The Cotton Loan*

1. Quoted in Philip Van Doren Stern, *The Confederate Navy: A Pictorial History* (New York: Da Capo Press, 1992), 157. John Slidell formed a close relationship with Emile Erlanger, which became even closer when his daughter Marguerite married the latter in 1864.
2. In her carefully researched article on the Erlanger Loan, Judith Gentry concluded that "the Confederates could not have negotiated a better contract than that made with Erlanger & Company, and a comparison of the Erlanger contract with offers from other firms removes all doubt of it" (Judith F. Gentry, "A Confederate Success in Europe," *Journal of Southern History, 36* [1970]:182).
3. At the time of the Loan, the (unofficial) Confederate exchange rate was $13.33 : £1 sterling, which would have made it worth $39,990,000. Using the U.S. exchange rate of $4.85 : £1 sterling, it was worth $14,550,000. The prospectus for the Loan is in the *Times*, March 20, 1863, the *Economist*, March 21, 1863, and is reprinted in *The Times Reports the American Civil War* (London: Times Books, 1975), 110–113.
4. Samuel B. Thompson, *Confederate Purchasing Operations Abroad* (Chapel Hill: University of North Carolina Press, 1935), 58.
5. *Times,* March 20, 1863.
6. Quoted in Richard Roberts, *Schroders: Merchants and Bankers* (Basingstoke: Macmillan, 1992), 66.
7. *Economist,* March 21, 1863.
8. Ibid.
9. Ibid.

10. Moran, vol. 2, 1137–1138.
11. *Times*, August 6, 1863.
12. There is a useful summary of Erlanger Loan quotations, taken from the *Index* and *The Times*, in Lester, app. II, 204–208.
13. *Times*, August 14, 1865.
14. Ibid., October 2, 1865.
15. Thomas J. Keiser, *The English Press and the American Civil War* (Reading University PhD thesis, 1971), 298.
16. A list of major Erlanger Loan bondholders, from John Bigelow, *Lest We Forget: Gladstone, Morley and the Confederate Loan of 1863* (New York, De Vinne Press, 1905), is reprinted in Lester, app. III, 209.
17. Quoted in *Times*, October 7, 1865.
18. Ibid., October 9, 1865.
19. *Morning Star*, October 9, 1865.
20. *New York Herald*, December 9, 1865. Sixty-six of the names had previously appeared in the *Index* as subscribers to General Jackson's statue, but none of them included men such as Vice-Admiral Sir Provo Wallis, John M. Chamberlain, Thomas G. Taylor, William B. Morgan, Joseph Joseph, Spencer Herapath and Joseph Sebag, who are known to have attended meetings of bondholders in the autumn of 1865.
21. *Times*, December 21, 1865.
22. Ibid., November 3, 1865.
23. *Morning Star*, October 3, 1865; reprinted in Bigelow, 8.
24. Ibid., November 15, 1866.
25. Daniel Grinnan, "Disposition of Confederate Funds," *Confederate Veteran* (July 1929):328–329. For an account of the post-war history of the Cotton Loan, see John C. Schwab, *The Confederate States of America, 1861–1865: A Financial and Industrial History of the South During the Civil War* (New York, C. Scribner's Sons, 1901), 37–39.
26. Gentry, 171.
27. Schwab, 36.
28. Ibid., 43; Gentry, 188.

8 — *Business with the Southern States*

1. The engineer who installed the machinery was a Mr. McFarland, whom both Capt. Huse and Major Anderson encountered at the London Armory Company in 1861, working as a Federal purchasing agent. *ORA*, ser. IV, vol. 1, 345. George Measom, *The Official Illustrated Guide to the South-Eastern Railway and Its Branches*, 1858 (reprinted by E & W Books Ltd., 1970), 132–136; Robert E. Gardner, *Small Arms Makers* (New York: Crown, 1963), *passim.*
2. Howard L. Blackmore, *A Dictionary of London Gunmakers, 1350–1850* (Oxford: Phaidon Christie's, 1986), 39. Jackson's pistol, still in its original case with all its accoutrements, is in the Museum of the Confederacy in Richmond, Virginia. Col. Gorgas's visit to London is mentioned in an advertisement in the *Index* (July 7, 1864), though it is not recorded in his diary. Robert Adams started up again in business in 1866 but died in 1870.
3. Blackmore, 130.
4. S.B. Saul, "The Machine Tool Industry in Britain to 1914," *Business History*, 10 (1968):26–27; Robert E. L. Krick, *Staff Officers in Gray* (Chapel Hill: University of North Carolina Press, 2003), 87; Frank E. Vandiver, *Ploughshares into Swords* (Austin: University of Texas Press, 1952), 174–176.
5. *Times*, December 7, 1861.
6. Adams to Seward, January 24, 1862, in *Foreign Relations, 1862*, 17.
7. Seward to Adams, June 2, 1862, ibid., 108.
8. Moran, vol. 2, 1090.
9. London consular dispatches, January 20, 1865.
10. *Foreign Relations, 1865*, vol. 1, 256–257, 348–350.
11. Moran, vol. 2, 1426. Taliaffero P. Shaffner was secretary of the North Atlantic Telegraph Company and also joint author of an *Illustrated Record of the International Exhibition of 1862.*
12. North to Hood, June 16, 1864, *ORN*, ser. II, vol. 2, 671–672. T. & C. Hood is an example of a firm which dealt with both sides: in December 1863, fifty 68-pounder guns they had supplied for the United States were proved at Woolwich Arsenal, then taken away by Naylor, Vickers & Co., who were acting as agents for the Federal government, and shipped to New York (Bulloch, vol. 1, 362).
13. London consular dispatches, November 25, 1864.
14. *London American*, August 13, 1862.
15. *Index*, October 1, 1863.
16. Ibid., October 22, 1863.
17. Ibid., September 3, 1863.
18. Sally C. Luscomb, *The Collector's Encyclopedia of Buttons* (New York: Crown Publishers, 1967), 46–48; Forrest, 163. A set of 24 gilded, brass Confederate Navy buttons, made by Firmin & Sons and still in their original box, is in the Museum of the Confederacy. The company, which is now based in Birmingham, still has some of the original button-stamping dies, though unfortunately not a complete set. Firmin also made swords, and one formerly owned by Flag Officer French Forrest (Douglas Forrest's father) is also in the Museum of the Confederacy.
19. *Index*, February 15, 1864; ibid., January 5, 1865. An estimated 550,000 pairs of shoes were imported, though English footwear was apparently thought to be no better than that issued by the Confederate government: "English-made shoes were ... lined with stiff paper, and after fording a few times, they came to pieces," one former soldier recalled (Philip Van Doren Stern, *An End to Valor: The Last Days of the Civil War* [Boston: Houghton Mifflin, 1958], 239–240).
20. Mark E. Neely, Jr., et al., *The Confederate Image* (Chapel Hill: University of North Carolina Press, 1987), 8; Lester, 162. In the event, the one-cent orange stamp was never issued.
21. *De La Rue Journal 1862–1865*, MS937, University of Reading Library. The rejected press was apparently transferred to Kent, Paine & Co. of Richmond, Virginia.
22. Lester, 161. The firm also printed paper currency ("greenbacks") for the Federal government.
23. Lorna Houseman, *The House That Thomas Built* (London: Chatto & Windus, 1968), 103; Stern, 306–307, 319.
24. Boaz, 9–10; *Dictionary of American Biography*, vol. 5, 121.

25. Mason to Benjamin, April 30, 1863, *ORN*, ser. II, vol. 3, 754–755.

26. *Index*, August 25, 1864; ibid., November 3, 1864; ibid., November 19, 1863.

27. *Times*, June 14, 1864. It was not only Confederate notes that were being forged: Benjamin Moran noted in his diary (December 13, 1862): "There is a gang of English rogues at Sheffield busily engaged in counterfeiting our Treasury notes."

28. Overend, Gurney turned out to be the owners of freight on Zachariah Pearson's steamer *Circassian*, which was captured off Cuba in May 1862. Their name also appears several times in correspondence published in Frank E. Vandiver's *Confederate Blockade Running through Bermuda, 1861–1865* (Austin: University of Texas Press, 1947).

29. Forrest, 40. James T. Soutter was the former president of the Bank of the Republic in New York and lived in Rome during the war; his daughter Sallie married Lieutenant Charles M. Fauntleroy, the last captain of the ill-fated CSS *Rappahannock*. Details of the proposed £15 million loan are in Thompson, 100–101.

30. *Foreign Relations*, 1864, pt. I, 582–583. The Atlantic Trading Company is not mentioned in *Lifeline of the Confederacy*, Stephen Wise's exhaustive study of blockade-running, and may never actually have commenced operations.

31. Charles Capper, *The Port and Trade of London: Historical, Statistical, Local and General* (London: Smith, Elder & Co., 1862), 182. The collapse of the banking house of Overend, Gurney in 1866 dealt shipbuilding in London a serious blow from which it never really recovered.

32. "Record of Performance and Experiences with Twin-screw Steamers built by J. & W. Dudgeon," in *"Transactions of the Institute of Naval Architects*, 1865, 209–213.

33. *Times*, September 4, 1863. The *Nutfield* was apparently named after the village in Surrey where Edgar Stringer was then living.

34. Scott Russell seems to have had Confederate links which went beyond just building blockade-runners. In April 1864 he approached Charles Francis Adams with what he claimed were Confederate terms for an armistice. Though Adams was naturally skeptical, the information was nevertheless conveyed, via his son, Capt. C. F. Adams, Jr., to Secretary of State W. H. Seward. The State Department went as far as approving an unofficial liaison officer, but he was unreliable and the effort collapsed the following month (*The Letters of Henry Adams, vol. 1, 1858–1868* [Cambridge, MA: Belknap Press, 1982], 434).

35. Mrs. Georgiana Walker, wife of Confederate agent Major Norman Walker, traveled as a passenger in the *Index* from Bermuda to London in June-July 1864, in what was to be its last trip as a blockade-runner, and described the experience in her journal; the trip took 22 days. Details of individual blockade-runners are in Wise.

36. Moran, vol. 2, 1109.

37. *Survey of London*, vol. 37, *North Kensington* (London: Greater London Council, 1973), 168; *Builder* (1865), 677.

38. *Foreign Relations, 1873*, vol. 3, "American-British Claims Committee," 117–123; W. R. Hooper, "Blockade Running," *Harper's New Monthly Magazine* (December 1870):105.

39. *Times*, July 28, 1863. See also October 30, 1863, January 16, 1864, February 6 and 20, 1864, March 7 and 12, 1864, April 25, 1864.

40. Ibid., February 10, 1864. Samuelson was the builder of the *Eugenie*, which was also purchased for the Confederate Ordnance Bureau. Later in 1864, his own firm collapsed and he was forced to sell out to a joint-stock company, which itself went into liquidation in 1866.

41. Collie to Wharncliffe, June 27, 1868, in Wharncliffe Muniments, WhM 461.

42. *Times*, November 29, 1865.

9 — Artistic Reflections, Literary Echoes

1. "From the Diary of John R. Thompson," *Confederate Veteran* (March 1929):100. Most of these plays have never been published, but there are manuscript copies in the Lord Chamberlain's Plays Collection in the Department of Manuscripts at the British Library in London. See also Allardyce Nicoll, *History of English Drama, vol. 5, Late Nineteenth Century Drama, 1850–1900*, 2nd ed. (Cambridge, UK: Cambridge University Press, 1959).

2. *Times*, May 2, 1863; *Index*, April 9, 1863.

3. *Times*, March 25, 1863.

4. Ibid., November 23, 1861, August 10, 1863; *London American*, January 22, 1862. McClellan himself visited London in February 1865 and stayed at the Westminster Palace Hotel.

5. Forrest, 53–54. Lieut. King subsequently served on the CSS *Georgia*.

6. *Times*, June 20, 1865; ibid., July 10, 1865. "General Tom Thumb" (Charles S. Stratton) was a famous American midget who came to England several times. Most of the other Civil War personalities were removed in or before 1869; Madame Tussaud's has no record of a figure of John Wilkes Booth, so it is not known how long he was there.

7. *Illustrated London News*, March 7, 1863.

8. *Times*, November 7, 1863. This was presumably painted by or in association with New York artist Frederic Church, who is known to have contributed to at least one other panorama.

9. Ibid., November 9, 1863.

10. Ibid., November 10, 1863.

11. Ibid., January 10, 1862.

12. *Index*, August 25, 1864.

13. Ibid., December 10, 1863.

14. Ibid., December 8, 1864.

15. Neely, 20–21, 119, 195; *Index*, May 25, 1865.

16. Ibid., June 25, 1863.

17. *Times*, May 26, 1863, May 29, 1863. This phenomenon is examined by Charles P. Cullop in "English Reaction to Stonewall Jackson's Death," *West Virginia History*, 29 (1967):1–5; see also John D. Bennett, "General Jackson's Statue," *Crossfire*, December 2004, 25–26.

18. Moran, vol. 2, 1167.

19. Hotze to Benjamin, June 6, 1863, *ORN*, ser. II, vol. 3, 784.

20. *Index*, April 26, 1864. This may also have been the photograph used by Foley for his statue.

21. Ibid., December 24, 1863. "Volk" was probably

the Bavarian-born sculptor Frederick Volck. The original bust is now in the Confederate White House at Richmond. A plaster statuette of Robert E. Lee, based on photographs, was also made by the Richmond sculptor Edward V. Valentine, while studying in Berlin in 1864, and sent to England to be sold for the Southern cause, possibly at the Liverpool Bazaar in October of that year (Ex inf. Valentine Richmond History Center.)

22. Peyton, vol. 2, 39–40.
23. *Illustrated London News,* January 9, 1864.
24. E. Lawrence Abel, *Singing the New Nation* (Mechanicsburg, PA: Stackpole Books, 2000), 104–105, 112–113, 316, 318.
25. *Times,* August 20, 1864, quoted in Michael Hammerson, "The American Civil War Comes to Belsize Park," in *Belsize 2000: A Living Suburb* (London: Belsize Conservation Area Advisory Committee, 2000), 60.
26. They are listed in the *British Museum Catalogue of Printed Maps, Charts and Plans,* vol. 14 (London: British Museum, 1967), 634–638.
27. The full title was the *Monthly Packet of Evening Readings for Younger Members of the English Church.* The articles are not mentioned in Mary Elizabeth Massey's *Refugee Life in the Confederacy* (Baton Rouge: Louisiana State University Press, 1964), perhaps because she was unaware of them or maybe doubted their authenticity.
28. Royden Harrison, "British Labour and the Confederacy," *International Review of Social History,* 2 (1957):79, 104.
29. Samuel P. Day, *Down South,* vol. 2 (London: Hurst & Blackett, 1862), 196.
30. William W. Malet, *An Errand to the South in the Summer of 1862* (London: Richard Bentley, 1863), 187. There is a parallel account of Malet's visit, written by Elizabeth Collins, who was his sister's maid (*Memories of the Southern States* [Taunton, Somerset, UK: J. Barnicott, 1865]).
31. Allan Nevins et al. (eds.), *Civil War Books: A Critical Bibliography,* vol. 1 (Baton Rouge: Louisiana State University Press, 1967), 91; Constance C. Harrison, *Recollections Grave and Gay* (New York: Charles Scribner's Sons, 1911), 133.
32. William C. Corsan, *Two Months in the Confederate States,* ed. B. H. Trask (Baton Rouge: Louisiana State University Press, 1996), xii; *Index,* June 25, 1863.
33. Catherine C. Hopley, *Life in the South,* vol. 1 (London: Chapman & Hall, 1863), vi–vii.
34. Ibid., vol. 2, 404.
35. *Saturday Review,* May 6, 1865.
36. Fitzgerald Ross, *Cities and Camps of the Confederate States,* ed. Richard B. Harwell (Urbana: University of Illinois Press, 1997), xviii–xix.
37. *All the Year Round,* March 19, 1864. The two pamphlets only contained selections from George T. Fullam's journal; the full text, edited by Charles G. Summersell, was not published till 1973.
38. Robin and Carol Wichard, *Victorian Cartes-de-Visite* (Princes Risborough, Bucks, UK: Shire Publications, 1999), 62. In 1864 action photographs were not yet possible, though in his account of the battle, Frederick Edge claimed to have seen the negative of one made by a Cherbourg photographer called Rondin (*Notes & Queries,* April 23, 1910).
39. Moran, vol. 2, 1308.
40. Walker, 53.

41. Ibid., 104. In her journal Mrs. Walker makes no mention of Belle Boyd, who was also in London at this time and actually living nearby; well-bred Southern ladies are unlikely to have approved of her flamboyant behavior and predilection for male company.
42. Wharncliffe to Greenhow, September 5, 1864, in Wharncliffe Muniments, WhM 461.
43. Spence to Wharncliffe, October 31, 1864, in Wharncliffe Muniments, WhM 460. Mrs. Greenhow's body was found the next day on the beach near Fort Fisher by Thomas Taylor, who was engaged in blockade-running for the Anglo-Confederate Trading Co. of Liverpool.
44. Collie to Wharncliffe, November 9, 1864, ibid.
45. Moran, vol. 2, 1346–1347.
46. These quotations are all taken from Sala's Introduction, which is dated May 17, 1865.
47. *Illustrated London News,* February 25, 1865.
48. Sala declined to put his name to the English edition, for reasons which are not apparent, though it appeared on the American one, published in New York later that year.
49. Quoted in *Belle Boyd in Camp and Prison,* ed. Curtis C. Davis (New York: Thomas Yoseloff, 1968), 48.
50. Ibid., 48–49.
51. Ibid., 50. Despite these lackluster reviews, she seems to have done quite well as a result of her literary venture. In April 1868, in a letter to a friend, she speaks of expecting "some 7. or 8. thousand dollars coming to me from the sale of my Book." Quoted in Sharon Kennedy-Nolle's introduction to *Belle Boyd in Camp and Prison* (Baton Rouge: Louisiana State University Press, 1998), 4.
52. Charles E. Shain, "The English Novelists and the American Civil War," *American Quarterly,* 14, no. 3 (1962):420–421 (Copyright the American Studies Association).

10— Support for the South?

1. Bulloch, vol. 1, 294.
2. Maury to Franklin Minor, January 21, 1863; Williams, 404.
3. Forrest, 43–44.
4. Robert G. H. Kean, *Inside the Confederate Government: The Diary of Robert Garlick Hill Kean*; ed. Edward Younger (Baton Rouge: Louisiana State University Press, 1993), 129. J. E. Ward was a former U.S. minister to China.
5. Peyton, vol. 2, 101; 39–40.
6. Moran, vol. 2, 1022.
7. Adams to Seward, July 11, 1862; *Foreign Relations, 1862,* 133. Adams to Adams, Jr., December 25, 1862, Ford, vol. 1, 220–221; Adams to Adams, Jr., September 25, 1863, ibid., vol. 2, 85.
8. Forbes was in England on a secret mission for the Federal government (Douglas H. Maynard, "The Forbes-Aspinwall Mission," *Mississippi Valley Historical Review,* 45 (1958):73.
9. *New York Tribune,* October 15, 1875, quoted in Philip Ziegler, *The Sixth Great Power: Barings 1762–1929* (London: Collins, 1988), 214.
10. London consular dispatches, July 18, 1862.
11. Ibid., August 7, 1863.
12. Hotze to Benjamin, July 23, 1863, *ORN,* ser. II, vol. 3, 849; Ford, vol. 2, 58–63.

13. Hotze to Benjamin, October 31, 1863; Thompson, 74. Spence claimed $45,000 — just over £9,000 — as compensation for his losses.
14. Gilliat to Barret, April 24, 1863, quoted in Lester, 41.
15. *Times,* January 16, 1863.
16. John W. Raimo, *A Guide to Manuscripts Relating to America in Great Britain and Ireland,* Rev. ed. (London: Mansell Publishing, 1979), 58.
17. *Times,* October 9, 1862.
18. Sir William Gregory, *Autobiography,* ed. Lady Gregory (London: John Murray, 1894), 215–216.
19. Ella Lonn, *Foreigners in the Confederacy* (Chapel Hill: University of North Carolina Press, 2002), 357–358. Robert Bourke described his visit in *Blackwood's Magazine,* December 1861, 755–767. Thomas Conolly's diary was published as *An Irishman in Dixie,* ed. Nelson D. Lankford (Columbia: University of South Carolina Press, 1988).
20. *House of Commons Parliamentary Debates,* July 10, 1863.
21. H. Adams to C. F. Adams, Jr., March 15, 1862; Ford, vol. 1, 120–121.
22. *Cassell's Illustrated Family Paper,* March 28, 1863.
23. H. Adams, 186.
24. *House of Commons Parliamentary Debates,* June 30, 1863.
25. Sir John Trelawny, *Parliamentary Diaries, 1858–1865,* ed. T. A. Jenkins, Camden, 4th ser., vol. 40 (London: Royal Historical Society, 1990), 260. Lindsay confirmed Roebuck's version of their meeting with the Emperor in a letter to the *Times,* July 4, 1863.
26. *House of Commons Parliamentary Debates,* June 30, 1863. In his diary, Gladstone recorded the books he was reading and during the Civil War they included: James Spence, *The American Union* (November 23, 1861); Alexander Beresford-Hope, *A Popular View of the American Civil War* (December 13, 1861); John Cowell, *Southern Secession* (January 25, 1862); James Spence, *On the Recognition of the Southern Confederacy* (August 12, 1862); and Arthur Fremantle, *Three Months in the Southern States* (January 2, 1864).
27. H. Adams to C. F. Adams, Jr., July 3, 1863; Ford, vol. 2, 43.
28. *Illustrated Times,* July 4, 1863.
29. Collie to Wharncliffe, January 23. 1865, in Wharncliffe Muniments, WhM 461.
30. Moran, vol. 2, 904. An article in the *Spectator* (October 5, 1861), for example, claimed that American news from Reuters was biased towards the Confederates.
31. *Die Presse,* November 14, 1862, quoted in John Laskey, "Marx and Engels on the Civil War," *Crossfire* (December 2003), 24. Edward B. Hamley, "Our Rancorous 'Cousins'," *Blackwood's Magazine,* November 1863, 637; Peyton, vol. 2, 39–40.
32. Adams to Seward, July 23, 1863, in *Foreign Relations, 1863,* vol. 1, 319.
33. Perhaps demonstrated by the fact that George E. Seymour, one of the proprietors of the pro-Northern *Daily News,* was included in the list of Confederate bondholders. Henry Adams was a contributor to both the *Morning Star* and the *Daily News.*
34. *London American,* December 4, 1861.
35. Semmes, 348–349.
36. Hammerson, 60.
37. Raimo, 59.
38. *Foreign Relations, 1863,* vol. 1, 19–24, which reprints the complete text of the association's pamphlet.
39. Ibid., 18.
40. Moran, vol. 2, 1329.
41. *Times,* October 12, 1864.
42. Collie, who undoubtedly made a great deal of money out of the Civil War, seems to have been prone to munificent gestures: through Governor Vance, he donated $20,000 for the relief of the North Carolina poor (*Papers of Zebulon Baird Vance,* vol. 1, liii).
43. Southern Independence Association of London, *Address to the Public,* in Goldwin Smith, *Letter to a Whig Member of the Southern Independence Association* (London: Macmillan, 1864), 34–35.
44. Ibid., 35–36.
45. Ibid., 35.
46. John Bigelow, "The Confederate Diplomatists," *Century Magazine* , May 1891, 123.
47. Hotze to Benjamin, March 12, 1864, *ORN,* ser. II, vol. 3, 1061.
48. *Times,* December 23, 1864; ibid., December 26, 1864.
49. Taylor to Wharncliffe, January 5, 1865; Warwick to Wharncliffe, January 6, 1865; Arco to Wharncliffe, January 12, 1865; Hampson to Wharncliffe, January 17, 1865, in Wharncliffe Muniments, WhM 461. Another disabled Confederate soldier who visited London was William H. Brawley, a South Carolinian who had lost his left arm at the battle of Fair Oaks in 1862. He arrived in London in June 1864 and in his diary he recorded meeting Commissioner Mason and seeing the sights; his diary was edited by Francis R. Brawley and published in 1970.
50. Hotze to Benjamin, September 26, 1862, *ORN,* ser. II, vol. 3, 534.
51. Joseph M. Hernon, Jr., "British Sympathies in the American Civil War," *Journal of Southern History,* 33 (1967):362.
52. Donald Bellows, "A Study of British Conservative Reaction to the American Civil War," *Journal of Southern History,* 51 (1985):505–526.
53. Quoted in deKay, 131.
54. *Bee-Hive,* April 11, 1863, quoted in Royden Harrison, "British Labour and the Confederacy: A Note on the Southern Sympathies of Some British Working Class Journals and Leaders During the American Civil War," *International Review of Social History,* 2 (1957):99.
55. E. D. Adams, 133.
56. Harrison, 101.

Epilogue

1. William Webb returned to his native state of Virginia, where he died in 1881. (William A. Young, Jr., "Treasures from the Attic: The Colonel's Bootjack & the Commander's Watch Chain," *Crossfire,* August 1997, 13–15.)
2. Daniel E. Sutherland, "Exiles, Emigrants and Sojourners: The Post-Civil War Confederate Exodus in Perspective," *Civil War History,* 31 (1985): 252. Paris acted as a magnet for Americans both during and after the Civil War, and particularly for artists; men like Thomas Eakins and Winslow Homer flocked there, as *Americans in Paris 1860–1900,* a recent exhibition at London's National Gallery demonstrated.

3. George Augustus Sala was an admirer of the American actress Kate Bateman, who was then playing in London, and knew her father, the theatrical impresario, Col. Hezekiah L. Bateman. Sala may have introduced him to Belle Boyd, and got her an introduction to the stage (Sigaud, 186).

4. For an account of the Confederate community at Leamington, see John D. Bennett, "A Popular Place with Rebels," *Crossfire*, April 2005, 23–24.

5. "United States of America v. Prioleau," *Times*, July 7, 1866, December 21, 1866, and June 18, 1867; Wise, 223.

6. "United States of America v. McRae," *The Law Reports, Equity Cases*, vol. 4, 1867, 327–340; *Chancery Appeal Cases*, vol. 3, 1867, 79–92; *Equity Cases*, vol. 8, 1869, 69–77; Daniel Grinnan, "Disposition of Confederate Funds," *Confederate Veteran* (July 1929):328.

7. William C. Davis, "The Conduct of Mr Thompson," *Civil War Times Illustrated*, May 1970, 5–7, 43–47. It seems likely that Thompson had considerably more than this; he went back to America in 1869, and when he died in 1885 was estimated to have been worth at least $500,000.

8. Morse to Seward, November 30, 1865, in *Foreign Relations,* 1866, vol. 1.

9. *Times*, November 24, 1875.

Appendix E — Southern Independence Association of London

1. *Index*, January 14, 1864, which also prints the Association's constitution.

Appendix F — The British Jackson Monumental Fund

1. *Index*, July 2, 1863; this differs somewhat from the list in *ORN*, ser. II, vol. 3, 828.

Bibliography

Primary Sources: Unpublished

De La Rue Collection, #MS937, University of Reading.
De La Rue Private Day Book 1862, National Postal Museum, London.
Jackson Memorial Account, Coutts & Co., London.
London Consular Dispatches, 1861–1865, #M528, John Rylands University Library, Manchester (microfilm).
James Heyward North Diary, #862, Southern Historical Collection, Wilson Library, University of North Carolina at Chapel Hill (microfilm).
Wharncliffe Muniments, #WhM 460 & 461, Sheffield City Libraries.

Primary Sources: Published

Adams, Henry. *The Education of Henry Adams, an Autobiography*. Boston: Houghton Mifflin, 1961. Originally published in 1918.
Anderson, Edward C. *Confederate Foreign Agent: The European Diary of Major Edward C. Anderson*, ed. W. Stanley Hoole. University, AL: Confederate Publishing, 1976.
Barron, Samuel. "Diary from 1863 to 1865." *ORN*, ser. II, vol. 2, 813–821.
Bigelow, John. "The Confederate Diplomatists." *Century Magazine* (May 1891), 113–126.
_____. *Lest We Forget: Gladstone, Morley and the Confederate Loan of 1863*. New York: De Vinne Press, 1905.
Boyd, Belle. *Belle Boyd in Camp and Prison*, ed. Curtis C. Davis. South Brunswick, NJ: Thomas Yoseloff, 1968. Originally published in 1865.
Bulloch, James D. *The Secret Service of the Confederate States in Europe; or, How the Confederate Cruisers Were Equipped*, ed. Philip van Doren Stern. 2 vols. New York: Thomas Yoseloff, 1959. Originally published in 1883.
"Caleb Huse." *Confederate Veteran* (May 1905), iii.
Ferguson, Emma H. "Sketch of Major Ferguson." *Confederate Veteran* (March 1899), 99–100.
Ford, Worthington C., ed. *A Cycle of Adams Letters, 1861–1865*. 2 vols. London: Constable, 1920.
Forrest, Douglas F. *Odyssey in Gray: A Diary of Confederate Service, 1863–1865*, ed. William N. Still, Jr. Richmond: Virginia State Library, 1979.
Grinnan, Daniel. "Disposition of Confederate Funds." *Confederate Veteran* (July 1929), 328–329.
"Major Huse of the Secret Service." *Confederate Veteran* (February 1905), 65–66.
Mason, Virginia. *The Public Life and Diplomatic Correspondence of James Murray Mason, With Some Personal History by His Daughter*. Roanoke, VA: Stone Printing & Manufacturing Co., 1903.
Moran, Benjamin. *The Journal of Benjamin Moran, 1857–1865*, ed. Sarah A. Wallace & Frances E. Gillespie. 2 vols. Chicago: University of Chicago Press, 1948.
Morgan, James M. *Midshipman in Gray: Selections from Recollections of a Rebel Reefer*, ed. R. Thomas Campbell. Shippensburg, PA: Burd Street Press, 1997. Originally published in 1917.
Murray's Modern London 1860. Moretonhampstead, Devon: Old House Books, 2003.
Official Records of the Union and Confederate Armies in the War of the Rebellion (ORA), 4th ser. Vols. 1–3. Washington, DC: 1900.
Official Records of the Union and Confederate Navies in the War of the Rebellion (ORN), 2nd Ser. Vols. 2–3. Washington, DC: 1921–1922.

Papers Relating to the Foreign Relations of the United States. Washington, DC: 1861–1865.

Pardon, George F. *The Popular Guide to London and Its Suburbs*. London: Routledge, Warne & Routledge, 1862.

Peyton, John L. *The American Crisis; or, Pages from the Notebook of a State Agent During the Civil War*. 2 vols. London: Saunders, Otley, 1867.

Richardson, James D. *Messages and Papers of the Confederacy, Including the Diplomatic Correspondence, 1861–1865*. 2 vols. Nashville, TN: U.S. Publishing, 1905.

Semmes, Raphael. *Memoirs of Service Afloat During the War Between the States*, ed. John M. Taylor. Baton Rouge: Louisiana State University Press, 1996. Originally published in 1869.

Thompson, John R. "From the Diary of John R. Thompson." *Confederate Veteran* (March 1929), 98–100.

Trelawny, Sir John. *Parliamentary Diaries, 1858–1865*, ed. T.A. Jenkins, Camden, Fourth Series, vol. 40. London: Royal Historical Society, 1990.

Walker, Georgiana G. *The Private Journal of Georgiana Gholson Walker, 1862–1865; with Selections from the Post-War Years, 1866–1876*, ed. Dwight F. Henderson. Tuscaloosa, AL: Confederate Publishing, 1963.

"William L. Yancey's European Diary, March-June 1861," ed. W. Stanley Hoole. *Alabama Review*, 25 (1972), 134–142.

Secondary Sources

Adams, Ephraim D. *Great Britain and the American Civil War*. 2 vols. London: Longmans, 1925.

"An American in London." *Times Literary Supplement*, June 30, 1950.

Barton, Peter. "The First Blockade-Runner and Another Alabama." *Mariner's Mirror*, 81 (1995), 45–64.

Beers, Henry P. *The Confederacy: A Guide to the Archives of the Government of the Confederate States of America*. Washington, DC: National Archives and Records Administration, 1998. Originally published in 1968.

Bennett, John D. "Benjamin Moran's Journal." *Crossfire, The Magazine of the American Civil War Round Table* (UK), August 1998, 8–9.

———. "A Confederate Link with Chelsea." *Crossfire*, March 1999, 24.

———. "General Jackson's Statue." *Crossfire*, December 2004, 25–26.

———. "A Popular Place with Rebels." *Crossfire*, April 2005, 23–24.

Boaz, Thomas. *Guns for Cotton: England Arms the Confederacy*. Shippensburg, PA: Burd Street Press, 1996.

Brogan, Hugh, ed. *The Times Reports the American Civil War: Extracts from the Times, 1860–1865*. London: Times Books, 1975.

Callahan, James M. *The Diplomatic History of the Southern Confederacy*. Baltimore, MD: Johns Hopkins Press, 1901.

Caskie, Jaquelin A. *The Life and Letters of Matthew Fontaine Maury*. Richmond, VA: Richmond Press, 1928.

Cochran, Robert T., Jr. "Witness to a War." *National Geographic*, April 1961, 453–491.

Collyer, C. "Gladstone and the American Civil War." *Proceedings of the Leeds Philosophical and Literary Society*, 6 (1948–1952), 583–594.

Coulter, E. Merton. *Travels in the Confederate States: A Bibliography*. Baton Rouge: Louisiana State University Press, 1994. Originally published in 1948.

Crapster, Basil L. "Thomas Hamber, 1828–1902: Tory Journalist." *Victorian Periodicals Newsletter*, 8 (1975), 115–124.

Cullop, Charles P. "Edwin De Leon, Jefferson Davis's Propagandist." *Civil War History*, 8 (1962), 386–400.

———. "English Reaction to Stonewall Jackson's Death." *West Virginia History*, 29 (1967), 1–5.

———. *Confederate Propaganda in Europe, 1861–1865*. Coral Gables, FL: University of Miami Press, 1969.

Davis, William C. "The Conduct of Mr. Thompson." *Civil War Times Illustrated* (May 1970), 5–7, 43–47.

———. "Confederate Exiles." *American History Illustrated*, June 1970, 31–43.

deKay, James Tertius. *The Rebel Raiders: The Astonishing History of the Confederacy's Secret Navy*. New York: Ballantine Books, 2002.

Delaney, Norman C. "'When Can You Start?': The Strange Occupation of James Bulloch." In *Raiders and Blockaders: The American Civil War Afloat*. Washington, DC: Brassey's, 1998, 1–12.

Diamond, William. "Imports of the Confederate Government from Europe." *Journal of Southern History*, 6 (1940), 470–503.

Dubose, John W. *The Life and Times of William Lowndes Yancey*. Birmingham, AL: Roberts & Son, 1892.

Dufour, Charles L. *Nine Men in Gray*. Garden City, NY: Doubleday, 1963.

Gentry, Judith F. "A Confederate Success in Europe: The Erlanger Loan." *Journal of Southern History*, 36 (1970), 157–188.

Goff, Richard D. *Confederate Supply*. Durham, NC: Duke University Press, 1969.
Griffiths, Dennis. *Plant Here the Standard*. London: Macmillan, 1996.
Hammerson, Michael. "The American Civil War Comes to Belsize Park." In *Belsize 2000: a Living Suburb*. London: Belsize Conservation Area Advisory Committee, 2000, 58–66.
Harris, S.H. "John L. O'Sullivan Serves the Confederacy," *Civil War History*, 10 (1964), 275–290.
Harrison, Royden. "British Labour and the Confederacy: A Note on the Southern Sympathies of Some British Working-Class Journals and Leaders During the American Civil War." *International Review of Social History*, 2 (1957), 78–105.
Hearn, Chester G. *Gray Raiders of the Sea*. Baton Rouge: Louisiana State University Press, 1992.
Hendrick, Burton J. *Statesmen of the Lost Cause*. New York: Literary Guild of America, 1939.
Henry, William W. "Kenner's Mission to Europe." *William and Mary Quarterly*, ser. I, vol. 25 (1916), 9–12.
Hernon, Joseph M., Jr. "British Sympathies in the American Civil War: A Reconsideration." *Journal of Southern History*, 33 (1967), 356–367.
Houseman, Lorna. *The House That Thomas Built: The Story of De La Rue*. London: Chatto & Windus, 1968.
Jameson, J.F. "London Expenditures of the Confederate Secret Service." *American Historical Review*, 35 (1930), 811-824.
Jenkins, Brian. "Frank Lawley and the Confederacy." *Civil War History*, 23 (1977), 144–160.
_____. "William Gregory: Champion of the Confederacy." *History Today*, (May 1978), 322–330.
Jordon, Donaldson, & Edwin J. Pratt. *Europe and the American Civil War*. Boston, MA: Houghton Mifflin, 1931.
Keiser, Thomas J. *The English Press and the American Civil War*. Unpublished doctoral dissertation, Reading University, 1971.
Lester, Richard I. *Confederate Finance and Purchasing in Great Britain*. Charlottesville: University Press of Virginia, 1975.
_____. "An Aspect of Confederate Finance During the American Civil War: The Erlanger Loan and the Plan of 1864." *Business History*, 16 (1974), 130–144.
_____. "The Procurement of Confederate Blockade Runners and Other Vessels in Great Britain During the American Civil War." *Mariner's Mirror*, 61 (1975), 255–270.
Logan, Kevin J. "The Bee-Hive Newspaper and British Working-Class Attitudes Towards the American Civil War." *Civil War History*, 22 (1976), 337–348.
London Times. The History of the Times: The Tradition Established, 1841–1884. London: Times, 1939.
Lonn, Ella. *Foreigners in the Confederacy*. Chapel Hill: University of North Carolina Press, 2002. Originally published in 1940.
"The Lost Shipment." *De La Rue Journal* (July 1951), 18–20.
Luraghi, Raimondo. *A History of the Confederate Navy*. London: Chatham Publishing, 1996.
Markham, John. "The Rise and Fall of Hull's Ambitious Mayor." *Select* (October/November 1988), 88–90.
Maurer, Oscar. "Punch on Slavery and Civil War in America." *Victorian Studies*, 1 (1957), 5–28.
Maynard, Douglas H. "The Forbes-Aspinwall Mission." *Mississippi Valley Historical Review*, 45 (1958), 67–89.
_____. "The Confederacy's Super-Alabama." *Civil War History*, 5 (1959), 80–95.
Merli, Frank J. *Great Britain and the Confederate Navy, 1861–1865*. Bloomington: Indiana University Press, 2004. Originally published in 1970.
Morton, Brian N. *Americans in London*. London: Queen Anne Press, 1988.
Neely, Mark E., Jr., Harold Holzer, & Gabor S. Boritt. *The Confederate Image: Prints of the Lost Cause*. Chapel Hill: University of North Carolina Press, 1987.
Nevins, Allan, James I. Robertson, & Bell I. Wiley, eds. *Civil War Books: A Critical Bibliography*. 2 vols. Baton Rouge: Louisiana State University Press, 1967–1969.
Oates, Stephen B. "Henry Hotze: Confederate Agent Abroad." *Historian*, 27 (1965), 131–154.
Owsley, Frank L. *King Cotton Diplomacy: Foreign Relations of the Confederate States of America*, 2nd ed. Chicago: University of Chicago Press, 1959.
Owsley, Harriet C. "Henry Shelton Sanford and Federal Surveillance Abroad, 1861–1865." *Mississippi Valley Historical Review*, 48 (1961–1962), 211–228.
Priestley, Charles. "Confederates in Paris: Slidell, Benjamin and the Shameless Jezebel of Secession." *Crossfire* (September 2001), 14–16.
_____. "Batavian Grace: A.J.B. Beresford Hope: An Example of English Upper Class Support for the Confederacy in the American Civil War." *Crossfire* (August 2002), 18–22.
_____. "Cleaning Tremlett's Grave." *Crossfire* (December 2003), 18.
_____. "Did Semmes Sleep Here? 71 Euston Square, London." *Crossfire* (April 2004), 24–25.
_____. "France's Opportunity: An Englishman's Plea for French Intervention." *Crossfire* (April 2005), 13–16.

Robbins, Peggy. "Caleb Huse, Confederate Agent." *Civil War Times Illustrated* (August 1978), 30–40.

Robinson, William M., Jr. *The Confederate Privateers*. Columbia: University of South Carolina Press, 1994. Originally published in 1928.

Schwab, John C. "The Confederate Foreign Loan: An Episode in the Financial History of the Civil War." *Yale Review*, 1 (1892), 175–186.

_____. *The Confederate States of America, 1861–1865: A Financial and Industrial History of the South During the Civil War*. New York: Scribner's & Sons, 1901.

Shain, Charles E. "English Novelists and the American Civil War." *American Quarterly*, 14 (1962), 399–421.

Sigaud, Louis A. *Belle Boyd: Confederate Spy*. Richmond, VA: Dietz, 1944.

Smith, Van Mitchell. *British Business Relations with the Confederacy, 1861–1865*. Unpublished doctoral dissertation, University of Texas, 1949.

Spencer, Warren F. *The Confederate Navy in Europe*. Tuscaloosa: University of Alabama Press, 1997. Originally published in 1983.

Stern, Philip Van Doren. *Secret Missions of the Civil War*. New York: Bonanza Books, 1990. Originally published in 1959.

Sutherland, Daniel E. "Exiles, Emigrants and Sojourners: The Post-Civil War Confederate Exodus in Perspective." *Civil War History*, 31 (1985), 237–256.

Thompson, Samuel B. *Confederate Purchasing Operations Abroad*. Gloucester, MA: Peter Smith, 1973. Originally published in 1935.

Todd, Richard C. *Confederate Finance*. Athens: University of Georgia Press, 1954.

Vanauken, Sheldon. *The Glittering Illusion: English Sympathy for the Southern Confederacy*. Worthing, Sussex, UK: Churchman, 1988.

Vandiver, Frank E. *Confederate Blockade Running Through Bermuda, 1861–1865: Letter and Cargo Manifests*. Austin: University of Texas Press, 1947.

_____. *Ploughshares into Swords: Josiah Gorgas and Confederate Ordnance*. College Station: Texas A&M University Press, 1994. Originally published in 1952.

Weller, Jac. "The Confederate Use of British Cannon." *Civil War History*, 3 (1957), 135–152.

_____. "Imported Confederate Shoulder Weapons." *Civil War History*, 5 (1959), 157–181.

Williams, Frances L. *Matthew Fontaine Maury: Scientist of the Sea*. New Brunswick, NJ: Rutgers University Press, 1963.

Wise, Stephen R. *Lifeline of the Confederacy: Blockade-Running During the Civil War*. Columbia: University of South Carolina Press, 1991. Originally published in 1988.

Young, William A., Jr. "Treasures from the Attic: The Colonel's Bootjack & the Commander's Watch Chain." *Crossfire* (August 1997), 13–15.

Index

Abel, Prof. Frederick 97–98
Abel fuses 97–98
"Action off Cherbourg" 127
Acton, Sir John, MP 146
Adams, Charles Francis 28, 33, 36–38, 63–64, 75–76, 79–85, 97, 103, 136, 143, 146, 150
Adams, Henry 33–34, 36, 43, 136, 140–142
Adams, John 6
Adams, John Quincy 28
Adams, Robert 95–96
Address to the British Public (London Confederate States Aid Association) 146
Address to the Public (Southern Independence Association of London) 148–149
Adelphi Theater, Strand 18, 56
Advance (blockade-runner) 61
Agrippina (bark) 63
Ajax, CSS 64
Alabama, CSS 63, 67–69, 77, 82, 84, 110, 113, 123, 127, 153
Alabama: A Nautical Extravaganza 18, 111
Alabama and the Kearsarge 127
Alabama claims 93
Alar (steamer) 72
Albemarle Street, Piccadilly 12, 28
Albert, Prince Consort 23
Albert Memorial, Hyde Park 24, 115
Albion Trading Co. 103
Aldridge, Ira 6
Alexandra (steamer) 82, 86
Alexandra, Princess of Wales 24
Alexandria, Virginia 154
Alhambra Palace, Leicester Square 19
All Saints' Church, Margaret Street 40
All the Year Round 39, 118, 127
"American Affairs" 47
"American Blockaded Ports" 123–124
American Crisis 144, 154
American Disruption 39–40
"American Generals" 123–124
American Notes 110
American Union 39, 48, 101, 118
Amnesty, United States 152
Anderson, Major Edward C., CSA

52, 54–56, 60–61, 63, 66–68, 84–85, 96, 152
Anderson, Capt. J.W. 127
Anderson, John 23
Annie Childs (blockade-runner) 67
Antietam, battle of 137
Arabia (steamer) 70
Archer, Asst. Engr. E., Confederate States Volunteer Navy 85
Arco, James D. 150
Argyll Rooms, Great Windmill Street 19
Arkansas, CSS 123
Arklow House, Connaught Place 148
Armstrong & Co., Newcastle-on-Tyne 96
Armstrong guns 97
Army & Navy Club, Pall Mall 69
Army Stores and Clothing Depot, Northamptonshire 52
Arnold, Matthew 146
Ash, James 103, 106
Ashbridge & Co., Liverpool 103
Ashburton, Lord 60
Aspinwall, William H. 68, 80
Atalanta (blockade-runner) 103, 105–106
Athenaeum 39, 46, 132
Atlanta, CSS 152
Atlantic Trading Co. 103
Audubon, John J. 6
Austin Friars 107

Bacon & Co. 114, 117
Bahama (steamer) 63, 85
Baltimore 154
Bank, Confederate 103
Bank of England 74, 157
Banvard, John 20
Baring Bros. 27
Barnett & Sons 83, 95
Barney, Cdr. Joseph N., CSN 77
Barron, Flag Officer Samuel, CSN 69, 76–77, 153
Barrow, Col. Robert H., CSA 134
Bates, Joshua 27
Bath, Marquess of 34, 91, 140, 148
Bath House, Piccadilly 60
Battersea Park 20
Battery Wagner, South Carolina 122

"Battle of Gettysburg" 121
Beasley, Benjamin 95
Beauregard, Gen. Pierre G.T., CSA 101, 140, 153
Bedgebury Park, Kent 157
Bee-Hive 150–151
Begbie, Thomas S. 75, 82–83, 103, 107, 158
Belgravia 7, 9
Belle Boyd in Camp and Prison 132
Belsham, Robert R. 140
Benjamin, Judah P. 38–39, 41, 43, 47, 49, 60, 87, 94, 102, 114, 136, 149–150, 152, 155–156
Bennett, Alfred W. 113
Bennett & Wake 82
Bensusan, Thomas 102
Bentley & Son 124–125, 128
Beresford Hope, Alexander J. 39–40, 92, 114–115, 148, 157
Bermuda (blockade-runner) 56, 101
Berners Hotel, Berners Street 73–74
Bethnal Green, factory explosion at 24
Bible Society of the Confederate States 102
Bibles 101–102
Bigelow, John 41, 93
Birmingham 54
Birmingham Small Arms Co. 96
Bishopsgate station 15
Bissell, Thomas 95
Black Angel 132
Blackmore, R.D. 134
Blackwall 106
Blackwood & Sons 124, 127
Blackwood's Magazine 120, 124, 127, 135, 148
Blakely, Capt. Alexander T. 85, 97
Blakely guns 97
Blakely Ordnance Co. 97
Blamphin, Charles 116
Blanchard's restaurant, Soho 12, 136
Bledsoe, Albert T. 45, 154
Blockade, Union 3, 25, 31–32, 34, 49, 121, 136, 140
Blockade-running 56–57, 59, 61, 67, 79–80, 101, 103–109
Blondin, Charles 19
Bloodgood, M. Hildreth 58, 152

Bloomsbury 7
Bold, Thomas 70, 73
"Bonnie Blue Flag" 50, 116
Bookbinders' Union 150–151
Boosey & Sons 116
Booth, Edwin 18
Booth, John W. 18, 112
Boots and shoes 99
Border and Bastille 125
Bostwick, A.W. 48
Boucicault, Dion 56
Bourke, Hon. Robert 120, 140, 148
Bouverie Street 45, 99
Bowles, James 10
Bowman, William 59
"Boy of the Rappahannock" 116
Boyd, Belle 125, 130–132, 154
Bradbury & Evans 124
Braidwood, James 23
Breach, James 9, 12
Breckinridge, Maj. Gen. John C., CSA 152, 156
Brewer, H.O. 43, 103
Brewer & Co. 116
Briggs, Thomas 24
Bright, John, MP 141
Brighton 157
Britannia Theater, Hoxton 18, 111
British & Foreign Bible Society 102
British Honduras (Belize) 156
British Jackson Monumental Fund 114–115
British Swiss Legion 41
Britton, Mr. 54
Brixton Prison 23
"Brown, Capt." 75
Brown, Governor Joseph E. 25, 60–61
Brunswick Hotel, Jermyn Street 132
Buckland Crescent, Belsize Park 68, 144, 147
Buckley, Frederick 116
Buckley, Joseph 102
Buckley, Victor 84
Buckstone, John B. 18
Bull Run, first battle of 30, 124
Bulloch, Cdr. James D., CSN 36, 38, 52, 54–56, 62–70, 76–77, 82–85, 135, 144
Bulwer-Lytton, Edward 146
Bunch, Robert 26
Bunting, J.G. 82
Burford's Panorama, Leicester Square 20
Burlington Arcade, Piccadilly 16
Burlington Hotel, Cork Street 9, 58, 76
Burton, James H. 96–97, 155
Bury Street, St. James's 12, 41, 72
Butler, Maj. Gen. Benjamin, USA 111, 134
Buttons 99

Calais 73–75, 82
Calhoun, John C. 99
Cambridge House, Piccadilly 37, 139
Camilla (yacht) 66
Campbell, Alexander 52
Campbell, Dugald F. 93
Campbell, Lord 34, 49, 92, 140, 148

Campbell, Robert B. 45
Campbell, Lt. William P.A., CSN 73
Canton (Pampero) 68
Capper, Charles 104
Career of the Alabama 127
Carlyle, Thomas 146
Carter, Lt. William F., CSN 64, 72–73
Carteret, Felix 87
Cassell's Illustrated Family Paper 123
Catlin, George 6
Causes and Consequences of the Civil War 46
Cecil, Lord Eustace 140
Cecil, Lord Robert, MP 40, 122, 139–140, 148
Central Criminal Court, Old Bailey 74
Chameleon (blockade-runner) 106
Chancellorsville, Battle of 114
Chapman, Lt. Robert T., CSN 68, 72, 102
Chapman & Hall 125, 127
Charing Cross station 16
Charleston Mercury 25
Charleston, South Carolina 37, 90, 121–123, 142
"Charleston Under Fire" 122
Charlotte (blockade-runner) 103
Chase, Thomas H. 80–81
Chattanooga, battle of 90
Cherbourg 111, 127
Chesham Place, Belgravia 35
Chesnut, Mrs. Mary B. 32–33
Chesterfield, Lady 130
Cheyne Row, Chelsea 146
Chichester, Bishop of 150
Chickamauga, CSS 105
Chorley Wood, Hertfordshire 157
Christian Brotherhood 145
Church of England clergy 144
Church Times 144
Church's Historical Panorama, St. James's Hall 112–113
City of London 7, 88
City of Richmond (blockade-runner) 77
"Civil War in America" 112–113
Clanricarde, Marquess of 150
Clarendon Road, Notting Hill 53
Clark, Governor Henry T. 60
Clarke, Charles H. 134
Clarke, H.G. 117
Clements, Nelson 61
Clerkenwell House of Detention 23
"Close of the American War" 122
Cobden, Richard, MP 34, 151
Cold Bath Fields Prison, Clerkenwell 22–23
Coleman & Co. 73–75
Coles, Capt. Cowper, RN 63, 66
Colleen Bawn 56
Colletis (steamer) 67
Collie, Alexander 61, 105–108, 115, 130, 142, 148, 158
Collie, William 158
Collie & Co. 57, 91, 107
Collier, Sir Robert 93
Colline, Victor 116

Collins, Henry G. 7
Collins' Illustrated Atlas of London 7
Colt, Samuel 6
Commons, House of 139–142
Condor (blockade-runner) 107, 130, 153
"Confederate Raid" 116
Confederate's Daughter 18, 111
Confederate Secession 140
Confederate States Commercial Agency 41–42
Confederate States Exchange Rooms 99
"Confederate Struggle and Recognition" 122
"Confederate War March" 116
Conolly, Thomas, MP 140
Conscription, Confederate 140
Consulate, United States 80, 82
Consuls, British 140
Conway, Rev. Moncure D. 36
Cooper, James F. 6
Cooper, Mr. 64
Coote, Charles 116
Cora: or, The Slaves of the South 111
Corbett, Capt. Peter 65
Cornhill Magazine 49, 121, 123
Corsan, William C. 125, 142, 158
Corsan, Denton & Burdekin, Sheffield 125
Cotton embargo 25
Cotton famine 24
Cotton Loan, Confederate 37, 58, 68, 87–94, 103, 156
Court of Exchequer, Westminster 82
Court of Queen's Bench, Westminster 75
Coutts Bank, Strand 115
Covent Garden Theater 17
Cowell, John W. 34, 39
Cowell, William 10
Cramer, Beale & Wood 116
Crane Court, Fleet Street 45
Cremorne Gardens, Chelsea 74
Crenshaw, Capt. William G., CSA 57–58, 61, 74, 77, 155
Crossan, Lt. Thomas M., CSN 61, 154
Crowder, Maynard, Son & Lawford 88
Cruise of the Alabama 127
Cruise of the Alabama and the Sumter 128
"Cruise of the Confederate Ship 'Sumter'" 121
Crystal Palace, Hyde Park 6
Crystal Palace, Sydenham 20, 55
Cubitt Town 57, 64, 105–106, 158
Curtis & Harvey 54
Cushman, Charlotte 18

Daily News 45, 92, 127, 144
Daily Telegraph 16, 45, 132, 144
Dallas, George M. 26, 28
Davidson, Lt. Hunter, CSN 77
Davis, President Jefferson 25–27, 34, 37, 41, 46, 77, 99, 101–102, 112–113, 115, 118, 120, 123–125, 135, 137, 148, 155
Davis, Joseph E. 27

Davis, Mrs. Varina H. 117, 124
Day, Samuel P. 124–125, 142
Day & Son 114
Dayton, William L. 36
Deane, Adams & Deane 95–96
"Death of Stonewall Jackson" 116
Deerfoot 23
De Hoghton, Sir Henry 148
Delane, John T. 91
De La Rue, Victor 114
De La Rue & Co. 99, 101
De Leon, Edwin 49, 54, 120–121, 139, 154
Denbigh (blockade-runner) 103
Denny & Co., Dumbarton 64
Deptford 106
Devonshire Street 146
"Diary of a Confederate Boy" 118
Dickens, Charles 7, 39, 78, 110, 118
Diplomatic recognition, Confederate 3, 27, 30, 32, 34, 38, 46, 49–50, 70, 119, 140
Disraeli, Benjamin 134
"Dixie" 32, 74, 116
"Dixie's Land Gallop" 116
"Dixie's Land Polka" 116
Domestic Manners of the Americans 110
Donoughmore, Earl of 140, 148
Dorrell & Son 127
Dover 75
"Down Among the Cotton" 116
Down South; or, An Englishman's Experiences at the Seat of the American War 124
Down South; or, Life in the Cotton Fields 111
Drake, Frank 121
Drayton, Henri 111–112
Dudgeon, John & William 57, 64, 105, 158
Dudley, Thomas H. 63, 68, 80
Duncombe, William E., MP 139
Dunning, T.J. 150–151
Dyke, Mid. James H., CSN 77

Eardley, Sir Eardley 57
Eardley, Lady Florence 57
Early Closing Assocation 16
East India Co. 62
Eastern Counties Railway 15–16
"Echoes of the Week" 132
Economist 87–88
Economist (blockade-runner) 56, 80
Edge, Frederick M. 127
Edith (blockade-runner) 105
Edward, Prince of Wales 24
Egyptian Hall, Piccadilly 20
Elopement: A Tale of the Confederate States 134
Emancipation, Confederate 37–38, 45
Emancipation Proclamation, Lincoln's 3, 137, 143, 151
Emerson, Ralph W. 6
Emmett, Daniel D. 116
Engineer Bureau, Confederate 60
England and the Disrupted States of America 47
Enrica (CSS *Alabama*) 63

Erlanger, Emile 87–88, 90, 94, 103
Errand to the South in the Summer of 1862 124, 158
European Trading Co. 103
Eustis, George 32
Euston Hotel 10
Euston Square 69
Euston station 15, 85
Evans, Lt. William E., CSN 68, 72
Evans' Supper Rooms, Covent Garden 19, 74
Evening Herald 144
Evening Standard 144
Evening Star 144
Exeter Hall, Strand 23–24, 151
Express 144
"Extracts from the Journal of a Refugee in Georgia" 122

Facey, T.G. 150
"Fairfax, Miss L." 134
Falcon (blockade-runner) 107
Falmouth, Cornwall 54, 128
Farmer, Henry 116
Fauntleroy, Lt. Charles M. 73
Fawcett, Preston & Co., Liverpool 63
Fearn, Capt. John W., CSA 28, 33, 36, 54, 130, 132, 153
Federals and Confederates 111
Fenchurch Street station 15
Fenton's Hotel, St James's Street 9, 33
Ferguson, Mrs. Emma 57
Ferguson, Major James B., CSA 57
Fergusson, Sir James, MP 34, 139–140
Ferté, Jean F.J. de la 99
Ficklin, Major Benjamin F., CSA 57, 99, 101
Field, Inspector Charles F. 78
Fiery Cross 132
Fingal (blockade-runner) 56, 67, 79, 85
Finsbury Square 143
Firmin & Sons 99
Fishmongers' Hall, King William Street 30–31
Fitzroy, Rear Adm. Robert, RN 70
Fitzroy Square 81
Flamingo (blockade-runner) 107
Fleet Street 9, 45, 48, 142, 144
Fletcher, Lt. Col Henry 121
Flora (blockade-runner) 105
Florida, CSS 63, 67, 69, 77
Florida (steamer) 76
Foley, John H. 102, 115, 134
Forbes, George 116
Forbes, John M. 68, 80, 136
Foreign Enlistment Act 4, 63, 65, 74–75
Foreign Office 137, 146
Forrest, Asst. Paymaster Douglas F., CSN 15, 73–74, 77, 99, 112, 135, 153
Forrest, Edwin 6
Fort Fisher, North Carolina 37, 97–98, 130
Fort Sumter, South Carolina 37, 113, 122

Fortnightly Review 120
Foster & King 116
Fourteenth Amendment 108
La France (steamer) 64
Francis, Henry 113
Franco-Confederate treaty, abortive 36
Franklin, Benjamin 5
Franklin, battle of 36
Fraser, Trenholm & Co., Liverpool 3, 56–58, 62, 65, 82, 85, 88, 94, 97–98, 102, 107, 156
Fraser's Magazine 46
Fredericksburg, battle of 113, 117–118
Freeman, William 45, 134
Fremantle, Lt. Col. Arthur J.L. 121, 124, 134, 158
Freshfields & Newman 88
Fullam, George T. 127
Fuller, Hiram 45–46, 154

Galveston, Texas 155
Garibaldi, Gen. Giuseppe 24
Garroting Act 21
Geddes, C.W. 82
"General Jackson Schottische" 116
Gentry, Judith F. 94
Georgia, CSS 70, 72–73, 77, 142
Gettysburg, battle of 90, 124, 136, 142
Gilliat, Algernon 64
Gilliat, John S. 34, 137, 148, 157
Gilliat & Co. 87–88, 102, 107
Giraffe (blockade-runner) 101
Gladiator (blockade-runner) 56, 80
Gladstone, William E., MP 15, 37, 49, 91, 137, 142, 150, 156
Glaisher, James 5
Glasgow 68–69, 75–76, 82
Globe 144
Gold, Confederate 156
Gompertz, M. 112
Goody & Jones 99–100
Gorgas, Col. Josiah, CSA 51–52, 54, 56, 96–97
Gospel Oak train crash 23
Grand Transformation Scenes in the United States 154
Grant, Lt. Gen. Ulysses S. 97
Grattan, Thomas C. 47
Graves, Lt. Charles I., CSN 74
Gray, Charles W. & Wentworth 109
Gray, W.F. 82
Graz, Austria 155
Great Exhibition of 1851 6
Great Northern Hotel, King's Cross 10
Great Northern Railway 16, 81
Great Russell Street, Bloomsbury 60
Great Seal of the Confederacy 102, 115
Great Western Hotel, Paddington 10
Great Western Railway 16
Grecian Theater, City Road 111
Greek War of Independence 88
Green, Charles 54–55
Green Park 20
Greenhithe, Kent 55, 77
Greenhow, Mrs. Rose O. 59, 81, 128–130, 148, 153

Greenmore, John 19
Greenock, Scotland 67, 79
Greenwich 106
Greenwich Park 20
Greenwood & Batley 96–97
Greg, Percy 47, 134, 157
Gregory, William H., MP 27, 34, 92, 115, 139–141, 148, 157
"Grigson, Mr." 72
Grosvenor Hotel, Victoria 10, 74
Grosvenor Square, Mayfair 130
Gunboats, Confederate 64
Gun's American Agency, Strand 43

Half Moon Street, Piccadilly 12, 24, 28–30, 52, 60
Haliburton, Thomas C., MP 139
Hamber, Thomas 41, 47, 157
Hamburg 85
Hamilton, Archibald 52, 56, 157
Hamley, Major Edward 121, 143
Hammond, Edmund 137
Hampson, T. 150
Hampton Roads peace conference 37
Hardinge, Lt. Samuel W., USN 130, 132
Harriet Pinckney (steamer) 81, 107, 128
Harrison, Mrs. Constance 124
Hartington, Marquess of 140
Hartwell, Robert 151
Haseltine, George 48
Hatchett's Hotel, Piccadilly 10, 52, 66
Havas News Agency, Paris 49
Hawk (steamer) 75–76, 82–83
Hawkins, Edward 21
Haxell, Edward N. 10
Haxell's Hotel, Strand 10, 50
Haymarket 19, 56
Hayward, William S. 132, 134
Hazlewood, Colin H. 18, 111
Helen (blockade-runner) 103
Helm, Major Charles J., CSA 54
Hemy, Henri F. 116
Her Majesty's Theater, Haymarket 17–18
Hercules, CSS 64
Heroine of the Confederacy 134
Hewitt, Capt. William N.W., RN 130
Highgate Cemetery 24
Highland Falls, New York 155
History of the United States to Reconstruction 157
Hobson, Lt. Charles L., CSA 74
Hoge, Rev. Moses D. 101
Holborn Casino, High Holborn 19, 56
Holcombe, Lt. Isaac C., CSN 77
Holland, Sir Henry 34, 70
Holloway Prison 23
Holyhead, Wales 67, 85
"Home Life in a Confederate State" 122
Hood, Gen. John B., CSA 122
Hood, Thomas & Charles 98
Hopkins, John B. 44–46, 99, 157
Hopley, Catherine C. 125, 127, 140

Hopwood, John L., MP 139
Horsemonger Lane Gaol, Southwark 22–23
Hot Springs, Virginia 153
Hotze, Henry 33, 39–41, 43, 45–50, 56, 58, 88, 103, 112, 114, 130, 136, 139, 149–150, 154–155
Houghton, Lord 91
Household Words 78
"How We Broke the Blockade" 121
Hoyer & Ludwig 99
Hull 108, 158
Hunt, Thornton 47
Hunted to Death 132
Hunter, Robert M.T. 30, 34, 40
Hurst & Blackett 124
Huse, Major Caleb, CSA 51–54, 56–61, 63, 66, 74, 84–85, 96–97, 101, 107, 130, 135, 152, 154–155
Hyde Park 9, 20, 115

Illustrated London News 105–106, 112, 116–118, 121, 123–124, 132
Illustrated Times 33, 142
Index 12, 37, 43–50, 98–99, 103, 111, 114–115, 132, 134, 148, 154
Index (blockade-runner) 59, 106
Indian Empire (steamer) 108
International Exhibition of 1862 23–24
Irvine, Mrs. 57
Irving, Washington 18
Isaac, Campbell & Co. 52, 54, 56–58, 61, 69, 74, 78, 91, 93, 99, 103, 107–108
Isaac, Samuel 52, 55–56, 107–108, 158
Isaac, Saul 52, 108, 158
Isle of Wight 156, 158
Islington 7, 9
It's Never Too Late to Mend 18
Ivanhoe (blockade-runner) 103

Jackson, Lt. Gen. Thomas J., CSA 96, 114–116, 121, 123, 127, 132, 134
James, Thomas & George 10
Jansen, Capt. Marin H. 70
Japan (CSS *Georgia*) 70
Jefferson, Joseph 18
Jermyn Street 10, 54, 60, 66, 84–85
Jewell, J. 116
Johnston, Gen. Joseph E., CSA 114, 140
Johnston, T. & J. 103
Jones, Frederic 127
Jones, George 54
Jones, John B. 58
"Jones, Sarah L." 125
Jones, Loyd & Co. 88
Junior United Service Club, Charles II Street 69
Juno (blockade-runner) 103

Kean, Robert 135
Kearsarge, USS 63, 69, 111, 127
Kell, Lt. John M., CSN 69, 107, 153
Kenner, Duncan F. 37–38, 154
Kennon, Lt. Beverley, CSN 134
Kensington 158
Kensington Gardens 20

Kensington Palace Gardens 107, 158
Kerr, James 54, 96
Kerrison, Sir Edward, MP 34, 139
Kew Gardens 20
Kilbourne, Wisconsin 154
King, Lt. Charles, Jr., CSN 112
King, Thomas B. 25, 152
King's Cross station 16
Kirwan, Daniel J. 12
Knight, John A. 48
Knox, Lt., CSN 76
Koppel, Thomas 113
Kramer, M. 102

Ladd, William 98
Ladies' London Emancipation Society 50
Lady Sterling (blockade-runner) 103, 106
Lady's Newspaper 17
Laird, John, MP 91, 139
Laird & Sons, Birkenhead 63
Laird rams 3, 63–64, 77, 82, 86, 142
Lamar, Lucius Q.C. 36, 153
Lancaster, Charles W. 95–96
Lane, Sam & Sara 18
Langham Hotel, Portland Place 12
"Last Days of the Confederate Government" 118
"Last Six Days of Secessia" 120
Laurel (steamer) 66
Laurence, Son & Pearce 88
Lawley, Francis 120, 122, 127
Lawley, Robert 122
Lawrence, George A. 125
Layard, Sir Austen 137, 146
Leadenhall Street 107
Leamington Spa 37, 59–60, 155
Lee, General Robert E., CSA 38, 57, 90, 96, 114, 116, 120–121, 123, 136–137, 142–143
Legation, United States 28–30, 81, 132, 146
Leisure Hour 123
Leno, J.B. 151
Lest We Forget 93
Letters on Slavery 46
Lewis, John 16
Libby Prison, Richmond 12
Life in the South 125
Lincoln, President Abraham 90, 112, 120, 134, 151
Lindsay, William S., MP 28, 92, 139, 140–142, 148, 156
Lindsay & Co. 68, 81, 87–88, 103, 141
Little Bookham, Surrey 158
Little St. James's Street 70, 72
Liverpool 3, 4, 51–52, 54, 56–57, 60, 62–64, 66, 72, 76, 83, 85, 92, 102, 107, 154–157
Liverpool, Confederate bazaar at 37, 150
Lloyd (steamer) 108
Lloyd, J.T. 117
Lloyd's American Railroad Map 117
Lloyd's Map of the Southern Confederacy 117
Log of the Alabama and the Sumter 128

Logan, Celia 134
Lombard Street 104
London: American presence in 6; apartments 12; bridges 12–13; casinos 19; clubs 17; concert rooms 20; criminals 22; department stores 16; drainage system 6, 24; events in 23–24; extent of 5, 8; fogs 7; from a balloon 5; garroting outbreak 21; guidebooks 9, 12, 22; horse buses 13; horse cabs 13–14; hotels 9–12; maps & atlases 6–7; music halls 18–19; newspapers 45, 143–144; nightlife 19–20; parks 20; population of 5; prisons 22–24; railway terminals 15; residential districts 7, 9; restaurants 12; rooming houses 12; shipbuilding 104–105; shopping arcades 17; shops 16; slums 9; steamboats 5; street crime 21; street entertainers 21; street names 6; street vendors 11, 21; streetcars 13; theaters 17–18; trades 9; traffic congestion 21; underground railway 6
London American 48, 98, 111, 144
London & Birmingham Railway 15
London & Blackwall Railway 15
London & Greenwich Railway 15
London & North Western Railway 15, 81
London & South Western Railway 16
London Armory Co. 51, 52, 54–55, 83, 95–96
London Bridge station 15, 56, 74–75
London, Brighton & South Coast Railway 15–16
London, Chatham & Dover Railway 16, 64, 105
London Confederate States Aid Association 146
London Confederate States Commercial League 98
London Emancipation Society 50
London Journal 3, 123
London Labour and the London Poor 21
"London New York Herald" 144
London Pavilion, Tichborne Street 18, 74
London Reader 123
London, Tilbury & Southend Railway 15–16
London Trades Council 150
Longstreet, Lt. Gen. James, CSA 57
Lonsdale, Christopher 116
Lord Mayor's banquet 34
Lords, House of 140
Lost Cause 154
Lothian, Marquess of 140, 148
Louisa Ann Fanny, CSS 64–65, 77, 86
Lowther Arcade, Strand 17
Lungley, Charles 106
"Lying List" 92–93
Lynx (blockade-runner) 57

Macarthy, Harry 116
Mackintosh, Henry F. 45
Macmillan & Co. 142
Macon, Georgia 153
Maffitt, Lt. John N., CSN 63
Magoffin, John 82
Mail steamers 4
Malet, Rev. William W. 124, 144, 158
Mallory, Stephen R. 62–63, 67–68, 77, 125
Manassas, first battle of 30, 124, 132, 134, 143
Manassas, second battle of 150
Manchester Guardian 47
"Manhattan Letters" 41
Mann, A. Dudley 25–28, 30–33, 35, 40, 52, 60, 66, 91, 143, 149, 155
Mann, W. Grayson 28
Mansion House 34
Map Showing Operations under Grant, Sherman and Thomas 118
Maps, Civil War 117
Marion & Son 113
Marmion (blockade-runner) 103
Martin Chuzzlewit 110
Marx, Karl 24, 143
Mary Augusta, CSS 64, 77
"Maryland: A Confederate March" 116
"Maryland, My Maryland" 116
"Maryland Quadrille" 116
Marylebone 7
Mason, James M. 30–34, 36–39, 43, 46, 54, 57, 59, 68–70, 74, 76, 87–88, 90, 97, 102, 112, 120, 135, 139, 152, 154
Matthews, Charles 55
Maury, Cdr. Matthew F., CSN 69, 71–72, 74–75, 77, 98, 125, 130, 135, 144, 148, 153
Maury, Matthew, Jr. 70, 77
Maury, Lt. William L., CSN 70, 72
May, Thomas 107
Mayfair 7, 9
Mayhew, Henry 17, 19, 21–22, 55
McClellan, Maj. Gen. George B., USA 90, 112, 137
McCormick, Cyrus 6
McFarland, C. 54
McFarland, James E. 32, 59
McGill, Lt. John, Confederate States Volunteer Navy 85
McLean, Melhuish & Haes 113
McRae, Colin J. 58–59, 88, 103, 107, 152, 156
Meade, Richard 56
Mediation, British 3, 141–142
Melita (steamer) 69, 107
Memminger, Christopher 59, 94, 103
Memoirs of Service Afloat 128, 144, 153
"Memoirs of the Confederate War" 121, 127
Mercantile Trading Co. 103, 105, 107
Mercedita, USS 101
Merrimac (blockade-runner) 108
Merrimack, USS (CSS *Virginia*) 113, 123

Mersey Tunnel 158
Metropolis Road Commissioners 15
Metropolitan Police 22
Metropolitan Railway 15, 24, 74
Metropolitan Tabernacle, Elephant & Castle 23
Midland Railway 16
Millbank Penitentiary 23
Miller & Sons, Liverpool 63
Milton, Governor John 125
Minna (blockade-runner) 81
Mitchell's Newspaper Press Directory 44–45
Mobile, Alabama 153
Modern Greece (blockade-runner) 108
Monitor, USS 113, 123
Montgomery, Alabama 153
"Month with the Rebels" 120
Monthly Packet 122
"Month's Visit to Confederate Headquarters" 121
Montreal 154
Moore, Governor Thomas O. 61
Moran, Benjamin 26, 30, 34, 38, 46, 48, 56, 75, 80, 82, 90, 97–98, 106, 114, 128, 132, 136, 143–144, 148, 152
Morgan, Mid. James M., CSN 70, 72, 153
Morley, John 91
Morley's Hotel, Trafalgar Square 10, 51, 74, 90
Morning Advertiser 144
Morning Chronicle 78
Morning Herald 41, 50, 124, 132, 144, 157
Morning Post 41, 45, 91, 130, 144
Morning Star 32, 45, 91–93, 144
Morris, Lt. Charles M., CSN 74
Morse, Freeman H. 66, 68, 76, 78–79, 80, 82–83, 85, 95, 97–98, 136, 156
Mortlake, Surrey 157
Morton, John M. 111
Motley, John L. 7
El Mounassir 64
Muller, Franz 24
Murdaugh, Lt. William H., CSN 144
Murray, John 122
Murray's Modern London 5
My Diary North and South 124
My Imprisonment 128
My Lord and My Lady 55

Napoleon III, Emperor 36, 38, 128, 141
Nashville, CSS 60, 76, 98, 101, 120
Nashville, battle of 37
Navy Department, Confederate 57, 62, 66–68, 84
Negretti & Zambra 98
Neutrality, Proclamation of 4, 28, 95, 136
New Army Map of Virginia 117
New Bond Street 71, 74
New Orleans 111, 134, 154
New Plan 59, 107
New York 154–155

New York draft riots 123
New York Evening Post 154
New York Herald 120, 143
New York Times 91
New York Tribune 136
Newcastle-on-Tyne 137
Newgate Prison 22–24
Newhaven, Sussex 72
Nonconformist clergy 146
North, Cdr. James H., CSN 66–69, 77, 82, 98, 144, 153
North America (steamer) 62
North and South 46
North Heath (blockade-runner) 103
North London Railway 16, 24
Northfleet, Kent 106
Norton, Mrs. Caroline 34
Notting Hill 10, 24
Nunn, Joshua 80
Nutfield (blockade-runner) 106

Observer 18
O'Connor, Florence J. 134
Old Capitol Prison, Washington 125, 128, 130
Olustee, CSS 106
Olympic Theater, Wych Street 18, 55, 110
Once a Week 123
Ordnance Bureau, Confederate 51, 57, 59, 96, 108
Oreto (CSS *Florida*) 63
Oscar, Prince 34
Osnaburgh Street, Regent's Park 115
O'Sullivan, John L. 45–46, 130, 154
"Ouida" (M.L. de la Ramée) 134
Our American Cousin 18, 110
Our Cruise on the Confederate States War Steamer Alabama 127
"Our Queen Varine" 116
"Our Rancorous Cousins" 121
Overend, Gurney & Co. 76, 103–104, 108
Owl (blockade-runner) 140
Oxenford, John 55
Ozanne, Rev. T.D. 125

Pacific (steamer) 81
Paddington station 16
Page, Capt. Thomas J., CSN 77
Palace Hotel, Buckingham Gate 12
Pall Mall 100
Palmerston, Lady 130
Palmerston, Lord 24, 37–38, 41, 49, 60, 138–139, 150
Pampero (*Canton*) 68
Panoramas, Civil War 112–113
Paris 27–28, 30, 32, 36, 38, 49, 54, 57–60, 66, 69, 76, 87, 93, 101, 152, 154–156
Parker, Joseph 148
Parliament 139
Peabody, George 6, 23–24, 28, 61
Peace petition (Society for Promoting the Cessation of Hostilities in America) 148
Peace the Sole Chance 46
Peacocke, George M.W., MP 139
Pearson, Zachariah C. 74–75, 103, 108, 158

Pearson & Co., Hull 108
Peel, Frederick, MP 139
Pegram, Cdr. Robert B., CSN 76–77, 144, 146
Pembroke, Edward 103, 105
Pentonville Prison 23
"Perils of a Spy" 154
Peterhoff (steamer) 108
Petersburg, Virginia 38, 90
Peyton, Col. John L., CSA 60, 116, 135, 143–144
Photographs, Civil War 113
Physical Geography of the Sea 70
"Picket of the Potomac" 116
Pile, Spence & Co., West Hartlepool 108
Pilkington, James 21
Pimlico 7
Pinchon, William 64
Pitcher, Henry S. 66
Planché, J.R. 55
La Plata (steamer) 32
Plays, Civil War 110–111
Plymouth 4
Pollaky, Ignatius P. 78–80
Polygraphic Hall, Strand 111
Porter's Knot 55
Portraits, Confederate 114
Postage stamps, Confederate 99
Princess Royal (blockade-runner) 81
Princess's Theater, Oxford Street 18, 74
Printing House Square 144
Prints, Confederate 113–114
Prioleau, Charles K. 65, 156
Prisoners-of-war, Confederate 150
Pritchard, Mr. 66
Propaganda, Northern 41, 48
Propaganda, Southern 39–50
"Prospects of the Confederates" 122
Prosser, William 102
Ptarmigan (blockade-runner) 107
Punch 18, 21, 25, 32, 118–120, 135, 141, 143–144
Purchasing agents: Confederate 51–60, 62–73; state 60–61

Quarterly Review 39, 122
Quartermaster's Bureau, Confederate 57
Quilter, Ball, Jay & Co. 58

Randall, James 116
Ransford, Edwin 111
Rappahannock, CSS 73–75, 77, 82, 158
Reade, Charles 18
Reagan, John H. 99
Rebel Privateer 134
Recognition: A Letter to Lord Palmerston 46
Recollections of a Naval Life 153
Recollections of a Rebel Reefer 153
Redfern, James 115
Reform Club, Pall Mall 60
Regent Street 16, 19, 148
Regent's Park 7, 20
Reinhart, Benjamin F. 114
Reuter's News Agency 4, 142–143

Revell's Fine Art Gallery, Leadenhall Street 114
Richardson's Hotel, Covent Garden 56
Richmond Enquirer 98
"Richmond on the James River" 123
Richmond Park 20
Richmond Record 50
Richmond Sentinal 94
Richmond, Virginia 38, 90, 154–155
Rideout, W.J. 91
"Ridge, Samuel P." 130
Ridgway, W. 127
Rip Van Winkle 18
Robinson, Capt. John M., CSA 60
Robinson, Peter 16
Robson, Frederick 18, 55
Roebuck, John A., MP 139, 141, 143, 149, 156
Roosevelt, President Theodore 156
Ross, Capt. Fitzgerald E.T. 121, 124–125, 127, 134, 142, 158
Ross & Co. 54
Rost, Pierre A. 25–27, 30, 32–33, 35, 52, 154
Rothschild & Sons Ltd. 88
Royal Academy, Piccadilly 115
Royal Arcade, New Oxford Street 17
Royal Lyceum Theater, Wellington Street 18
Royal Opera Arcade, Haymarket 17
Royal Small Arms factory, Enfield 96–97
Royal Victoria Theater (Old Vic), Lambeth 18, 111
Rumble, William 75
"Run through the Southern States" 121
Russell, Henry 111
Russell, Lord John 24, 27, 30, 32, 34–36, 63–64, 97
Russell, John S. 106
Russell, William H. 124, 134, 140
Russell Square, Bloomsbury 67

Sackville Street, Piccadilly 24, 59, 70, 129–130
Sadler's Wells Theater, Finsbury 18
Sage, Bernard J. 75
St. Bride's Wharf, Wapping 82
St. James's Church, Piccadilly 24, 130–131
St. James's Hall, Piccadilly 24, 46, 112–113, 151
St. James's Park 20
St. James's Street 85
St. Mildred's Court, Poultry 98
St. Peter's Church, Belsize Park 24, 144–146
Sala, George A. 16, 132–133
Sampson, M.B. 91
Samuelson, Martin, Hull 108
Sanderson, James M. 12
Sanford, Henry S. 78–80, 83–84
San Jacinto, USS 31–32
Saturday Review 40, 47, 92, 127
Saunders, Otley & Co. 114, 125, 127, 132
Savannah, Georgia 37, 152
Savile House, Leicester Square 24

Savile Row 24, 41–42, 50
Sayers, Tom 24
Schroder, J. Henry 103, 115
Schroder & Co. 70, 87–88, 90, 94
Schulze, Adolphe 127
Schwab, John C. 94
Scoville, Joseph A. 41
Scylla (CSS *Rappahannock*) 73
Sea King (CSS *Shenandoah*) 65–66
Sea Queen (steamer) 108
Secret History of Confederate Diplomacy Abroad 154
Secret Service of the Confederate States 156
Semmes, Capt. Raphael, CSN 63, 69, 77, 107, 127–128, 144, 153
Senac, Paymaster Felix, CSN 74
Senac, Ruby 155
Seven Days' Battles 120–121, 136, 137
Seward, William H. 37–38, 41, 78–80, 83, 90, 92–93, 97, 136, 143, 148, 150, 156
Seymour, Edward 120
Seymour, John 74
Shaffner, Taliaffero P. 98
Shaw, Kathleen 146
Sheerness Dockyard 73, 75
Sheffield 158
Shenandoah, CSS 65–66, 77, 86
Shepperton Manor, Middlesex 157
Shiloh, battle of 134
Shoolbred, James 16
Signal Bureau, Confederate 98
Silver & Co. 98
Sinclair, Cdr. George T., CSN 68–69, 77, 144
Sinclair, Hamilton & Co. 52, 54, 56, 60–61, 67, 82
Slavery, attitudes to 26, 33, 36, 39–40, 46, 50, 118, 122, 124–125, 137, 144, 149
Slidell, John 30–33, 36, 49, 57, 87–88, 112, 120, 155–156
Smith, Goldwin 149–150
Smith, Maj. Gen. Gustavus W., CSA 140
Society for Promoting the Cessation of Hostilities 148, 150
Society for the Relief of Distress 150
Songs, Confederate 116
"South American Confederation" 123
South as It Is 125
South Eastern Railway 15–16
South Place Chapel, Finsbury 36
South Vindicated 46
Southampton 4, 26, 32, 58, 60, 120
Southborough, Kent 157
Southern Field and Fireside 50
Southern Illustrated News 50
Southern Independence Association of London 93, 148–150
Southern Literary Messenger 50
Southern lobby 139
Southern Prisoners' Relief Fund 37, 115
Southern Review 154
Southern Secession 39
Southerner Just Arrived (play) 18, 110

Southwick (steamer) 60, 80
Soutter, James T. 103
Spectator 92, 132
Spence, James 39–40, 46–49, 59, 88, 91, 101, 115, 118, 122, 128, 130, 136–137, 149, 157
Spottiswoode, George A. 45
Springbok (steamer) 93, 107
Spurgeon, Charles 23
Stafford House, St. James's 34
Standard 41, 45–47, 50, 127, 144, 154–155, 157
Stanford, Edward 6
Star of the South 132
Statesman's Yearbook 142
Staunton, Virginia 154
Stephen, Leslie 110
Stephen & Sons 65
Stiles, Cdr. Edward C., Confederate States Volunteer Navy 75
Stock Exchange 88
Stonewall, CSS 64, 77
Stonewall Brigade 140
Stonewall Jackson 127
Stonewall Jackson Memorial Account 115
"Stonewall Jackson Quadrille" 116
Stowe, Mrs. Harriet B. 110
Straker & Sons 101,
Strand 45
Stratheden House, Knightsbridge 49
Stratton, Mrs. Lavinia 112
Stringer, Edgar P. 61, 68, 103, 105–106, 108, 157
Stuart, Maj. Gen. James E.B., CSA 116–117, 127
Sturgis, Russell 27
Sumter, CSS 69, 72, 123
"Sunny Days Will Come Again" 111
Sunnyside, Georgia 153
Supplies for the Confederate Army 155
Surrey Theater, Blackfriars Road 18
Surveillance, Federal 78–86
Sutherland, Duke of 34
Swisher, John 61
Symonds, Capt. T.E., RN 105
Syren (blockade-runner) 106

Talisman (blockade-runner) 103
Tallahassee, CSS 106
Talley, Asst. Paymaster Daniel, Confederate States Volunteer Navy 76, 85
Tavistock Hotel, Covent Garden 10, 74
Taylor, Joseph 150
Taylor, Tom 18, 110
"Ten Days in Richmond" 120
Tenniel, John 119
Tennyson, Alfred 146
Texas State Military Board 61
Thackeray, William M. 121
Thames, River 15
Theater Royal, Drury Lane 18, 111
Theater Royal, Haymarket 18, 55
Thompson, George 140
Thompson, Jacob 156
Thompson, John R. 50, 111, 127, 146, 154
Thompson, Lydia 111

Thompson, William 26
Thomson, James & George, Glasgow 68
Three Letters from a South Carolinian 49
Three Months in the Southern States 124, 158
Tilton, Mr. 61
Times 12, 30, 34, 36–39, 45–47, 60, 64, 68, 81, 88, 90–93, 97, 103, 108–109, 111–114, 120, 124, 127, 130, 136–137, 144, 148, 150, 155
Tinsley Bros. 125
Tooley Street fire 23
Torpedoes 98
Tothill Fields Prison, Westminster 23
El Tousson 64
Toxteth Park Cemetery, Liverpool 156
Train, George F. 13, 15, 48
Transatlantic telegraph 4
Trelawny, Sir John, MP 141
Tremlett, Rev. Francis W. 68, 130, 144–148, 157
Tremlett, Louisa 146
Trenholm, George A. 62, 103
Trent incident 3, 31–32, 97, 118, 144, 146
Trollope, Mrs. Frances 110
Troup, George 150–151
Turner Bros., Hyde & Co. 99
"Tuscarora" (poem) 120
Tuscarora, USS 63, 120
Tussaud's Waxworks, Baker Street 20, 74, 112
Twelve Songs of the American War 116
Two Months in the Confederate States 125–126, 158
Tyburnia 7, 9

Uncle Tom's Cabin 18, 33, 110
Uniforms, Confederate 99
Union, Disunion and Reunion 46
Union Street Congregational Chapel, Southwark 146
United Daughters of the Confederacy 156
Universal Trading Co. 103
Upper Seymour Street 33

Vance, Governor Zebulon B. 60
Vicksburg, surrender of 90, 136, 142–143
Victor, HMS 73
Victoria (blockade-runner) 121
Victoria, Queen 23
Victoria Docks 64–65, 75, 82, 83
Victoria Park 20
Victoria station 16
Vincennes, USS 69
Virginia Military Institute, Lexington 154
Virginia Volunteer Navy 75, 85
Visit to the Cities and Camps of the Confederate States 121, 125, 127, 158
Vize, Thomas 150
Vizetelly, Frank 118, 121–122, 124, 127

"Voice from the South" 60
Volck, Frederick 115
Volunteer Navy, Confederate States 75
Von Borcke, Lt. Col J.A.H. Heros, CSA 121

Wachusett, USS 63
Waddell, Lt. Cdg. James I., CSN 66
Waddington, Rev. Dr. John 146
"Waif from Dixie" 118
Walker, Mrs. Georgiana G. 59–60, 128–130, 155
Walker, Leroy P. 40, 60
Walker, Major Norman S., CSA 59–60, 64, 128, 155
Walker & Sons 115
Wandering Minstrel 55
War Department, Confederate 57–58, 98
"War Song of Dixie" 116
Ward, J.E. 135
Ward & Lock 134
Waresboro, Georgia 153
Warrior, HMS 55, 66
Warwick, William S., 150
Washington, DC 153
Waterloo station 16
Webb, Cdr. William A., CSN 152

Webster, Benjamin 18
Weed, Thurlow 41
Weiner, Carl 116
Weller, Edward 6
Wellington Street 144
West Hartlepool 56, 108
West India Docks 107
Westminster Palace Hotel, Victoria Street 10, 12, 28, 70
Weston, Major J.A., CSA 101
Weston, Capt. Plowden C.J., CSA 124
Wetter, A.P. 43
Wharncliffe, Lord 91, 108, 130, 140, 142, 148–150, 157
Wharncliffe House, Curzon Street 149
White, John 61, 154
"White Republican" 46
Whiteley, William 16
Whiteside, James, MP 139
Whittle, Lt. William C., Jr., CSN 65–66, 76
Whitworth & Co. 68, 96
Whitworth guns 97
Wigan, Horace 18, 110
Wigfall, Louis T. 155
Wigg, George 103
Wilkinson, Lt. John, CSN 105

Williams, James 45–46, 130, 155
Williams, Joseph 116
Wilmington, North Carolina 37, 57, 64, 76, 142, 153
Wilson, John 60
Wilson & Sons 99
Wimbledon Common 55, 102
Winchester, Virginia 155
Witt, John G. 50, 157
Wolseley, Lt. Col. Garnet 120–121
Wood, Sir W. Page 90
Wood's Hotel, High Holborn 10, 65
Woolley's New Map of the Confederate States 117
Woolwich Arsenal 54–55, 96–98
Wright, Richard 65
Wrottesley, Lord 70
Wyatt, Matthew D. 107
Wyld, James 20, 117
Wynn, William 74
Wyon, Joseph S. 102

Yancey, William L. 25–28, 30–31, 33, 35, 40, 43, 52, 55–56, 60, 66, 153
Yeomans, James 98
Yonge, Charlotte M. 122
Yonge, Clarence R. 82

Zug, Switzerland 155

www.ingramcontent.com/pod-product-compliance
Lightning Source LLC
Chambersburg PA
CBHW081557300426
44116CB00015B/2914